CONVEYANCING

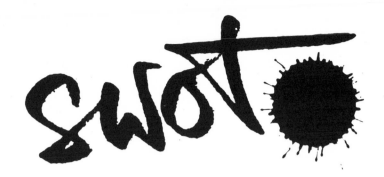

CONVEYANCING

BRIDGET WALKER, BA, Solicitor

Senior Lecturer in Law, Leeds Business School

Series Editor C.J. CARR, MA, BCL

BLACKSTONE PRESS LIMITED

First published in Great Britain 1992 by Blackstone Press Limited, 9-15 Aldine Street, London W12 8AW. Telephone 081-740 1173

ISBN: 1 85431 180 8

British Library Cataloguing in Publication Data
A CIP catalogue record for this book is available from the British Library

Typeset by Murdoch Evans Partnership, Tonbridge, Kent
Printed by Redwood Press Ltd, Melksham, Wiltshire

Cartoons drawn by Anne Lee

CONTENTS

PREFACE

Conveyancing is a word which strikes apprehension if not fear into the heart of every student. On occasions I have longed to teach family law or criminal law. So often I have been disappointed to walk along a corridor and overhear a group of students saying 'I love family law, it's my favourite subject'. If only occasionally they would say they 'love' conveyancing. Needless to say it has not yet happened to me and I doubt it ever will.

This book is not an attempt to convert you to the love of conveyancing. Nor do I expect you to sit down, having read this book, and say how much you enjoyed reading it. (I confess that I have always felt somewhat suspicious of people who enjoy reading anything other than a novel or a biography.) What I do hope though is that at the end of this book some of the dread of conveyancing will have disappeared and that you are able confidently to say that conveyancing was not as difficult as you thought it would be.

The author's preface is traditionally the place where thanks are extended to nearest and dearest, professionals and family, for their help. I am very grateful to many people for their help but my list became impossibly long. To all the unsung heroes and heroines I extend my very grateful thanks and to some my love.

Bridget Walker
Scales House Farm
November 1991

ONE

CONVEYANCING WITHOUT FEAR

On a radio phone-in the other day, the DJ discovered that the caller was studying law. Not content with asking what subject the student liked most, the question was put: 'What subject do you dislike most?'

'Conveyancing', said the caller.

Well, thanks! At a stroke those of us who teach and practise conveyancing had our social popularity publicly confirmed as about equivalent to that of dentists. Those of us who actually enjoy what we do must surely be classified as complete lunatics. Having said that, I am not about to regale you with tales of how I always loved land law and conveyancing and wanted to pass on my love of the subject to others. I did not. I have to confess that as a student I hated and was frightened of conveyancing. It was only when I went into practice and had to start sorting out actual conveyancing problems that I gained any confidence or real understanding of the subject. With my understanding grew an anger that what is, in essence, a reasonably straightforward subject, had been such a mystery (and misery) whilst I was studying it. This book is an attempt to short-cut the process which I went through. I make no apologies for the simplistic approach. If you are one of those few lucky students who find no problems with the subject then I am very pleased for you (and indeed somewhat envious). If you are, like me, a mere mortal, then I hope that some of what you read here will, even if you don't actually come to enjoy conveyancing, remove some of the fear of the subject so that you do experience 'success without tears'.

The nature of the subject

It is essential to realise, right at the beginning of your study, that conveyancing is a second-level subject. Unless you have a solid foundation of land law, then much of the subject will be a foreign language to you. You can study land law without conveyancing, but not conveyancing without land law. If you are studying conveyancing for a professional examination then land law will usually have been a compulsory element of your earlier study. How long ago was that, though? How much can you remember? And, if truth be told, how well did you actually understand it, or did you cram for the exam and somehow got through? If you are at all unhappy about your answers to any of these questions, then I suggest that before you start to study conveyancing you revise the basics of land law. You may also find, during your study of conveyancing that you need to come back to a basic land law text and refresh your memory. If you go to one of the larger texts you may find yourself in tears before you start. MacKenzie and Phillips, *A Practical Approach to Land Law*, is a text that I can recommend. It is well written, easy to read, and small enough not to make your arms ache if you read it in bed or in the bath!

In addition to brushing up on your land law, you may have to adapt to a new approach to your studies. In some conveyancing courses you may find that there is a bias to academic issues. If this is so and you have already successfully studied any academic law, the types of questions which may be set should not present you with any particular problems. You will need to ensure that you have a good grounding in the basic principles and that you have done the necessary reading and study required by the syllabus. Beyond that, the techniques which you have acquired in your earlier study should stand you in good stead. It is much more likely though that the course you are studying places the emphasis on the practice of conveyancing. Conveyancing is essentially a practical subject. You will need to know the theory behind the practice but also be able to follow the theory through to see the practical effects. At the end of most of the chapters in this book you will find a section on answering examination questions, the nature of which may be different to anything you have encountered so far. With these and tutorials or seminars you should not find adapting to the new style of questions and answers too harrowing. If, when reading this book, you come across a term which is unfamiliar you may find it helpful to refer to the glossary at the end of the book.

Effective studying

Getting a perspective on the subject

Most students find themselves experiencing one of two types of problem:

(a)   They may not be able to see the wood for the trees (in that all the detail seems clear and understandable but the overall scheme of things remains a mystery).
(b)   They may not be able to see the trees for the wood (in that the overall scheme of things seems clear but getting to grips with the detail is a real problem).

Both problems are equally frightening. The answer seems to be:

(a)   Before you start to look in any detail at a conveyancing transaction try to familiarise yourself with the objectives of the transaction and an outline of the stages involved.
(b)   Whenever you start a new section of your study, ask yourself where the topic fits into the overall transaction. Once you have established that, jump in with both feet and try to get to grips with the detail.

(c)   At the end of the topic, just to make sure you are not losing your way, look again to see where it fits into the overall transaction.

Key issues

Another common problem in studying conveyancing is an inability to recognise key issues. Students often say after an exam, 'I could have explained that point but I didn't notice it'. A useful technique is, throughout your study, to try to think in terms of key legal issues:

(a)   When you are studying a topic try to break it down into a number of:

(i)   issues
(ii)   problems
(iii)   possible solutions.

(b)   Throughout your reading and tutorial and exam preparation, make a note, as you go along, of the ways in which the key issues have been presented. How did the question draw your attention to it? Was it in the narrative or the documents provided with the narrative? What facts were supposed to push you to consider that particular issue?

By the time you reach the examination, not only will you have a list of factual scenarios surrounding each key issue which might possibly come up in the exam but also you will have significantly increased your awareness of such issues and be more likely to spot them in the exam.

(c)   Whenever you have to tackle a tutorial test or examination question, stop after each sentence and ask yourself, 'What, if any, is the key issue that I am being pushed towards?'

Developing skills

As well as understanding the legal issues involved, most conveyancing courses now recognise that in a practical subject you must examine skills as well as understanding.
    A lawyer who is able to understand the problems but cannot cope with the practicalities of letter writing or drafting will have a very limited practice indeed. Although the skills must always be backed by a sound basis of law, most of those which are examined in conveyancing really amount to whether or not you can communicate effectively. Whether these skills come naturally or whether they need considerable time to be developed varies from person to person. One thing is certain though, and that is that these skills cannot be developed by cramming. You must work at them steadily throughout your course. Remember to use common sense and plain English as your guides and with written answers ask yourself two questions:

(a)   Who, primarily, is going to be reading this and what do they need to know? For example, if you are asked to draft a letter to a client you may need to include some points of law, but your letter should explain the law, not recite it. If clients could be expected to understand legal issues without the medium of a lawyer, you would not need to be employed at all.

(b)   Is there anything else which the person reading this wants to know? For example, if you are asked to draft a letter to a client, over and above what they need to know, you may have been given some specific instructions about matters which they would like you to explain to them.

The building bricks approach

There are some subjects which you can approach on a topic-by-topic basis. There is no real need for an overall perspective and, if you are doing an exam where there is a choice of questions, you can reasonably safely concentrate on some topics more than others. You may also find that if you miss lectures and tutorials for a while, you can carry straight on and pick up what you missed at the end of the course. The building bricks can stand independently of one another and you may be able to look at them out of order (see figure 1.1).

Figure 1.1

| Topic 1 | | Topic 2 | | Topic 3 |

Conveyancing is not like that. The building bricks stack one upon the other. If you miss a topic, or do not fully understand it, you cannot safely go on to the next topic. Each topic relies on you understanding the ones before it and, indeed, on being able to appreciate the overall transaction or the way a tower is constructed with building bricks (see figure 1.2).

Figure 1.2

| Topic 3 |
| Topic 2 |
| Topic 1 |

Using this book

In studying any legal subject it is important not to forget what are the lawyer's 'raw materials', i.e., statutes, cases and statutory instruments. It is very easy when studying a second level subject like this to think that these raw materials have become less important. It is true that there is not a great emphasis in this book on common law authorities. That does not mean that they are unimportant, but rather that many of the concepts being dealt with will have been studied in land law and at this stage you should simply be refreshing your memory as to the principles. Statutory provisions too are looked at in fairly general terms. The aim is to give you a sound basis of understanding which you can then develop further on your own or in tutorials. In any specific problem the general concepts should be simply your first port of call. Having considered the position in terms of basic principles there is then no substitute for reading the actual statutory provisions and the cases.

You may find that keeping a keen eye out for articles on conveyancing in the professional journals will give you the edge in an examination on both academic and procedural questions. Even if they do not actually help to answer one of the questions in the exam, the more you can read, the more likely it is that the different elements of the subject will slot into place in your work.

Precedents may be a new phenomenon for you. There are many good books of conveyancing precedents which are used on a regular basis by practitioners. As a student you should use them with care. I would recommend that you first try to draft in your own words. Once you have actually done the drafting, then look at a precedent together with your own draft and break each down into its key elements. Having done that, compare the two and ask:

(a)   Can each key element in the precedent be paraphrased in the same terms as my draft? If yes, then yours has probably done the job, albeit not in such fancy language.

(b)   Have I missed any of the key elements? If yes, what are they and what is their legal effect?

If you have worked through this process you will not find the practitioner's task of adapting or modifying precedents to the circumstances of a particular case quite so much like a children's party game of pinning the tail on the donkey.

Textbooks too have a role to play in your study. There are many weighty academic works on conveyancing and title which you may find useful. With all of them, though, you must be careful not to impale yourself on some thorny and detailed problem to the detriment of an appreciation of the basic scheme of things and your overall confidence with the subject.

This book is not designed to replace study from journals, cases and texts, but to supplement them. Ideally it should be read before you start your study. The relevant chapter should be read before you approach each new subject area. Whenever you get that sinking feeling of losing your way, being left behind, or something going over your head, come back to this book to re-establish your confidence and your sense of perspective.

TWO

EXAMINATIONS

Preparing for the exam

One of the biggest fears with conveyancing exams is the documentation which may accompany the questions. I was invigilating in one examination when the students were asked to check their papers to see that all 16 sheets were there. A collective gasp was heard and the temperature rose by at least one degree. To a certain extent I can understand the panic. Being given pages of documentation to read through in an examination is far worse than simply being given questions which, you will know at a glance, you either can or cannot answer. There are two things that you can do to help alleviate your fear. One is to realise that everyone sitting the exam will be under the same pressures. The second is to practise reading contracts, conveyances, transfers etc. and extracting the important information from them. If left to the last minute this type of exercise will not only panic you, but it will also show little or no results. It is important to practise this throughout the course and in the early stages of your revision.

You should use past papers to help in your revision and in practising exam technique. Frequent testing and practising seem to be two of the keys to developing an ability to identify issues from sometimes substantial documentation. However, a word of warning also needs to be sounded. If you are using past papers with the suggested answers, do remember the following points:

(a)   That paper will not be the one in your exam.
(b)   If you are not extremely disciplined in not looking at the answers until you have completed the whole paper you will be unlikely to gain anything from the exercise. The best way to learn is from your own mistakes. When you look at the answers they seem so obvious.

Revising

I cannot stress enough the importance of a step-by-step approach to conveyancing. It is always tempting to leave things to the last minute and to cram for an exam. You may, in the past, even have done it quite successfully. I certainly used this method on occasions during my degree. When it comes to conveyancing, though, you must think differently. Fortunately I learned that about a quarter of the way through my conveyancing course and was able to make up for lost time. I am certain I would not have coped if I had left it until the last minute as I did with some other subjects.

If you have worked your way steadily through the course then revision should be a matter of fine tuning rather than learning the fundamental principles.

Many revision techniques are little more than common sense and not every technique will work for every student. Try to experiment before tests and mock exams to find the method which works best for you.

A revision timetable

Preparing a revision timetable always used to calm my nerves but I seldom managed to stick to it with the vigour or rigour I had anticipated. It certainly helps to make a revision timetable so that you can see the size of the problem at the beginning and discipline yourself accordingly. Be careful, though, that once you have made the timetable it does not then become your downfall. Watch out for two possible pitfalls:

(a)   Working yourself into exhaustion by sticking slavishly to an overambitious timetable.
(b)   Allowing yourself to become depressed and lose confidence because you have not kept to the timetable.

In either case, remember that you are far more likely to fail through panic, loss of confidence, exhaustion or depression than because of missing half an hour or an hour's revision.

Memory techniques

Revision can be helped by various techniques which can assist memorising. Using mnemonics or revision index cards or colour coding can all help. The trick which I find most helpful is to break all the topics down into key issues in respect of each point. I list the points which need to be remembered (both the elements of the problem itself and the solutions). I then learn the points, but also learn the *number* of points relating to each issue. When under pressure I can then remember how many points I have to deal with. I don't know why it works, but knowing how many points there are seems to help to bring them back. This method may not work for you. Throughout the course, you could experiment with all the different tricks to find out which works best for you and then use it in your final revision.

Last-minute revision

Try to plan your revision to leave you two or three days, without any 'formally planned' revision, when you can check up on things that you have difficulty remembering or about which you are unhappy.

You may, for various reasons, in fact end up using that time to do last-minute cramming. You may not have been able to get to grips with something earlier; you may be too nervous to *stop* revising, or you may, despite all the warnings, have left things too late. If your last-minute revision does have to involve more than reassuring yourself then don't despair. Instead:

(a)   Break the subject down into a manageable number of topics, perhaps 10 or 12.
(b)   Break each topic down into no more than six key areas.
(c)   Break each key area down into no more than six key words.

Do this in writing and as neatly as possible. Use plenty of paper so that the layout is not cramped. Having done that, take a fresh sheet and try to reconstruct the lists from memory. If you cannot remember then check your master copy. If you are still not reassured then simply repeat the exercise until you are.

The exam itself

On the day of the exam, if you are anything like me, even when you are sure you know your subject, you probably wake up with that sick, stomach-churning feeling. The first trick I employ is to expect to feel sick. Somehow, saying to yourself, 'I feel sick, but so what', reduces the feeling to a matter of little consequence rather than something panicking.

What about when you actually get into the exam? Below are some of my observations based on both my own experience of exams and of preparing students for, and invigilating and marking exams.

The first few moments

The first moments in an exam room seem to set the tone for the whole exam. Those awful few minutes before you can actually start the exam seem like an eternity. Most people's breathing during this period is scarcely perceptible. I recommend that, during this time, you make yourself take five (counted) breaths. Deep ones, in through the nose and out through the mouth. You may think it's silly, but why not give me the benefit of the doubt — you've got to breathe anyway during that time and you've got nothing else to do. You might even feel better.

Reading the paper

As with any exam paper, remember to read *all* of it before you start any of your answers. If the paper includes a number of documents this becomes even more important but even more difficult to do. Disciplining oneself to read something through cooly and calmly when others around you have started writing is hard. Try to remember that even if your understanding of the law is first class, if you get the facts wrong you cannot hope to do well.

Attitudes to reading through documents differ. A very few people can read and remember without taking notes or underlining. Others go to the other extreme and either highlight or underline just about everything. To my mind doing this defeats the whole object of underlining. When you have finished, the documents look just as confusing as when you started. A useful compromise is to highlight only key words and to make a note on a piece of scrap paper of the issues which arise from the documentation. This has the added advantage that you will end up with a note of all the key issues on one piece of paper.

When looking at the questions you may find it useful to underline the operative words. For example, if the question says: 'What advice would you give your client and what further enquiries would you make', there are two parts to this, the *advice* and the *further enquiries*. Underlining these words should address your mind successfully at the outset to the relevant issues.

Make sure also that you actually do what the question tells you. If it asks you to '*draft and explain* the special conditions you would include in the contract', don't make the mistake of *describing* and explaining.

Writing your answers

As a student I was bored to death with being told to plan my answers. I never really felt that I could afford the time. If you can afford the time, then ideally you should plan them in writing. If you haven't time, you must do the same thing in your head. A well-structured answer, with the same information, will usually score more highly than an unstructured one. You are displaying to the examiner a clear understanding of the issues and an ability to communicate your understanding.

The first steps to structuring your answer involve an appreciation of four stages:

(a)   *Identifying* to the examiner the material in the exam paper which gives rise to the issue.
(b)   *Explaining* to the examiner what the legal problem or issue is.
(c)   *Discussing* the possible solutions.
(d)   *Concluding* what would be the appropriate course to take.

Students often make the mistake of missing out on the simple explanation of the basic problems. Often it is the brightest students who do this because they say it seems too obvious. One solution to this problem is to think carefully to whom you are explaining the matter. If you have to explain the matter to the examiner then a sensible starting-point is to assume that the examiner is a reasonably intelligent individual who has had a legal training but knows little or nothing about conveyancing. This will usually ensure that you explain the basic principles of the subject without a full exposition of the English legal system. If you are asked to address your answer to someone other than the examiner (e.g., you are asked to write to your client) then, unless you are told that the person has some special expertise, try to explain the legal issues in terms that anyone could understand. If, to produce that understandability you have to simplify more than you would like, then by all means put a note at the end of the answer stating the law and explaining to the examiner why you have put it in such simplistic terms.

Remember, above all, that the examiner can only mark what is on the paper. All the thought processes which you went through to reach a conclusion can only be credited if you put them down in writing. If two students each simply write down their conclusion to a problem, without any explanation, the student whom the examiner thinks 'knew it really' will score no more marks than the one whom the examiner thinks hit upon the correct conclusion by accident.

Freezing

Something that all of us dread in exams is that moment when your mind goes blank, your head spins and you cannot remember anything. You have 'frozen'. If you are lucky it won't happen to you. If it does, how do you cope with it?

The first thing to do is to stop. Don't look at or think about the paper, but take those breaths again. Once you have done that, look at the basic facts. Write them down in note form and point by point. Then, ask yourself if they suggest any legal issues at all. If so, write them down in note form and point by point. See if any of the issues will convert into a diagram form. Often a non-verbal layout can jog your memory again.

All of this will probably trigger something into action. If it does not then, as calmly as possible, leave the question and come back to it later. If still nothing happens write down anything at all sensible which you have thought of for that question and move on. It is upsetting but you will be by no means the only person in the exam to have that problem and you may still have a good chance of getting through.

THREE

THE AIMS AND OBJECTIVES OF A CONVEYANCING TRANSACTION

Before you embark on any study of conveyancing it is essential to appreciate two basic things:

(a)   What conveyancing is.
(b)   If you are a solicitor acting in a conveyancing transaction, what it is that you are trying to do.

A conveyancing transaction is composed of various stages. Without some appreciation from the start of what those stages are and how they fit into the scheme of the whole transaction it will be very difficult for you to understand the purpose of what you are doing.

What is conveyancing?

First then, what is conveyancing? It is the transfer of estates and interests in land by document. An 'estate' or an 'interest' in land, is an abstract and intangible concept. Because the transfer is of the estate or interest and not of the thing itself (which is tangible), ownership of it must be supported by documentation. If the estates and interests are to be 'legal' rather than equitable then those documents must nearly always be in the form of deeds. If, like many students, you have just switched off because I have mentioned estates and interests and law and equity, and you keep saying that you 'never really got to grips with what those meant in land law anyway', then switch back on. The concepts may need some revision but esentially they are not difficult.

There are only two legal *estates*, the 'fee simple absolute in possession' (more commonly called the 'freehold') and the term of years absolute (more commonly called the 'leasehold').

There are only five legal *interests* which are set out in the Law of Property Act 1925, s. 1(2). The ones which you are most likely to come across are the legal easement and the legal mortgage.

Table 3.1

Legal	Equitable
2 legal estates 5 legal interests	Everything else

There are therefore only seven legal estates or interests (see table 3.1). If you identify someone as having an interest in land and it is not one of those seven things, it *must* be equitable (see table 3.1). The distinction between law and equity is one which you must not forget as how a right is classified will affect both the owner of the right and the buyer of the property for whom you may be acting.

The second and very basic distinction which you have to remind yourself about is the distinction between rights which amount to what a lay person would call 'ownership' of the property and those called 'third-party rights' which are basically rights of other people over land which they do not 'own'. Obviously in a conveyancing transaction both of these types of rights are going to be important.

If, for example, your clients are proposing to buy a semi-detached house, Cherry Trees, from Mr Sellers, it is going to be important to check that Mr Sellers actually owns the property and can sell your clients the right to own it.

It will also be important for your client to know if any third parties have rights over the property which might affect your clients' enjoyment of it. For example, does Mr Sellers's neighbour, Mr Nosey, have a legal easement to walk across the garden of Cherry Trees to get to the back lane? If he does then even though Mr Sellers can sell your clients the right to own and occupy the property it will be subject to Mr Nosey's right and your clients may not want to buy the property under those circumstances.

Not only will it be important to know what rights other third parties have over Cherry Trees but it is also important to know, as owner of Cherry Trees, what rights your clients would have as third parties over other property such as Mr Nosey's property. For example, suppose there is a shared driveway which is wide enough for one car and built partly on Mr Nosey's land and partly on Cherry Trees. If Mr Nosey turns nasty and tells your clients that they cannot use 'his half' of the driveway, do they have any right to insist on using it?

Objectives of a conveyancing transaction

Having decided what conveyancing is, it is then necessary to consider what a professional adviser is trying to do in a conveyancing transaction. The objectives will depend largely on who the adviser is acting for.

Acting for sellers

If your clients are selling all of the land which they own, your objective is simply to achieve a transfer of the whole of what your clients own in return for the purchase price. Also you will want to make sure that your clients are not either under-representing what they own, and so perhaps not getting the best price, nor representing that they own more than they do, and so leaving themselves liable to be sued for damages.

If your clients are selling only part of the land which they own then your objective is to sell all that the clients want to sell and no more. For example, as we shall see when looking at drafting the contract, it is important to ensure that the buyers do not, unbeknown to the sellers, acquire any easements by operation of law.

Acting for buyers

If you are acting for buyers of property your objective is to ensure that the property is successfully transferred to your clients in return for the price that they pay. You also want to make sure that the property is what the clients think they are buying. You are therefore going to have to check:

(a)   Whether the extent of the property which the sellers are selling is the same as the buyers think they are buying. Here you will be checking not only the physical extent of the land but also rights such as rights of way which are believed to pass with the property.

(b)   Whether the sellers own what they say they own and can transfer it.

(c)   Whether anyone else has any rights which could affect the buyers' enjoyment of the property. Are there any third-party rights affecting the property?

In many conveyancing transactions solicitors may find there is another party involved in addition to the buyers and sellers. Most buyers of a domestic property buy the property not simply with cash but with the aid of a mortgage, that is, they borrow money (usually from a bank or a building society) in return for which loan they grant a charge over the property. The charge will usually entitle the building society or bank ('the mortgagee') to repossess the property and sell it in order to get its money back if the buyers default on the agreed payments.

A solicitor may be asked to act for a mortgagee. It is also possible that the solicitor may be asked to act for the mortgagee and the buyer at the same time.

Acting for a mortgagee

The objectives in acting for the mortgagee are similar to the objectives when you are acting for the buyers. It is simply that the angle from which you are looking at the matter is different. The buyers want to buy a property which they can use and enjoy living in without any unacceptable interference from anyone else. The mortgagee wants the property which it is accepting as security for the loan to be resaleable in the event of the buyers defaulting on the mortgage. The solicitor for the mortgagee therefore needs to check:

(a)   Whether the extent of the property is the same as that over which the mortgagee thinks it is getting security.

(b)   Whether the sellers own what they say they own and can transfer it to the buyers so that the buyers can give a charge over it.

(c)   Whether anyone else has any rights over the property which could affect the resaleability of the property. Are there any third-party rights affecting the property?

In addition to checking the property, and the sellers' right to sell it, the mortgagee will also want to check that it will be able to get its money back from the property if the buyers default. Partly this will involve checking the condition and value of the property by the mortgagee instructing a surveyor to inspect the property. Partly it will involve checking out the buyers' creditworthiness by the mortgagee making enquiries about the buyers' status. Also the mortgagee will want to make sure that, if the buyer defaults on the repayments of the mortgage, the mortgagee will be the first person with a claim on the property. This is going to involve the mortgagee's solicitor in certain additional matters:

(a)   Checking whether the buyer is bankrupt or threatened with bankruptcy. If there are bankruptcy proceedings in progress then it would be unsafe for the mortgagee to lend money to that buyer as, whatever the value of the property, the mortgagee could not be sure of getting its money back.

(b)   Ensuring the protection of the mortgagee's charge. The mortgagee's solicitor must ensure that the mortgagee's charge is protected so that if the buyers create any other charges over the property the mortgagee's charge will take priority.

The stages of a conveyancing transaction

Now you have some basic idea of what it is that you are trying to do in the conveyancing transaction, you need to understand the different stages of the transaction and have some ideas of the position of the parties at each stage and what is going to happen during that stage.

There are five basic stages to a conveyancing transaction:

(a)   Pre-contract.
(b)   Contract.
(c)   Pre-completion.
(d)   Completion.
(e)   Post-completion.

The detail of each of the stages is discussed further in the rest of this book. The following is a general outline.

(a)   *Pre-contract*. At this stage there are no binding obligations on either party. They are still negotiating and either party could back out of the proposed transaction without incurring any liability to the other. This is where the buyers' solicitors will:

(i)   carry out various searches and enquiries;
(ii)   check that the draft contract gives the buyers what they think they are going to buy;
(iii) (under the usual modern practice) check to see that the sellers can actually sell what they are contracting to sell.

(b)   *Contract*. The stage where a legally binding contract is made between the parties. This stage involves knowing, amongst other things, exactly how to go about making that contract.

(c)   *Pre-completion*. This is the stage where, if the buyers' solicitors have not already checked the evidence of title (or proof of ownership) then they will check it, and ask questions about anything with which they are not happy and which does not conform with the draft contract. At this stage there are also special searches to be done and the drafting of documents to attend to.

(d)   *Completion*. This is when the sellers' solicitors hand over to the buyers' solicitors the deed which transfers the property to the buyers (and any other relevant deeds), and the buyers' solicitors hand over the balance of the purchase price.

(e)   *Post-Completion*. At this stage there may be notices to deliver and they buyers' title must be registered at the Land Registry. Also if there is a mortgage then matters relating to the protection of the mortgage must be dealt with.

It is easy to be confused about who is responsible for which matters during the course of the conveyancing transaction. Often in the study of conveyancing it will help you to imagine yourself in a real office and dealing with the practicalities of the situation. Table 3.2 is an attempt to lead you through the very basic and practical communications involved in a simple transaction which does not involve any mortgages.

Table 3.2

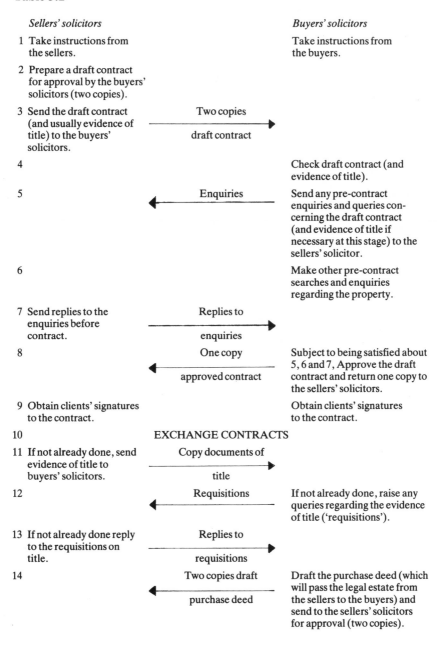

Sellers' solicitors		*Buyers' solicitors*
1 Take instructions from the sellers.		Take instructions from the buyers.
2 Prepare a draft contract for approval by the buyers' solicitors (two copies).		
3 Send the draft contract (and usually evidence of title) to the buyers' solicitors.	Two copies ⟶ draft contract	
4		Check draft contract (and evidence of title).
5	⟵ Enquiries	Send any pre-contract enquiries and queries concerning the draft contract (and evidence of title if necessary at this stage) to the sellers' solicitor.
6		Make other pre-contract searches and enquiries regarding the property.
7 Send replies to the enquiries before contract.	Replies to ⟶ enquiries	
8	One copy ⟵ approved contract	Subject to being satisfied about 5, 6 and 7, Approve the draft contract and return one copy to the sellers' solicitors.
9 Obtain clients' signatures to the contract.		Obtain clients' signatures to the contract.
10	EXCHANGE CONTRACTS	
11 If not already done, send evidence of title to buyers' solicitors.	Copy documents of ⟶ title	
12	Requisitions ⟵	If not already done, raise any queries regarding the evidence of title ('requisitions').
13 If not already done reply to the requisitions on title.	Replies to ⟶ requisitions	
14	Two copies draft ⟵ purchase deed	Draft the purchase deed (which will pass the legal estate from the sellers to the buyers) and send to the sellers' solicitors for approval (two copies).

Seller's solicitors		*Buyers' solicitors*
15 Check and approve the draft purchase deed; return one copy to buyers' solicitors approved.	One copy ⟶ approved purchase deed	
16	⟵ Engrossed purchase deed signed by buyers	Engross the purchase deed and obtain buyers' signatures to it. Then send to sellers' solicitors.
17 Obtain sellers' signatures to purchase deed.		
18		Undertake certain pre-completion searches.
19	COMPLETION	
20 Account to client for sale moneys.		Register the transaction at the Land Registry.

FOUR

THE TWO SYSTEMS OF CONVEYANCING

In order to understand conveyancing it is essential to realise that there are two different systems existing side by side in English property law.

Unregistered title

The traditional system is known as unregistered title where proof of ownership of property is by a bundle of title deeds through which can be traced the different owners of the land over the years. This system sometimes requires a large number of title deeds to be kept in respect of a single property. It also requires that, every time the property is sold, the title deeds must be checked to ensure that the sellers are the true owners and that the property was properly conveyed in the past and whether there are any third-party rights which can be discovered from the deeds.

Whilst evidence of the sellers' title and many third-party interests may be found in the title deeds, nevertheless the buyers will also be bound by some of the third-party rights which cannot be found in the deeds. How the buyers can discover the existence of these interests depends on the nature of the interest and in particular whether the interest is registrable as a land charge under the Land Charges Act 1972. There are three possibilities:

(a) *The interest is registrable as a land charge.* In this case the interest must be entered on the Land Charges Register at Plymouth. If it is registered then whether or not the buyers checked the register they will take the property subject to that interest (Law of Property Act 1925, s. 198). If the interest is registrable but the owner of the interest has failed, for whatever reason, to register it then, in most circumstances, buyers of the property will take the property free of the interest whether or not they actually knew about it. (An example of this type of interest is a second mortgage not protected by deposit of title deeds.)

(b) *The interest is a legal interest and is not registrable as a land charge.* In most circumstances buyers of the property will take the property subject to this interest whether or not they knew about it. (An example of this type of interest is a legal easement such as a right of way.)

(c) *The interest is equitable and is not registrable as a land charge.* In this case the buyers are expected to make reasonable enquiries and investigations (including checking the title deeds and inspecting the property) and will be bound by any interest which they would have discovered had they made such reasonable enquiries and inspections. The buyers are also expected to make further enquiries and follow up matters which seem unlikely or suspicious. The buyers will be bound by this type of interest if they have notice of the interest. Notice may be 'actual notice' in that the buyers know about the interest, it may be 'constructive notice' in that the buyers should have known about the interest had they made the necessary investigations, or it may be 'imputed notice' in that the buyers' agent (e.g., solicitor) had actual or constructive notice of the interest. (An example of this type of interest would be an equitable interest under a trust arising out of a contribution to the property.)

Of course, if the buyers ask the sellers about any third-party interests and the sellers tell the buyers there are none then the buyers may be able to take action against the sellers but so far as the property itself is concerned the buyers may still have to take the property subject to the interest of the third party.

Registered title

The system which is gradually superseding unregistered title is the system of registered title. When the property is first recorded on the register, the land registrar checks the details of the property. If the registrar is satisfied that the title is in order then the current legal owners will be entered on the register as the registered proprietors. Once the title is registered the buyers need not concern themselves with whether the previous owners had the right to sell the land but simply check whether the sellers are the registered proprietors of the property. (The land registrar, having checked the title, will in effect guarantee the title. If the title should be incorrect then in most cases compensation will be available.) Once the title is registered the proof of ownership ceases to be the title deeds and becomes the register itself.

So far as third-party rights are concerned, when the property is first registered, the title deeds will be checked to see whether there is any evidence of these and if so they will also be recorded on the register. One of the major shortcomings of the system of registration of title is that not all third-party rights affecting the land will be found on the register. But at least anything which was discoverable from inspecting the deeds should appear there and the successive buyers of the property are relieved of the task of sifting through the documents looking for possible defects or third-party rights.

What interests will be registered?

Whenever a title to a property is registered the details of the property are recorded on a separate register and each title is allotted a title number by which the property can be referred to. It is necessary to know which estates or interests in property will be given their own separate title and which will appear as third-party rights on a title number relating to a more important interest. There are various rights which are capable of substantive registration (i.e., with their own title) but in practice it is very uncommon to encounter any other than the two legal estates: the fee simple absolute in possession and the term of years absolute. Even some terms of years absolute (leases) cannot be registered with their own title:

(a)   A lease with 21 years or less left to run cannot be registered as an estate.

(b)   A mortgage in the form of a lease in which there is a provision that the lease will end when the mortgage money is repaid (a provision for cesser on redemption) cannot be registered as an estate.

Usually other interests in land will appear in the register relating to the legal estate which they affect.

How does the transition from unregistered to registered title take place?

Since 1925 different areas of England and Wales have gradually been made compulsory registration areas. Once a compulsory registration order is in force for a particular area then the title to the property must be registered when there is next:

(a)   A conveyance on sale of freehold land (a deed of gift or an assent of the property by executors to a beneficiary would not give rise to the need for first registration).

(b)   The grant of a lease for a term of more than 21 years.

(c)   The sale of an existing lease with more than 21 years left to run.

Thus in order to discover when title should go through the process of first registration you should be asking yourself:

(a)   Is/was there a compulsory registration order in force? (If you are wondering whether a transaction in the past should have resulted in the title being registered this can be discovered, amongst other places by a search of the public index map at the Land Registry which we will look at in chapter 7. If the problem is a current one this is quite easily answered as from December 1990 the whole of England and Wales is a compulsory registration area.)

(b)   Has one of the transactions triggering the requirement for first registration taken place?

What will happen if you fail to register the title after a relevant transaction?

If the title to property is unregistered and not due for first registration then the legal estate to the property will pass on completion when the deed conveying the legal estate is delivered (see table 4.1).

Table 4.1

| | Before the transaction | | After completion | |
Example: A gives the	Legal	Equitable	Legal	Equitable
fee simple in				
The Manor to	A	A	B	B
B.				

If the title to the property is already registered then *any* transaction involving the legal estate requires to be registered as until registration takes place the deed (which in unregistered title is effective to convey the legal estate) will only pass to the buyer an equitable interest. The legal estate does not pass until registration (see table 4.2).

Table 4.2

| | Before the transaction | | After completion | | After registration | |
	Legal	Equitable	Legal	Equitable	Legal	Equitable
Example: A gives						
or sells the fee simple	A	A	A	B	B	B
in The Manor to B.						

If the title to the property is unregistered but due for first registration then the legal estate will pass on completion *but*, if an application for first registration is not made within two months of completion of the transaction then the legal estate will automatically revert to the seller leaving the buyer with only the equitable interest in the property (Land Registration Act 1925, s. 123; see table 4.3).

Table 4.3

| | Before the transaction | | After completion | | If no application is made for first registration within two months | |
	Legal	Equitable	Legal	Equitable	Legal	Equitable
Example: A sells the						
fee simple in The	A	A	B	B	A	B
Manor to B.						

If the two-month time-limit for first registration has been missed then it is possible to make a late application. The registrar may be prepared to overlook the fact of the legal estate having reverted to the seller and nevertheless register the buyers as the proprietors. This would have the effect of curing the title of the technical defect.

Classes of title

When application is made for registration, the registrar will give the property a class of title depending on the documents which have been provided to the registry. The class really reflects the quality of the title. As was mentioned earlier, once a title is registered, the registrar will effectively guarantee that title, although if there is a mistake in the title it is possible for the mistake to be rectified in certain circumstances. Where there has been a mistake on the part of the land Registry, then whether or not the mistake is rectified the person who loses out as a result of the mistake will usually be able to claim compensation. The class of title reflects the quality of the title in the extent of the 'guarantee' which the Land Registry offers. There are three possible classes of freehold title and four of leasehold title.

(a)   Absolute (the best form of title; may be freehold or leasehold).
(b)   Possessory (freehold or leasehold).
(c)   Qualified (freehold or leasehold).
(d)   Good leasehold.

Absolute title   If the title is registered with absolute title then this tells you that the registered proprietor holds the legal estate in the property subject to:

(a)   Entries on the register (any enforceable third-party rights which the registrar noted on the register at the time of registration).
(b)   Overriding interests (all registered titles are subject to a group of third-party interests known as overriding interests (Land Registration Act 1925, s. 70(1)) which do not appear on the register).

If the registered proprietor holds the estate on trust then it is held subject to any minor interests (which neither appear on the register nor fall within the category of overriding interests) of which the trustee has notice.

The registered proprietor of a leasehold estate holds it subject to the matters contained in or implied into the lease.

Possessory title   Possessory title is given where the people who wish to be registered as the proprietors of the property cannot offer the usual documentary proof of the title, for example, where the title deeds to the property have been lost or where the applicants claim to have acquired their title through possessing the property adverse to the interests of the true owners for at least the last 12 years. The applicants will be relying on possession of the property by them (and/or their predecessors) rather than evidence of title deeds.

The proprietor of an estate registered with possessory title holds it subject to the same matters as affect an absolute title but also:

(c)   Any adverse interest existing at the date of first registration.

Qualified title   The registered proprietor of an estate registered with qualified title holds it subject to the same matters as affect an estate with absolute title but also subject to some specific defects. The most common example is where there has been a breach of trust. For example, trustees who sell property to themselves or one of themselves will, unless given authority to do so, be in breach of trust. As a result of such a breach of trust the beneficiaries could require the sale to be set aside and the purchasing trustees could lose the legal estate. If the registrar believes this may be possible then the estate would be registered with qualified title which would indicate that the Land Registry were satisfied with the title but would offer no guarantee in respect of that particular point.

Good leasehold title   When one is buying a lease there are in theory two titles which need to be checked:

(a)   The buyers need to see that the sellers own the lease and that the lease itself is in order. This is done by checking the lease itself and checking the documents relating to the sales of that lease over either the whole life of the lease or at least the last 15 years of its life.

(b)   Also the buyers need to know that the person who granted the lease had the right to grant it and that the buyers are not going to lose the lease because the landlord had no right to grant the lease in the first place. Checking this involves checking the landlord's freehold title.

If, on the registration of a leasehold title the Land Registry is able to check the landlord's title either:

(a)   because it is already registered, or
(b)   because the tenant provided documentary evidence of it when applying for registration,

then, providing the Land Registry is satisfied with the title, the Land Registry will grant absolute title. If the Registry has been given no opportunity to check the landlord's title then they will grant a *good leasehold title*.

Registration with a certain class of title is not a once-and-for-all matter. The registrar may upgrade a title if satisfied that the registered proprietors have an acceptable title. For example a good leasehold title could be upgraded by producing the freehold title to the registry at some later stage, or upon the freehold itself being registered with absolute title.

Conversely if some defect in title is 'created' after the title is first registered then the title could be changed from absolute title to a lesser one. For example, if a trustee purported to buy trust property (which had previously been registered with absolute title) without the necessary authority then the title would be changed from absolute to qualified.

The importance of the class of title is that it will tell you what matters your client will buy the property subject to.

(a)   If the title you are offered is absolute then you must remember that matters, additional to the interests you can see on the register, the proprietor takes subject to (e.g., overriding interests). These will give you a clue to what matters you will be making enquiries about elsewhere.

(b)   If the title you are offered is anything other than absolute then you must be aware of the risk which has been identified. If, for example, the sellers are offering qualified title under the trust situation looked at above then your buyer clients must be made aware of the risk that they could lose the title to the beneficiaries of the trust. Even if your buyers are prepared to take that very considerable risk, if the buyers are buying with the aid of a mortgage, the mortgagee may not be prepared to take that risk.

Form of the register

Each title that is registered is given a separate register. If the buyers are buying without the aid of a mortgage then they will be given a copy of the entries on the register in the form of a *land certificate* which must be produced to the Land Registry when there is a transaction involving that property. If the buyers buy with the aid of a mortgage then the registered proprietors will not be given a land certificate but the mortgagee will be given a copy of the entries on the register in the form of a *charge certificate*. This must be returned to the land registry when the mortgage is discharged. If there is more than one mortgage then a charge certificate is issued to each mortgagee. If the sellers or anyone else want an up-to-date copy of the entries on the register then *office copies* of the entries on the register and the plan filed with that register can be obtained from the land registry on payment of a fee.

The register itself comprises three parts, all of which need to be checked by the intending buyer:

(a)   *The property register.* This contains a description of the land in words and by reference to a plan. It also states whether the estate is freehold or leasehold and if it is leasehold it will give brief details of the lease. There will also be mention of any rights which benefit the property which could be ascertained from the deeds.

(b)   *The proprietorship register.* This section of the register states the class of title and contains the name and address of the registered proprietor(s). There may also be indications of third-party interests on this section of the register such as a restriction or a caution.

(c)   *The charges register.* This section contains details of rights of third parties over the land. These rights include easements enjoyed by someone else over the land, covenants which will bind the registered proprietor(s), mortgages and leases affecting the property.

Third-party interests

Third-party interests relating to a registered title are of four possible types: interests registered with a separate title, registered charges, overriding interests and minor interests.

Interests registered with a separate title   Interests registered with a separate title include leases which are capable of separate registration. A note of these should appear on the freehold register.

Registered charges   Registered charges should appear in the charges section of the register. If not protected in this way the charge will be equitable and not legal and will not be binding on a purchaser of the property unless protected as a 'minor interest' (see below).

Overriding interests   Overriding interests are interests which do not appear on the register and yet bind the buyers of the property whether or not the buyers knew about them. Overriding interests can be either legal or equitable interests and are perhaps the major problem for conveyancers when dealing with registered title. The buyers' solicitor must make enquiries and investigations, beyond simply looking at the register, in order to find out whether any of these interests affect the property.

The list of overriding interests is to be found in the Land Registration Act 1925, s. 70(1). The most commonly encountered are:

(a)   Legal easements and profits (s. 70(1)(a)). Some easements will appear on the register but you have to remember that the register can include only those matters which are brought to the registrar's attention on application for registration. Certain easements will pass with a deed of transfer or conveyance by virtue of implied grant such as in *Wheeldon* v *Burrows* (1879) 12 ChD 31. Because these easements are implied they will not be stated expressly in the deed. Nevertheless they exist and they will bind a purchaser of the land over which they are exercised even though they do not actually appear on the register.

(b)   Rights acquired or in course of acquisition under the Limitation Act 1980 (Land Registration Act 1925, s. 70(1)(f)). This means that buyers will be bound by the rights of anyone who can prove to be in adverse possession of the property. Of course if the period of possession is less than 12 years then the buyers may bring proceedings to regain possession of the property. However, if the period is already over 12 years (or if the period is less than 12 years but the buyers take no action before the trespasser has been in possession for 12 years), then the right may be lost. If the right is lost the buyers' registered title will be worth very little to them as of course even absolute title is expressed to be subject to any overriding interests.

(c)   The rights of any person in actual occupation or in receipt of rents and profits (s. 70(1)(g)). This is perhaps the most commonly encountered problem for the buyers of property and the effect is to ensure that buyers should make every effort to find out *who* is in occupation of the property and ask those people directly what interest, if any, they have in the property. If an occupier who is asked fails to disclose his or her interest then that occupier's rights will cease to bind the buyers. There are some important points to remember about this very common and often examined area:

(i)   The person claiming an overriding interest must have rights relating to the land *coupled* with either actual occupation or receipt of rents and profits. Occupation on its own without any rights in the property does not amount to an overriding interest.

(ii)   'Actual occupation' must be given it ordinary meaning (*Williams & Glyn's Bank Ltd* v *Boland* [1981] AC 487). Presumably therefore what is required for actual occupation may differ depending on the type and physical state of the property. A different level of occupation will be appropriate to a garden than to a house; or to a modernised property than to a ruined shell of a house due for renovation.

(iii)   If the owner of an interest is able to establish actual occupation or receipt of rents and profits then the extent of the enquiries made by the buyers (unless actually made of the person in actual occupation) is irrelevant. The buyers will not be protected from the overriding interest simply because they made extensive enquiries and acted in good faith. The enquiries may give the buyers a right to bring action against the sellers but not to take free of the interest.

(iv)   Some rights are, by statute, specifically excluded from being capable of being overriding interests and therefore if they are capable of being protected at all they must appear on the register. Most notable of these interests which cannot be protected by occupation are the interests of a beneficiary under a strict settlement and a spouse's statutory right of occupation under the Matrimonial Homes Act 1983.

(d)   Local land charges (s. 70(1)(i)). Charges appearing on local land charges registers will be binding on the buyers whether they know about the charge or not. It is therefore vital in registered title as well as unregistered title for the buyers to search the local land charges register.

(e)   Leases granted for a term of 21 years or less (s. 70(1)(k)). These shorter leases are, as we have seen, not registrable in their own right but are binding on the buyers regardless of whether any note of them appears on the register of the landlord's title.

Minor interests   Interests which are not registrable in their own right, which do not appear as a registered charge on the charges register and which do not amount to overriding interests under the Land Registration Act 1925, s. 70(1), must amount to minor interests. Minor interests will not bind buyers of the property unless protected by a note on the register. There are four forms of note which may be used to protect minor interests:

(a)   *Notice in the charges register.* The type of interests protected in this way include restrictive covenants, the interests of a buyer under a contract for sale, and spouses' statutory rights of occupation. With the exception of a spouse's right of occupation, the land certificate must be deposited at the Land Registry before a notice may be entered (i.e., usually this method requires the cooperation of the registered proprietor). The effect of this type of entry is that a buyer of the registered title takes subject to the interest so far as it is valid.

An example of this type of entry is: '14 January 1986. A conveyance of this title dated 2 April 1984 and made between X(1) and Y(2) contains restrictive covenants. A copy of these covenants is set out in the schedule annexed'.

(b)   *Caution recorded in the proprietorship register.* The type of interest protected in this way includes the interests of a buyer under a contract for sale or an agreement for a lease. Unlike the procedure for registering a notice the land certificate is not required to be deposited at the Land Registry. The effect of a caution is that the cautioner will be given notice before any dealing in the title is registered, and so the cautioner will be given an opportunity to explain what interest the cautioner has in the property before the buyer is registered as proprietor.

An example of this type of entry is: 'Caution dated 4 December 1990 registered on 14 December 1990 in favour of MN'.

(c)   *Restriction in the proprietorship register.* This is commonly used to protect interests arising under a trust. The restriction tells the buyer the manner in which a dealing must be undertaken and, providing the buyer complies with the restriction, the buyer will take free of any interests under the trust.

An example of this type of entry is: 'No disposition by a sole proprietor of the land (not being a trust corporation) under which capital money arises is to be registered except under an order of the registrar or of the court'. This looks confusing but the bottom line is that there is a form of trust and that any sale must not only be by all the registered proprietors but also there must be at least two people selling the property for the buyer to take the property free of any trust interests. In other words, if the registered proprietor is the last surviving trustee and is not a trust company then that registered proprietor must appoint another trustee to act with him or her to receive the sale moneys.

(d)   *Inhibition in the proprietorship register.* This type of note is usually placed on the register as a result of a court order. The effect will be for the time being to place a complete prohibition on dealing with the property.

Common examination problem areas

1   When checking copies of the register in registered title there are certain key things to remember:

(a)   Check that the physical description and plan accord with what you understand the property to be. Also check that the rights which you expect the property to have the benefit of appear on the property register.

(b)   Check the class of title. If it is anything less than absolute title then there are risks involved which should be explained to your client.

(c)   Check that the registered proprietor is who you think it should be. If the registered proprietor is an unexpected person (alone or in conjunction with the expected person) then, although there is likely to be a simple explanation, it is going to need explaining and sorting out.

(d)   Check whether there are any third-party rights mentioned on the register and whether they are acceptable or can be removed.

(e)   Remember that the register does not show the full extent of all third-party rights. There is that very wide-ranging category of overriding interests which will not appear on the register but will bind anyone who buys the property.

2 Protection of interests under a trust. It is very common for examination questions to suggest that there may be a resulting or constructive trust in respect of the property, for example, where the seller's mother is living in the property and contributed to the initial purchase price even though the property was ultimately registered in the seller's name alone. The question of the interest under the trust for sale is in law quite straightforward but you should be aware of the following points:

(a)   If the registrar was aware of the trust he would have entered a restriction on the proprietorship register. (If he was not told about the mother's contribution and the trust then no restriction would appear.) If a restriction appears it will tell the buyers the procedure which must be followed to ensure that the buyers take the property free of the mother's interest.

(b)   Even if there were no restriction on the register the buyers could be bound by the interest if the mother were in actual occupation of the property as her interest would be an overriding interest under the Land Registration Act 1925, s. 70(1)(g).

(c)   An equitable interest under a trust for sale is capable of being an overriding interest by virtue of the mother being in actual occupation (*Williams & Glyn's Bank Ltd* v *Boland* [1981] AC 487) but if overreaching takes place the interest will cease to be overriding and binding on the buyers but will become instead an interest in the proceeds of sale (*City of London Building Society* v *Flegg* [1988] AC 54).

(d)   Overreaching will operate if the buyers pay the purchase money to all the trustees (registered proprietors) and there are at least two of them (or if there is only one then it is a trust corporation). Then the interest of the seller's mother under that trust can safely be ignored as it is overreached and converted into an interest in the proceeds of sale of the property. The buyers will not be bound by the interest of the mother and will take the property free of them (see table 4.4).

Table 4.4

Legal	Equitable	Legal	Equitable
Seller	Seller and mother	Seller and another	Seller and mother
Sale to	(Mother's interest protected under Land Registration Act 1925, s. 70(1)(g))	Sale to	(Mother's interest overreached and turned into an interest in proceeds of sale)
Buyers	Buyers and mother	Buyers	Buyers

A note of warning should also be sounded here so that you do not start your studies with any misconceptions. *Not all interests can be overreached.* Overreaching is found most commonly in relation to interests under trusts. Check first whether the interest is capable of being overreached.

3   Students often have problems with confusing the principles of registered and unregistered title. You must make sure that you keep the two systems separate. It is often helpful to make sure that you take a note of the different rules on two separate sheets of paper and even in different coloured ink just to make sure that you do not let the two systems merge or slip together in your mind.

A particular area which causes problems is the confusion of the idea of notice and overriding interests protected by actual occupation. The problem arises out of a superficial similarity of the rules. Let us take for example again the interest of a beneficiary under a trust for sale. It is true that in both registered and unregistered title interest is capable of being overreached if the sale moneys are paid to all the trustees and there are at least two of them (or if only one that one is a trust corporation). If overreaching takes place then whether the buyers had notice of the interest or whether the owner of the interest was in actual occupation is irrelevant. If overreaching does not take place any apparent similarity is deceptive and the following points should be borne in mind:

(a)   In unregistered title the buyers will be bound by the equitable interest if they had notice of the interest. Notice will be implied if, amongst other things, there is any *evidence* of the interest or the existence of the owner of the interest to be found on inspecting the property.

In registered title, whether there is evidence is irrelevant. The question is whether the owner of the interest was in actual occupation *not* whether the buyer could reasonably have discovered the occupation.

(b)   The rule in registered title in the Land Registration Act 1925, s. 70(1)(g), is much wider than the doctrine of notice in that it protects those in receipt of rents and profits as well as those in actual occupation. There is no parallel rule in unregistered title in the doctrine of notice.

FIVE

TAKING INSTRUCTIONS

This stage of a conveyancing transaction is one which is regarded as extremely straightforward by practitioners. Once you have been in practice, some parts of this section would seem so obvious as to not be worthy of being included in an examination. Yet traditionally it causes problems for students regardless of whether or not they have experience of working in the conveyancing department of a solicitor's office. Apart from the heavily examined professional practice points in this area (which have their own peculiar pitfalls) the main problems seem to arise because:

(a)   This area usually requires students to state the obvious, e.g., when taking instructions you must take a note of your client's name and address. At this you are probably groaning and looking exasperated. To some extent I agree with you, it is a ridiculously obvious point, but on the other hand, you will look very silly indeed if, having taken detailed and otherwise competent instructions from your client about the sale of a property, you do not actually know the client's name. You will have to wait until the client gets in touch with you to find out why you have not written as promised before you can put the matter right.

(b)   Most examination questions in this area require you to have learned the subject area and to apply it to the particular facts of the question. In other words students who fail to appreciate the relevance of a factual scenario may know the subject-matter very well but not make best use of it.

What matters you should take instructions on depends on:

(a)   who you are acting for, and more particularly
(b)   what you are told in the factual situation of the question.

You then need to consider:

(a)   What information do you need from your clients?
(b)   On what matters do your clients need advice?
(c)   What arrangements or enquiries do you need to undertake after the initial interview?

Although the particular requirements of each case may be different there will be broadly similar matters to be dealt with in many conveyancing transactions. Set out below is a useful checklist of matters which you can expand upon in an examination question.

Acting for the sellers

Information required

(a) Names and addresses:

(i)   of your clients,
(ii)   the buyers and their solicitors,
(iii) the estate agents.

(b) Details of the property:

(i)   the address,
(ii)   whether it is freehold or leasehold,
(iii) if it is a sale of part of your clients' property, whether the estate agent has prepared an accurate plan.

(c) Is the property subject to a mortgage? If so the deeds or charge certificate will be with the mortgagee and you will need:

(i)   details of the account number so that the deeds or charge certificate may be obtained,
(ii)   to know the approximate amount outstanding on the mortgage so that you can advise on financial arrangements in respect of the transaction,
(iii) to establish whether there is any second or third mortgage and if so you will need similar details.

(d) Price:

(i)   What price is being asked, or has been offered for the property?
(ii)   Has anyone paid a preliminary deposit and if so how much and to whom?
(iii) Are any chattels to be included in the sale and is any additional price being paid for them? And are any fixtures to be removed from the property? (It would seem sensible at this stage to ask your client to complete a standard fixtures and fittings form which schedules the fixtures and fittings in the property.)

(e) Related transactions and timing:

(i)   Have your clients and the buyers discussed any proposed completion date(s) or alternatively are there any preferred dates?

(ii)   Are your clients also buying another property in which case do the sale and the purchase have to be synchronised?

Advice to your client

(a)   *Financial arrangements.* In most domestic conveyancing transactions your clients will be both sellers and buyers. They will be selling one house and buying another. In this situation the solicitors must be able to advise the clients on the overall financial position over the two transactions. More detailed discussion of examination questions in this area is to be found at the end of this chapter and a more detailed examination of the issues is included below in 'acting for the buyer' but broadly speaking you must consider two things:

(i)   If your clients are also buying a property, the short-term problem of financing a deposit. If your clients are buying a more expensive property than the one they are selling then they will receive less deposit on their sale than they have to pay out on their purchase.

(ii)   The overall financial effect of the clients' related transactions, i.e., on completion will there be enough money left to pay everything that needs to be paid? For example, can all the mortgages be repaid with the proceeds of sale?

(b)   *Estimate of costs.* Obviously when advising your client on the financial aspects of the transaction, advice should also be given on the likely amount of your fees and disbursements.

(c)   *Capital gains tax (CGT) liability.* In most domestic conveyancing transactions CGT liability will not be a problem as a gain made on the disposal of a dwelling-house and grounds up to half a hectare will be exempt providing it was occupied as your clients' only or main residence throughout their period of ownership. Certain periods of absence can be ignored but mention of any period away from the property should put you on warning to consider the reason for the absence, the length of time involved and whether the exemption will therefore be unavailable or only available in part. Similarly if it is mentioned that the property has been used for business purposes this may give rise to loss of the exemption in respect of at least part of the gain.

(d)   *Sale of part of the sellers' property.* If your clients are selling only part of their property there are more specific matters which must be considered with them. It is very important that you have an accurate plan of the property which is being sold and the property which your clients are retaining. You should also be considering with your clients, and advising them on, easements and covenants.

If the concepts of easements and covenants are simply a hazy memory to you then you should check before proceeding further with your study that you remember the basic common law and statutory principles from land law (for example the rule in *Wheeldon* v *Burrows* (1879) 12 ChD 31 and the Law of Property Act 1925, s. 62). If the contract is using the Standard Conditions this will have the effect of excluding the buyers' right to light or air over the land retained by the sellers but also of entitling both buyers and sellers to have included in the purchase deed such easements as would have passed by operation of law to a buyer.

Example. S owns a large house and barn shown on the plan below. S is selling the house (plot A) and keeping the barn (plot B). Throughout S's ownership he has used the track shown T to get from the barn to Low Lane and he has used the path shown P to get from the house to High Lane (see figure 5.1).

Under the open contract rule B (the buyer of plot A) would be likely to obtain an implied grant of a right to use the path but S as the owner of the retained plot B could not expect to receive any similar right by implication to use the track.

Using the Standard Conditions not only could B expect to obtain a right to use the path but S could expect to be entitled to a right to use the track.

Figure 5.1

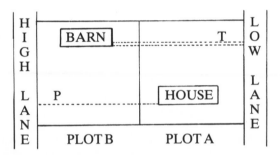

The question of what easements the sellers wish to reserve and what easements they wish to grant to the buyers should be discussed fully with your clients and appropriate provisions included in the contract. It is certainly arguable that neither the Standard Conditions and certainly not the open contract position should be relied upon but rather that specific provision should be made in the contract detailing exactly what rights the buyers will receive over the sellers' retained land and what rights the sellers will keep over the land sold to the buyers.

The Standard Conditions contain no provisions with regard to new covenants to be imposed on the sale of part of the land. This is a matter for you to advise your clients on and include appropriate specific provisions in the contract. You should remember here to consider the enforceability of covenants against later buyers who will not themselves have been a party to the covenants. Broadly, in freeehold land, negative covenants require to be protected by registration (class D(ii) in unregistered title; on the charges register in registered title), positive covenants can only usually be enforced either on the equitable basis (for example, that a person who takes the benefit of a right of way cannot then claim not to be bound by a covenant to make a contribution towards the upkeep of the roadway) or alternatively by a chain of indemnity covenants.

Example. X owns plots F and G and sells plot F to B1. On that sale B1 gives a covenant to keep a boundary fence in good repair. Whilst B1 continues to own plot F, X can enforce the covenant directly against B1, but when B1 sells to B2, X cannot enforce the covenant directly against B2. The only way in which the covenant may be enforced against the current occupier is indirectly through a chain of indemnity covenants (see figure 5.2).

Figure 5.2

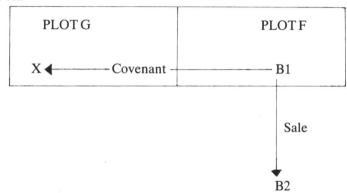

So if in the above example B1 covenanted 'for himself and his successors in title' and when he sold to B2, B2 covenanted to 'observe and perform' the covenant, then X cannot sue B2 but he can sue B1 who will then be able to sue B2.

The desired effect of 'persuading' B2 to perform the original covenant can often be achieved in this way. However, the system will break down if either someone in the chain forgets to take an indemnity covenant, or someone in the chain either cannot be found or, when found, is not worth suing. Your clients must be fully advised of the potential problems.

Arrangements and enquiries after the initial interview

(a)   Write to your clients. Following the initial interview you should write to your clients confirming their instructions and what has been discussed at the interview.

(b)   *Write to the buyers' solicitors.* If your clients have found buyers for the property a letter should be written to the buyers' solicitors confirming the position and advising them that you will forward a draft contract for approval in due course. You should also, at this stage, advise the buyers' solicitor whether or not you are proposing to adopt the National Protocol. (The National Protocol is looked at in chapter 18.)

(c)   *Obtaining the deeds.* If your clients have no mortgage then they may have left the deeds or land certificate at your office. Alternatively the deeds or land certificate may be with a bank for safe keeping in which case you should have obtained your clients' written authority to release the documents to you and this should now be sent to the bank together with a letter requesting the documents.

If, however, your clients have a mortgage then the deeds or charge certificate will be with the mortgagee and you must write to the mortgagee advising that you are acting in a proposed sale of the property and asking if the mortgagee is prepared to release the documents to you. Most institutional mortgagees such as banks and building societies will be prepared to release the deeds or charge certificate to a solicitor if the solicitor gives an undertaking to hold them to the mortgagee's order and either to redeem the mortgage or return the documents. Undertakings are a vital aspect of any conveyancing transaction and a heavily examined area of professional conduct which is discussed further below.

(d)   *Acting for a sole owner.* Sometimes you will be asked to act for a client who is the sole legal owner of property. If so then a question which should routinely be asked is whether anyone else lives in the property and has contributed anything towards its purchase or upkeep. If someone has done so then he or she may have an equitable interest in the property, so that the situation is that your client S holds the legal estate as trustee for S and someone else (say A) in equity (see table 5.1).

Table 5.1

Legal	*Equitable*
S (as trustee	S and A for S and A in equity)

If this is the case, appointing a second trustee to act with S to receive the purchase moneys will overreach the interest of A and turn it into an interest in the money (proceeds of sale) rather than the land and thereby allow the buyers to take the property free of A's interest.

More problematic than the equitable interest under a trust is where the sole owner of the property is married and encountering matrimonial difficulties. Your client's spouse, simply by virtue of being married to your client, will be entitled to a statutory right of occupation under the Matrimonial Homes Act 1983. To be effective, this right must be registered (as a class F land charge in unregistered title; as a notice on the land register in registered title). The Matrimonial Homes Act 1983, s. 4, will, if your client agrees to sell with vacant possession, imply a term into the contract for sale that your client will secure the release of any charge under the Act. If you suspect any such problems it may be wise to undertake a search against your own client at this stage and certainly the matter should be discussed fully with those concerned (and if necessary the other spouse take independent advice) rather than wait until later when your client is committed to a contract which he or she may then have difficulty in fulfilling.

(e)   *Searching for other mortgagees.* Sometimes your clients may seem unsure about what financial charges there are on the property. Often a central heating system, new kitchen or double glazing has been paid for with a loan from a finance company about which the clients have only the haziest idea. It may be sensible to undertake a search against your own clients at this stage so that all financial charges can be identified and quantified. The buyers will almost certainly be requiring them all to be repaid on or before completion and it is important that you know the extent of the liabilities now before your clients are committed to a contract.

Acting for the buyers

Information required

Much of the same information is required as when acting for the seller.

(a)   Names and addresses:

(i)   of your clients,
(ii)   of the sellers and their solicitors,
(iii)   of the estate agents.

(b)   Particulars of the property:

(i)   the address,
(ii)   whether it is freehold or leasehold,
(iii)   whether there is a plan of the property.

(c)   Price:

(i)   What price is being asked, or has been offered, for the property?
(ii)   Has anyone paid a preliminary deposit and if so how much and to whom?
(iii)   Are any chattels to be included in the sale and is any additional price being paid for them? Are any fixtures to be removed from the property?

(d)   Related transactions and timing:

(i)   Have your clients and the sellers discussed any proposed completion date(s) or alternatively are there any preferred dates?
(ii)   Are your clients also selling another property in which case do the sale and the purchase have to be synchronised?

(e)   Mortgages. Is a mortgage being obtained and if so from whom and for what amount?

Advice to the buyers

(a)   *Mortgages*. Mortgages are looked at in more detail in chapter 15. If your clients are obtaining a mortgage you may be asked to advise on the nature of different types of mortgage (e.g., an ordinary repayment mortgage as compared with an endowment mortgage). You should also be in a position to offer advice on income tax relief in respect of interest on the mortgage repayments.

(b)   *Financial   arrangements*.   In   most   domestic   conveyancing transactions your clients will be both buying and selling a house. It is therefore important to consider the financial situation of both the sale and the purchase together. The short-term problem of the deposit and the longer-term question of whether your clients will have enough to pay all the outgoings should be considered separately as they have different solutions.

(i)   *The short-term problem of financing a deposit*. In most contracts a deposit of 10 per cent of the total purchase price is payable on exchange of contracts. At this stage, your clients will not yet be entitled to the full amount of the sale proceeds of their own property nor will they be able to use any of a mortgage advance which may be being obtained on the new property. If your clients are buying a more expensive property than the one they are selling then they will receive less deposit on their sale than they have to pay out on their purchase. There are various possible solutions to this.

(1)   The sellers of the property which your clients are buying may agree to your clients paying a reduced deposit (usually subject to the contract providing that if completion does not take place on the contractual completion date the balance of the 10 per cent deposit becomes immediately payable).

(2)   The sellers of the property your clients are buying may agree to a reduced deposit being paid providing your clients obtain a deposit guarantee. In simple terms the buyers pay a premium whereupon the guarantor insurance company agrees to pay the full deposit if your clients should default. The guarantor will of course then attempt to recover the money from your clients but the sellers are sure of getting their money.

(3)   Your clients may be able to fund the shortfall from their own savings.

(4)   A bank may be persuaded to provide bridging finance for the period between exchange and completion, though the major disadvantages of this solution are the cost of arranging the loan and the cost of the interest payments.

(ii)   *The overall effect of the clients' related transactions*. On completion will there be enough money left to pay everything that needs to be paid?

Dealing with this part of the transaction involves nothing more complicated than listing the total expected receipts on both transactions (e.g., sale price of the property being sold and the mortgage advance on the property being bought) and also listing all the expected outgoings (including purchase price of the property being bought, amount required to redeem the mortgage(s) on the property being sold, your charges and any disbursements). If, having added up everything, there is not going to be enough money to cover the transaction then your clients must be advised and a solution found. Possible solutions may be:

(1)   Obtaining a larger mortgage advance.
(2)   Obtaining a second mortgage on the new property.
(3)   Your clients providing some savings to balance the figures.
(4)   Asking the sellers if they are prepared to reduce the purchase price.

Ultimately if a solution cannot be found then the bottom line is that your clients cannot afford to proceed with the transaction.

(c)   *Estimate of costs.* Obviously when advising your clients on the financial aspects of the transaction, advice should also be given on the likely amount of your fees and disbursements.

(d)   *The need for a survey.* If your clients are obtaining a mortgage then the building society or bank will usually arrange a survey of the property. The shortcomings of this survey should be explained to the clients. It may not necessarily be relied upon in all circumstances and in any event it will not be a full structural survey. It is a matter for your clients whether or not they wish to instruct a surveyor to carry out a further survey but in any event if the mortgagee's survey suggests anything at all untoward then the advice to your clients should be to investigate the matter further.

(e)   *Acting for more than one buyer.* If the property is being bought by two or more people then advice should be given on how the property is to be held. Even if all of them are to be legal owners (i.e., the legal estate is conveyed or transferred into their names) nevertheless there is the matter of equitable ownership to consider. In equity they may either hold as joint tenants or tenants in common. A solicitor acting for the buyers has a duty to advise them on the nature of a joint tenancy (i.e., that on the death of any one of them, the deceased's 'share' will pass automatically to the survivor(s) of them) and of a tenancy in common (that on the death of any one of them, the deceased's share will pass according to his or her will, or if none, the rules of intestacy). The solicitor also has a duty to advise them on which might be appropriate to their particular circumstances, e.g., if your clients tell you they have both been married before and have children by their earlier marriages whom they would like ultimately to benefit from the property, then a joint tenancy would clearly not be appropriate.

You should also consider, if they wish to hold as tenants in common, preparing a declaration of trust between them concerning the size of their relative interests. If A and B contribute £25,000 and £75,000 respectively they may wish their interests in the property to reflect that contribution. It is certainly desirable to have a declaration in case any dispute should later arise between the parties.

Arrangements and enquiries after the initial interview

(a) *Write to your clients*. Following the initial interview you should write to your clients confirming their instructions and what has been discussed at the interview.

(b) *Write to the sellers' solicitor*. At this stage a simple letter of introduction advising the sellers' solicitors that you are instructed and whether or not you are proposing to adopt the National Protocol is sufficient until the draft contract is received from them.

(c) *Pre-contract searches and enquiries*. If you have sufficient information to identify the property accurately prior to receiving the draft contract from the sellers' solicitors then pre-contrtact searches and enquiries can be undertaken (see chapter 7).

Professional practice points

There are several professional practice points to be aware of in this area, all of which seem to be popular topics for examination questions. If you know the rules thoroughly then they are easy to score high marks on but this really is one of the areas where a little learning is a dangerous thing. There are four main areas of professional practice which should be looked at separately:

(a)   Undertakings.
(b)   Contract races.
(c)   Conflict of interests.
(d)   Acting for more than one party in a conveyancing transaction.

Undertakings

There are certain elements which must be appreciated in relation to any undertaking given by a solicitor and so these elements are essential to any adequate examination answer:

(a)   A solicitor who gives an undertaking to do anything must be sure that it is within his or her power to perform it.

(b)   A solicitor who breaches an undertaking will be personally liable.

(c)   A solicitor who breaches an undertaking, will be professionally liable as it is a matter of professional misconduct.

Two common areas where undertakings can be examined are in relation to obtaining title deeds and obtaining bridging finance. If the undertaking relates to obtaining bridging finance then there are further points that the solicitor should bear in mind.

The lender may ask the solicitor to undertake to pay the net proceeds of sale to it on completion of the sale, out of which the lender will repay the loan which it has made and if there is anything left pass it on to the solciitor's clients. Care should be taken when considering an undertaking such as this:

(a)   The clients' written and irrevocable authority should be obtained before any such undertaking is given.

(b)   The undertaking should be to pay the 'net proceeds of sale' rather than any specified amount.

(c)   The undertaking should make it clear what is meant by 'net proceeds' and it should specify what deductions will be made (e.g., net proceeds after deduction of estate agents' commission, the amount required to redeem any mortgages which so far as we are aware currently do not exceed £x and the legal fees and disbursements relating to our clients' proposed sale and purchase).

(d)   The undertaking should be qualified in that it should be limited to payment of the net proceeds of sale 'if and when' received by the solicitor. This will prevent the solicitor from becoming liable to pay the proceeds of sale over if in fact the solicitor never actually receives them.

Contract races

'Contract races'

Sometimes your seller clients may tell you that it is very important to them that the property is sold quickly and that there are two or more people interested in it. Your clients may ask you to send out draft contracts to more than one potential buyer in the hope of producing a speedy exchange of contracts with one of them. It is permissible for you to do this but only if the direction made by the Council of the Law Society is strictly adhered to. The direction requires that:

(a)   The solicitor must obtain the sellers' authority to disclose the decision to send out more than one contract.
(b)   If the sellers refuse to give that authority the solicitor must refuse to act.
(c)   Having obtained the sellers' authority the decision must be disclosed to each of the solicitors acting for the prospective buyers (or personally to any prospective buyer who has not instructed a solicitor).
(d)   If the disclosure is made orally it must be confirmed in writing. Most examination questions in this area will ask little more of you other than that you know the *detail* of the direction, and that to fail to observe it would be a matter of professional misconduct.

Conflict of interest

There is an absolute prohibition on acting for more than one client where their interests conflict. This is a popular area for examination of professional conduct points and it is one which always causes students difficulties. It requires you to think the matter out for yourself and apply your own judgment and there is very little point in any lecturer or writer attempting to give examples as the examiner will always be able to think up a different set of facts for you to consider. The simplest thing to do if you are asked whether you can act for client A (say a buyer) and client B (say an institutional mortgagee) is to ask yourself:

(a)   Are there any points which are common to both clients and which I have to advise on whichever client I am advising?
(b)   Would the advice on those points differ depending on which client I am advising?

If the answer to both of these questions is yes it is likely that their interests conflict and you should not be acting for both clients.

Acting for buyers and sellers or mortgagor and mortgagee

This overlaps with the problem of conflict of interest but a common mistake is for students to think that the rule is the same. It is not. The principle that you may not act for more than one party where their interests conflict *always* applies. In conveyancing transactions there is an additional rule which prevents you from acting in a transaction at arm's length, for:

(a)   buyer and seller, or
(b)   lessor and lessee, or

(c)   mortgagor and mortgagee in a private mortgage (most mortgages from institutions engaged in the business of making loans and taking mortgages will not be private mortgages).

This rule prevents you from acting, for example, for buyer and seller *even where you think there is no conflict*. The only time you may act for both is if:

(a)   There is no conflict of interest, *and*
(b)   One of the exceptions set out in r. 6(1) of the Solicitors Practice Rules applies, i.e., the seller is not a builder or developer *and*

    (i)   the parties are associated companies,
    (ii)   the parties are related by blood, adoption or marriage,
    (iii)   both parties are established clients,
    (iv)   the consideration is less than £5,000,
    (v)   there are no other solicitors in the vicinity which the client can reasonably be expected to consult,
    (vi)   the parties are represented by two branch offices of a firm or associated firms which are supervised by different solicitors and in different localities *provided* that they have not been referred to the firm from another branch office or associated firm.

Common examination problem areas

1   **Questions on basic procedure.** A common problem in this area is either not stating the obvious points (like client's name and address, already mentioned) and/or not remembering them. You must make the obvious points. Either learn them by heart or if you cannot remember them imagine yourself in the office behind the desk and what you would say to the clients. It is amazing how memory or common sense deserts you in the exam room when all you can think about is what the examiner will think of your paper. Somehow miraculously if you think of being in the office and talking to a client, who is probably much more nervous than you are, the common sense reappears.

Another common problem in this area is, in your panic, only answering part of the question. Read the question carefully and answer it in the order in which the question is put as the mark scheme will often follow a similar order. For example, if the question says: 'What information would you obtain from your client and what further enquiries and arrangements would you make?', your answer should be split into two clear parts:

(a)   information you would need from your client,
(b)   enquiries and arrangements you would make.

It sounds obvious but all too often good students throw away vital marks by not taking a careful and logical approach to what the question is asking for.

2 *Financial arrangements questions.* A similar common problem arises here. Very often questions will ask what advice you will give your clients and what further enquiries you will make. If you fail to spot the two halves of the question, or even if you fail to organise your answer in two clear halves you will be throwing away marks.

Other common mistakes in this area are:

(a)   Not setting out your calculation clearly. Remember that the examiner is likely to be considering, amongst other things, how clearly you can explain the problem to your client. If the examiner is having to search around to find out whether you really understand the calculation, what hope is there for the client?

(b)   Wishy-Washy details of costs and disbursements. Imagine if you have clients in the office and you are about to tell them that there is not going to be enough money to complete the transaction because they had not taken account of your costs and the disbursements which you will have to pay which amount to about £2,000. The clients are going to want to know how that £2,000 is made up. You cannot simply say, 'well, this and that': you must be able to specify, for example:

Stamp duty at 1 per cent of the total purchase price.
Search fees.
Land Registry fees.
Your cost in acting for them in respect of the purchase and for the mortgagee in respect of the mortgage.

The examiner too will want to know that you do understand what has to be paid out and could explain it to your clients.

3 *Professional practice points.* Again a failure to pay attention to detail is usually the main cause of failure in these questions. In any question where you are asked to act for more than one person (e.g., two buyers or a buyer and an institutional mortgagee) remember to keep a keen eye out for possible conflicts of interest either in the narrative or as problems in the documentation itself.

If you are asked a question relating to acting for seller and buyer, make it clear that you know that there is a prohibition regardless of their being no conflict of interest. Make it clear that that prohibition is only overcome where there is no conflict of interest *and* one of the exceptions applies. Know the detail of the exceptions, e.g., related by blood, adoption or marriage will not allow you to act in an arm's-length transaction for the sellers and the buyer who is the unmarried partner of their daughter (no matter what you might think about the relevance or otherwise of a marriage certificate).

Whenever you deal with a matter of professional practice make it clear that you understand that a failure to observe the rules could result in disciplinary proceedings.

SIX

THE CONTRACT

Until the parties have entered into a legally binding contract there is unlikely to be any enforceable and legal relationship between them. At this stage either the buyers or the sellers will be free to back out of the proposed transaction without incurring any liaiblity to the other (although they will of course have their own costs to pay). Once a contract exists between the parties then any breach of that contract by either party is likely to result in the other being able to claim damages or, if the breach is serious enough, they may be entitled to withdraw from the contract ('rescind'). The remedies available for breach of contract are examined further in chapter 14. In the meantime we need to look at the process surrounding the formation of a contract to establish exactly when and on what basis the parties enter into a legally binding relationship.

Formalities

The basic requirements for formation of a simple contract are that there must be:

(a)   offer and acceptance,
(b)   consideration, and
(c)   intention to be legally bound.

These elements are essential in a contract for the sale of land, but they alone will not be sufficient to amount to a contract. Section 2 of the Law of Property (Miscellaneous Provisions) Act 1989, which came into force on 27 September 1989, provides that, a contract for the sale or other disposition of land or an interest in land must be made in writing. In other words an oral agreement for the sale of land is just an informal and unenforceable agreement and not a legally enforceable contract. The section not only specifies that the contract must be made in writing but also

(a)   that the agreed terms of the contract must all be included or incorporated into one document,
(b)   that incorporation of terms may be achieved either by setting the terms out in the document or by reference to some other document,
(c)   that the document must be signed by or on behalf of each party to the contract.

The normal practice in conveyancing transactions where solicitors are involved, prior to the coming into force of s. 2, has been to prepare two identical 'copies' of a contract and for the buyers to sign one copy and the sellers to sign the other. Once the contract was to become enforceable the part signed by the buyers would be sent to the sellers' solicitor and the part signed by the sellers would be sent to the buyers' solicitor. Section 2 has preserved this practice and provides that it will be acceptable if the contract is in the form of two identical copies (again incorporating all the terms) and provided each party signs one of the identical copies of the contract.

What contract will section 2 cover?

The provisions of the Law of Property Act 1989, s. 2, are undoubtedly far-reaching. The section covers contracts for the sale or disposition of an interest in land. Most contracts having anything to do with land will be covered by it. All the usual contracts for the sale and purchase of freehold property, the grant of a mortgage or the grant of an easement will certainly be covered. Section 2(6) also provides that an 'interest in land' includes an interest in the proceeds of sale of land and so a contract for the sale of an equitable interest in land (being, in theory, an interest in the proceeds of sale rather than any form of ownership of the land itself) would be caught by s. 2.

There are some notable exceptions to the formal requirements of s. 2. A contract for the grant of a lease not exceeding three years (which lease, despite being a legal estate, could itself be created orally by virtue of the Law of Property Act 1925, s. 54(2)) is not required to be in writing. Contracts made during the course of a public auction are also relieved of the requirement of being in writing and, in accordance with the existing law, the contract will be made when the auctioneer's hammer falls. Nor does s. 2 have any effect on the law relating to resulting, implied or constructive trusts. Such trusts may still arise as the result of oral agreements and negotiations.

The importance of incorporation

Section 2 of Law of Property (Miscellaneous Provisions) Act 1989 requires that all the agreed terms be included in the contract either expressly or, if they are contained in some other document, by an express term in the contract which refers to the other document and states that its terms are to be incorporated into the contract. What will the effect be if any of the terms agreed between the parties is not incorporated into the contract in one of the ways? Let us assume, for example, that there was agreement between the parties to a contract for the sale of a house that the buyers should buy the carpets and curtains for £2,000. That term was agreed in correspondence but was not expressly or by reference included in the contract itself. There are two main possibilities:

(a)   First the whole contract may fail. Section 2 requires that a valid contract must incorporate all the terms agreed between the parties. All the terms have not been included therefore there is no valid contract at all.

(b)   Alternatively, particularly as the term is not central to the whole transaction and there is separate consideration, the term may be construed not as a term of the contract for the sale of land but rather as a collateral contract which stands side by side with the main contract but is not actually part of it. This would allow the contract for the sale of land to survive despite the omission.

Obviously, solicitors should be sure that all the terms *agreed* between the parties are included in the contract and that there are no other terms agreed between the parties or in correspondence which might invalidate the contract. One additional safeguard (although it should be regarded as such and not as a substitute for careful drafting of the contract) is to include a term in the contract which says that the parties agree that the contract as signed represents *all* the terms agreed between the parties. If this is done there may be a problem in enforcing any term which has been omitted but it may also have the effect of saving the contract from being invalid.

Drafting the contract

In a conveyancing transaction, it is the sellers' solicitors who will have the title deeds or land or charge certificate and it is the sellers' solicitors who will be responsible for drafting the contract. The contract will be drafted in duplicate and both copies will be sent to the buyers' solicitors for approval. Here we look at what matters you should consider when drafting a contract. The essential things to bear in mind are:

(a)   Are you committing your clients to selling what they want and are able to sell and no more? If you commit your clients to selling more than they are capable of selling then your clients are at risk of being sued for breach of contract. If you commit your clients to selling more than they want to sell then they will be obliged to go through with the contract. Either way your clients will be looking to you for compensation for not carrying out their instructions properly.

(b)   Will the solicitors receiving the contract be able to understand exactly what their clients are committing themselves to buy and on what terms? In an examination it is important not to rely too heavily on precedents but rather to think about what it is that you are trying to do and draft the contract to the best of your ability. Once you have done it, read it through again as if you were the buyers' solicitor and ask yourself, 'From this document do I understand quite clearly what property my clients are buying and on what terms? Also ask yourself in respect of each clause, 'Is there any ambiguity here or are there any possibilities not covered?'

The contract, as we have seen, must embody all the terms agreed between the parties. It is possible to draft a contract in its entirety constructing your own clauses to cover all the aspects of the transaction. Most solicitors do not do this but make use of a standard form of contract by incorporating the 'Standard Conditions of Sale' into the contract. The Standard Conditions comprise nine fairly lengthy clauses which cover many of the more straightforward aspects of the transaction. It is usual to use these conditions but to vary them where they are inappropriate to the particular transaction with which you are dealing. There are three types of contractual term which you will come across:

(a)   *Special conditions.* These are terms which apply in respect of the particular transaction and which have been inserted either because the sellers' solicitor inserted them in the original draft contract or the buyers' solicitor subsequently insisted on them being included.

(b)   *Standard Conditions.* These are the standard terms drafted by the Law Society.

(c)   *Open contract position.* We have already seen what will be the position if a term agreed by the parties is omitted from the contract. However, there may be situations where the parties have included all the agreed terms (i.e., ones which they have discussed) but there are some matters which they failed to consider. For example, they may have agreed to the sale and purchase of the property but no one had actually discussed what documents the sellers would have to produce in order to prove that they owned the property. Under these circumstances the contract would be 'open' with respect to this particular matter and the 'open contract rule' would tell the parties what evidence should be provided.

So, in a contract which is drafted incorporating the Standard Conditions, when deciding whether special conditions, standard conditions, or open contract rules apply you must ask:

(a)   Is there a special condition to cover this particular point? If so then you must apply it. If not ask:

(b)   Is there a standard condition to cover this point? If so then you must apply it. If not:

(c)   Apply the open contract rule in respect of the particular point.

When looking at actually drafting the contract it is easiest, at least at first, to assume that you are drafting a contract incorporating the Standard Conditions and then ask what extra information and conditions peculiar to that particular transaction are needed and why.

There follows a selection of matters which can be dealt with in a contract.

Date

The place where the date of the contract is to be inserted is left blank at the drafting stage and completed on the date the contract is made (i.e., when contracts are exchanged).

Parties

The full names and addresses of the sellers and the buyers must be included to identify the persons who are committing themselves to the contract.

Particulars of the property

This part of a contract describes the subject-matter of the sale. What is it that your client are selling? As we have considered before, what is being sold is the intangible thing of the estate or interest in land rather than the land itself. It is therefore necessary to identify the estate, i.e., is it freeehold or leasehold? In the case of registered title you should also make it clear what class of title is being sold. In the absence of any express statement the sellers will be committing themselves to give absolute title.

Once you have identified the estate you then need to know in respect of what physical land the estate is held. So you need a description of the land. If the whole of a piece of property is being sold then the description is straightforward. The description will start with a postal address or some name by which the property can be identified (e.g., 25 High Street, Setterington, Seashire). This will normally be accompanied by a fuller description of the property often by reference to a plan. In the case of unregistered title, this fuller description can usually be found in an earlier conveyance of the property. A full description can either be repeated verbatim from the earlier conveyance or included by reference (e.g., 'which property is more particularly described in a conveyance dated 6 March 1984 and made between J. Fisher (1) and T. Tomkins (2)'). In registered title the reference is even simpler. The address of the property will be accompanied by a reference to the title number of the property (e.g., 'Registered at HM Land Registry under title number WYK 77345'). If the sellers are selling only part of the property which they own then a new description will be needed together with an accurate plan (see chapter 10).

The statutory definition of land includes not only the physical property but also any rights of which the property has the benefit. For example if X is buying No. 7 Maple Walk and the owner of No. 7 has a legal easement to use the driveway belonging to No. 9 then the right is a burden on No. 9 but of benefit to and part of the land of No. 7. It is therefore appropriate to include reference to any rights which benefit the property in the particulars. This can be done in one of two ways, either by repeating verbatim the words granting the right or by referring to a deed in which it is contained. The actual reference to the right can itself be included in the particulars (e.g., 'together with the right contained in a conveyance dated 4 April 1976 and made between S. Shotton (1) and B. Wilson (2)') or they can be set out in the special conditions, in which case the particulars will simply refer the reader to the special conditions (e.g., 'together with the rights referred to in special condition 5 of this contract').

Burdens on the property

If one is to include in the contract rights which benefit the property then it is also appropriate to make reference to the rights which third parties may have over the property being sold. How much you include in the draft contract depends on what the sellers are bound to disclose. There are certain matters which are the responsibility of the buyers to discover and there is no duty on the seller to tell the buyers. The extent of the sellers' duty of disclosure depends on the terms of the contract.

The open contract position (i.e., where there is no special condition and the Standard Conditions are not being used) is limited to defects in title which could not be discovered by inspection of the property (known as latent defects). The buyers are responsible for inspecting the property and checking for defects which are patent. There are obvious problems in deciding whether a defect is latent or patent. For example, a right of way is patent if there are physical signs of it such as a worn path but latent if there is no way it could have been discovered on inspection. The safest course for the sellers who want to avoid the possibility of litigation is to disclose all defects in title in the contract.

The position with regard to disclosure is different where the Standard Conditions are being used. Standard Conditions 3.1.1 says that the sellers sell the property free from encumbrances other than:

(a)   matters mentioned in the agreement and
(b)   adverse interests existing when the contract is made.

Standard Conditions 3.1.3 puts the sellers under a duty to disclose all adverse interests and anything in writing relating to adverse interests which they knew about before exchange of contracts. Adverse interests include public requirements, legal easements, entries on public registers (other than Land Registry or Land Charges Department registers) and overriding interests where the title to the land is registered. The finer detail of the condition is of importance to the buyers' solicitors. It is the key to knowing what the buyers may buy the property subject to, other than what is disclosed in the contract. There is room for debate about exactly what, bearing in mind Standard Conditions 3.1.1 and 3.1.3, the sellers are not bound to disclose. The safest course for the sellers' solicitor when drafting the contract is to be careful to disclose, by expressly drawing the buyers' attention to them in the contract, all encumbrances revealed by the deeds (or charge or land certificate) and all those not revealed by the deeds but which the sellers know of.

Capacity in which the seller sells

It is usual in a contract to state the capacity in which the sellers sell. If no capacity is included in the special conditions then Standard Condition 4.6.2 provides that the sellers sell as beneficial owners. The capacity is of importance as it will determine what covenants for title are included by implication in the final purchase deed (see chapter 10). The most commonly encountered capacities are:

(a)   *Beneficial owners.* This is only appropriate where the sellers are the only legal and equitable owners of the property.

(b)   *Trustees.* Appropriate where the owners hold as trustees (either under an express trust for sale or implied by statute where there is co-ownership) and they are not also the only equitable owners.

(c)   *Personal representatives.* Appropriate where the sellers are the executors or administrators of the last owner of the legal estate.

(d)   *Mortgagee.* Appropriate where the property is being sold by a mortgagee in exercise of its power of sale.

The sellers' solicitor should insert the capacity which is appropriate to the sellers' situation. If there are two or more sellers, who are also the only equitable owners of the property, then either trustees or beneficial owners would be appropriate. The sellers' solicitors would probably prefer their clients to convey as trustees but the buyers may well insist on them conveying as beneficial owners to ensure that more wide-ranging convenants for title are given in the purchase deed.

Completion date

In most conveyancing transactions there will be a particular date which will be convenient for the parties to complete the transaction. If the transaction is part of a chain of sales and purchases the completion date must also suit the other people in the chain. It is usual, on exchange of contracts, to insert the agreed completion date in the contract. If no completion date is otherwise mentioned in the contract then the Standard Conditions provide that the completion date is 20 working days after the contract is made (Standard Condition 6.1.1) and in any event, in the absence of other provision in the contract the Standard Conditions provide that time is not of the essence. This means that a failure to complete on the contractual completion date will be a breach of contract for which damages can be claimed but not a breach which will entitle the innocent party immediately to withdraw from the contract.

Contract rate

The contract rate is the rate at which compensation will be calculated in the event of a breach of contract by either party. Commonly the contract rate is between 3 and 5 per cent above the base rate of one of the major clearing banks. If the Standard Conditions are being used they define the contract rate as the Law Society's interest rate from time to time in force (Standard Condition 1.1.1).

Title

The sellers will prove their ownership of property and therefore their right to sell the property by means of their 'title'. There are two matters to consider here. First exactly what documents the sellers must show (what title will be 'deduced') and secondly how any defect in the title must be dealt with.

Title to be deduced

(a)   *Unregistered title*. In the absence of any provision in the contract the sellers' title must start with a good root of title at least 15 years old and from there an unbroken chain of ownership must be shown. In order to be a good root the instrument must:

(i)   deal with the whole legal and equitable interest (except any interests that can be overreached),
(ii)   contain an adequate description of the property,
(iii)   do nothing to cast doubt on the title.

The best root of title will be a conveyance on sale. Other documents which will be acceptable, providing they satisfy the requirements, will be an assent by personal representatives and a deed of gift (see further chapter 8).

The Standard Conditions do not vary the open contract rules at all.

It is possible to include a special condition varying the open contract rule and giving the buyer a shorter or a longer root. Neither is common as there is no need to give the buyer any longer title than the nearest good root which is over 15 years old and, the buyers will be unwise to accept a shorter root as there are certain risks in so doing (see further chapter 8). It is, however, usual to specify in the contract which document in that particular transaction will form the root of title.

(b)   *Registered title*. The open contract position is governed by the Land Registration Act 1925, s. 110. Section 110(1) requires the seller to provide the buyer with:

(i)   copies of the entries on the register,
(ii)   a copy of the filed plan, and
(iii)   copies of any document noted on the register which affects the land (e.g., rather than reproduce a list of restrictive covenants affecting the property the registrar may simply note that the property is affected by restrictive covenants contained in a certain document).

Section 110(2) also requires the sellers to provide, at their own expense, copies of documents relating to any matters as to which the register is not conclusive such as any documentary evidence there may be of overriding interests.

Standard Condition 4.2.1 simply restates s. 110(2) but is actually more generous to the buyers than s. 110(1) and requires any copies to be 'office' (i.e., official Land Registry) copies. The sellers cannot contract out if their minimum obligations under s. 110(1), but the provisions of s. 110(2) can be varied or excluded by special condition.

Defects in title   There may be matters in the sellers' title which are unsatisfactory. For example the property may have been sold subject to restrictive covenants stated in a document which has been lost. This situation is obviously unsatisfactory. The buyers will be buying a property subject to restrictive covenants which may be enforced against them but they will not know what they are unless and until they have breached them. Another example of a defect in the title would be where the property was conveyed from a trust by a single trustee. The interests of the beneficiaries under the trust could be binding on any later buyer of the land. If there are any such defects in the title the sellers' solicitors want to ensure that if the buyers enter into the contract they will not be able to claim that the sellers are in breach of contract for failing to show a good and defect-free title. The solution is to include a special condition telling the buyers what the defect is before they enter into the contract and making it clear that they take it or leave it on the basis. The wording of such a clause is, of course, a little more formal than that! For example, it might say:

The property is sold subject to restrictive covenants contained in a conveyance dated 15 October 1919 and made between M. Fletcher (1) and T. Jones (2). The seller has no copy of the covenants and the buyer shall assume there has been no breach of any of the covenants therein and shall raise no requisitions or objection in respect thereof.

Price

The contract must state quite clearly what the purchase price of the property is. The price being paid for any chattels must be considered at this point. The consideration for the chattels should be stated alongside the purchase price but in addition there should be a special condition identifying (either expressly or by reference to the fixtures and fittings form) which chattels are being sold.

Deposit

It is usual in the contract to state the amount of the deposit payable by the buyers on exchange of contracts. However, if there is no special condition in the contract then Standard Condition 2.2.1 requires a 10 per cent deposit to be paid. The open contract position (i.e., where the matter of deposit is not covered by the special conditions and the Standard Conditions are not being used) would be that no deposit at all would be payable on exchange.

The sellers' solicitors should also consider in what capacity they are to hold the deposit when it is paid to them on exchange. There are three possibilities:

(a)   The sellers' solicitor may hold the deposit as agent for the sellers. This would mean that the sellers could demand the deposit from the solicitors at any time. The advantage from the sellers' point of view is that it allows the deposit to be used on their own purchase.

(b)   The second possibility is that the sellers' solicitors could hold it as stakeholder in which case it is held for both buyer, and sellers and improper disposal of it to the sellers, would render the solicitors liable to the buyers.

(c)   The third possibility is a compromise between the two which is in fact included in the Standard Conditions. It allows the sellers' solicitor to hold the deposit as agent insofar as it is used as a deposit in a related property transaction (in other words the sellers can use the deposit for their own purchase but cannot use it for anything else). So far as the whole or any part is not used in a related property transaction the deposit must be held as stakeholder.

Indemnity covenants

If property is sold subject to a covenant then, in the absence of express provision to the contrary, statute will imply that the covenant is given by the covenantors on behalf of themselves 'and their successors in title'. The covenantors are therefore covenanting not only as to their own behaviour but also as to the behaviour of anyone who buys the property from them. If sellers have given a covenant on this basis then they will want an 'indemnity covenant' from their buyers which will enable the sellers, if they are sued by the covenantee, in turn to sue the buyers. Similarly when the buyers sell they will want to ensure that if they are sued by the sellers they can in turn sue the people who bought from them. An express condition in the contract will be needed to provide for the buyer to give such an indemnity covenant in the purchase deed. However, where the Standard Conditions are used, Standard Condition 4.6.3 provides for the buyers to give such a covenant.

Vacant possession

The open contract rule, i.e., in the absence of any other provision in the contract, is that the sellers must give vacant possession of the property on completion. If the Standard Conditions are used they provide for vacant possession to be given (Standard Condition 3.3.1). If vacant possession is not to be given then the contract should include a special condition to that effect. If the property is to be sold subject to tenancies then the contract should stipulate what evidence of them is to be provided to the buyers. If the

Standard Conditions are being used then the sellers are required by Standard Condition 3.3.2 to provide the buyers with full details and any documentation before exchange of contracts.

Care should be taken in considering whether the sellers can give vacant possession. An inability to give vacant possession and therefore a liability to damages is not limited simply to situations where there is an undisclosed tenancy but also extends to situations where vacant possession cannot be given because of the existence of a class F land charge (or notice in the case of registered title) and it may also be extended to cases where there is some other legal or physical impediment to the buyers entering into exclusive occupation of the property.

The special situation where only part of the sellers' property is being sold

If the sellers are only selling part of the property which they own then, as we saw in chapter 5, it is important for the sellers' solicitors to discuss with the sellers the question of easements to be granted to the buyers over the sellers' retained land, easements to be reserved to the sellers over the land being sold, and any new covenants that the sellers wish to impose on the property being sold.

The open contract rule and the Standard Conditions make no provision in respect of covenants in this situation. Each and every covenant which the parties are to be asked to enter into in the purchase deed must therefore be set out fully in special conditions.

The open contract position regarding easements is undesirable from the sellers' point of view in that:

(a)   it tends to favour the buyers rather than the sellers; and

(b)   the effects of the common law and statutory rules may be uncertain and may in some circumstances operate to grant rights which neither the buyers nor the sellers had ever expected the buyers to acquire.

The Standard Conditions improve upon the open contract position in that, as we saw in chapter 5, they give the sellers the benefit of much the same rules as the buyers. From the point of view of certainty, however, they are still not satisfactory. There may be matters which neither sellers nor buyers had thought about which could create easements by virtue of Standard Condition 3.4.2(b). It is much more satisfactory to discuss fully with the clients exactly what rights they need over the land being sold and exactly what rights they want the buyers to have over the land they are keeping and to provide expressly for them in the contract. In these discussions there are three matters which the sellers' solicitors should consider:

(a)   A special condition excluding the operation of the Law of Property Act 1925, s. 62, and the rule in *Wheeldon* v *Burrows* (1879) 12 ChD 31.

(b)   A special condition excluding the operation of Standard Condition 3.4.2(b).

(c)   The nature of the rights to be granted and reserved in the purchase deed and their extent.

Void conditions

There are certain matters in respect of which the sellers may not include special conditions as they will be void and therefore ineffective. These include:

(a)   Any condition attempting to exclude or limit the buyers' right to title under the Land Registration Act 1925, s. 110(1).
(b)   Any condition which attempts to prevent the buyers from objecting to the inadequacy of stamping on any of the documents of title.
(c)   Any condition which attempts to restrict the buyers' choice of solicitor.
(d)   Any condition which attempts to preclude the buyers from examining any power of attorney under which any of the documents of title is executed.
(e)   Any condition requiring the buyers to accept title made with the concurrence of those entitled to an equitable interest in the property where the seller could pass good title free of those interests simply by overreaching those equitable interests.

Perusing and approving the draft contract

Once the sellers' solicitors have drafted the contract they will send both copies of the draft contract to the buyers' solicitors for approval. The objectives of the buyers' solicitors differ from those of the sellers but essentially the skill and knowledge that is required is the same as that for drafting the contract. You must have:

(a)   An appreciation of the problems inherent in that particular transaction (for example, if the sellers are selling only part of their property the question of new easements should immediately spring to mind).
(b)   An understanding of the Standard Conditions and the open contract rules, whether they make provision for the particular situation and whether that provision is appropriate for the buyers or whether a special condition is required.

The only real difference is the viewpoint from which you look at those issues. You are looking to see what is in the buyers' best interests. What then are your objectives when acting for the buyers in approving the draft contract? You need to be sure of several things:

(a)   Is the property which the sellers will be contracting to sell exactly what the buyers want to buy? It may be, for example, that the physical extent of the property is not quite what the buyers had thought. For example, it may be that the sellers do not have any legal title to part of the garden but have used it with the permission of a neighbour for some years. The rights which benefit the property may not be adequate for your clients' needs. For example, although the sellers in fact drive their car to the house over an unmade road there may be no legally enforceable right to do so and the neighbours could legitimately prevent it at any time. The property may differ from what the buyers want to buy in that there may be third-party rights which limit the way in which the buyers could use the property. For example, it may be important to the buyers that there is a safe garden where their children can play. If you discover from looking at the title that a neighbour has the right to drive his car across the driveway which forms part of the garden then the property may not be so attractive to the buyers.

(b)   Do the details of the property accord with the clients' instructions, e.g., is the price stated correctly?

(c)   Are the terms of the contract itself acceptable or do they represent an unnecessary burden or risk to the buyers? For example, is the interest rate very high?

Specific matters which you should consider when persuing the draft contract include the following.

Description of the property

As suggested above, the physical description of the property should be checked to ensure that it is the same as your buyer clients want to buy. The legal description or estate should be checked. Your clients will not be pleased if, thinking they are buying the freehold, they discover later that they in fact bought the remaining 35 years of a 99-year lease. Any rights which benefit the property should be checked to ensure that they are adequate for the buyers' purposes. For example, is the right of way with vehicles as well as on foot? Is it for all purposes and at all times? These rights should also be checked to see whether they will involve the buyers in any expense. For example, will the right to use drains passing through an adjoining property also require the buyers to contribute towards their maintenance and if so on what basis?

Easements to which the property is subject

On a sale of the whole of the sellers' property there may well be easements which were granted prior to this sale which give neighbouring owners rights over the land which the buyers are proposing to buy. If so you must check whether these easements are acceptable to the buyers. Will they prevent the buyers using the property how they wish? For example, the buyers will be unable to put up a garden shed where it would obstruct a neighbour's easement of way over the back garden. You should also consider whether, particularly if a neighbour's right will cause wear and tear on the property, the buyers will be able to require the neighbour to contribute towards the cost. For example, if the neighbour's right is to use a driveway on the property, can he be required to contribute towards the cost of upkeep of the driveway?

Covenants which affect the property

There are three matters which the buyers solicitor needs to consider here:

(a)   The buyers' solicitor should consider the subject-matter of the covenants and whether they are acceptable to the buyers.

For example, a restrictive covenant preventing the use of the property for business purposes would be unacceptable if the buyers wished to convert part of the building into a workshop. Similarly a positive covenant that the buyers would maintain a 6-foot-high fence along one of the boundaries of the property could be expected to impose a considerable and possibly unacceptable financial burden on the buyers.

(b)   The enforceability of the covenants should also be considered. The situation other than where there is what is known as a Building Scheme is broadly:

(i)   *Positive covenants* are usually only enforceable by a chain of indemnity covenants. If there is a break in the chain of indemnity covenants then the covenant cannot be enforced against the buyers.

Figure 6.1

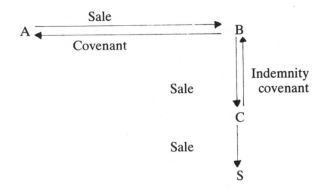

For example, in figure 6.1, A sells to B who covenants to maintain a fence along the boundary between the land bought by B and that retained by A. B then sells her land to C taking an indemnity covenant from him. C then sells to S but does not take an indemnity from him. If S is then selling to your clients there is little cause for concern. (A cannot sue your clients directly for any failure to maintain the fence.) The only way A could make your clients perform the covenant is by suing B who would then sue C who would then sue S who would then sue your clients. This, though, is not possible as the 'chain' is broken. A can sue B. B can sue C, but C cannot sue S as no indemnity covenant was given by S.

A break in the chain might also arise if it was not possible to find one of the members of the chain or if one of them is impecunious and not worth suing. In certain exceptional circumstances it may be possible to enforce a positive covenant other than through a chain of indemnities. For example, where the positive covenant is connected with a rentcharge, or where someone has a right of way over a neighbour's driveway subject to a positive covenant to maintain the driveway in good repair, that person will not usually be allowed to take the benefit of the right without also accepting the burden of the related covenant.

(ii) *Negative or restrictive covenants* may also be enforced by the chain of indemnity covenants if it remains intact but there is an additional method which may be open to the original covenantee. In the example above, if the covenant had been restrictive rather than positive (e.g., not to use the property for any purpose other than as a single dwelling) then A could have registered the restrictive covenant. In registered title it would have been entered on the register. In unregistered title it would have to be protected by registration as a class D(ii) land charge at the Plymouth Land Charges Registry. If A had so protected the covenant then A is likely to be able to sue your clients directly for any breach of the covenant.

(c) The buyers' solicitors must consider whether there has been any breach of an existing covenant.

If there has been no breach of any covenant so far then the buyers must simply decide whether the terms of the covenant are acceptable to them and if not whether they are enforceable against the buyers (either directly or indirectly). The situation is slightly different where there has already been a breach of an existing covenant. If, for example, the covenant has been breached by the sellers then the buyers will not want to indemnify the sellers in respect of liability for a breach which the sellers themselves caused. The buyers' solicitors should therefore be aware of the effect of Standard Condition 4.6.3 which would require the buyers to give the sellers a full indemnity covenant. Rather, the buyers' solicitors should insist, by the inclusion of a special condition in the contract, that this Standard Condition be modified and that the buyers should only give an indemnity in respect of *future* breaches of the covenant.

The situation is more serious than this where the covenant is a restrictive one which has been protected by registration. Here the original covenantee (in our earlier example, A) can enforce the covenant directly against the buyers. Modifying the indemnity clause will not therefore protect the buyers but there are other possibilities. Suppose, for example, the contract tells you that the property is sold subject to certain covenants in an earlier deed and the copy of the deed shows that one of the covenants is not to build anything other than detached dwellings on the property. You know that the property which your clients are buying is semi-detached. This is a prima facie breach of covenant. First you need to ask if the covenant is enforceable against your client. If it is not registered then an amendment to any indemnity covenant your client may be required to give may be sufficient protection. If it is registered than that amendment will not be sufficient. The matters to consider are:

(i)   Is it possible that a release of the covenant was obtained before the property was built? If so the situation will be satisfactory but evidence of that release will be required.

(ii)   Might an application to the Land Tribunal to release the covenant (see Law of Property Act 1925, s. 84) be successful?

(iii)   Can insurance be obtained? Often, particularly if there has been a considerable period of time since the breach occurred, it may be possible to obtain insurance against any action being taken by the original covenantor (or his successors in title) by the payment of a single premium.

New easements and covenants

When the sellers are only selling part of the property which they own, as we have seen in relation to drafting the contract, there needs to be some consideration of what, if any, new easements are to be granted to the buyers over the sellers' retained land and to be reserved to the sellers over the buyers' land. There are three possibilities:

(a)   No mention is made in the contract about easements, in which case the buyers will acquire certain easements under the common law and statute.

(b)   There is no special condition but the contract incorporates the Standard Conditions which provide for the sellers to acquire rights for the benefit of the retained land similar to those which the common law and statute would give to the buyers over the sellers' retained land.

(c)   There are special conditions excluding the open contract rule and the Standard Conditions and stating exactly what rights the buyers and sellers will have over each others' land after the sale.

For the sake of certainty, the third option is likely to be the most acceptable. The buyers must be sure that the rights which adjoining owners will get over the land which is being sold are acceptable and that the rights which the buyers will acquire over adjoining land are adequate. On the sale of part of the sellers' property, the easements and their terms may be open to negotiation. If the property is sold with the benefit of and subject to various existing easements the buyers must really decide whether they are happy with them on a 'take them or leave them' basis. If they do not like them the answer is not to proceed with the purchase as the easements are already in existence and it is unlikely that any change is possible. The situation is not the same with new easements: the sellers may be prepared to change the terms of any easements or consider the grant of extra ones.

New covenants may similarly be the matter of negotiation between buyers and sellers. Unlike the case of easements the buyers' only task is to check the terms of any which are specified in the special conditions. In the absence of any special conditions the buyers will not be subject to any new covenants.

Title

The contract may attempt to restrict the buyers' rights in respect of what title the sellers will show. It may also attempt to prevent the buyers from raising any objections to the title after exchange of contracts. If the latter condition is included in the draft contract it is of no real problem to the buyers except that they must ensure that all the documents of title have been fully checked and any problems with them sorted out before exchange of contracts.

A condition which attempts to restrict the title to be shown to buyers may be more problematic. For example if the condition were to require the buyers to accept as a root of title a document which was less than 15 years old this could have serious repercussions for the buyers. The effect would be that the buyers would be deemed to have notice of anything they would have discovered if they had investigated title for the full period and they will not be entitled to compensation in respect of any land charges registered before the root of title. Also, on application for first registration, the estate will not be registered with absolute title.

Capacity in which the sellers sell

When discussing the drafting of the contract, it was said that the sellers' solicitors must select the capacity most appropriate to the sellers position. We also saw that where the sellers were co-owners of the legal estate and also the only beneficial owners of the property they could sell either in their capacity as trustees (there is a statutorily implied trust for sale) or in their capacity as beneficial owners. From the point of view of the buyers it is preferable for the sellers to sell as beneficial owners as there will be four covenants for title implied at completion. In the case of a sale by trustees there is only one, i.e., that the sellers themselves have not created any incumbrance.

If the sellers are purporting to sell as beneficial owners where another person has a beneficial interest in the property then the buyers' solicitor should ask for this to be amended to trustees (and indeed if the seller is a sole seller the buyers' solicitor should insist on the appointment of a second trustee) so that the interests of the other person may be overreached.

Deposit

As we saw when looking at drafting the contract the question of how the deposit is held by the sellers' solicitors will be of importance to both parties. The buyers will want maximum possible security for the deposit which, if the sellers fail to perform the contract, they will want to be returned to them. If the contract provides for the deposit to be held as agent for the sellers there is considerable risk here. The sellers could demand the deposit from their solicitors at any time before completion and could spend the whole amount on whatever they chose (perhaps a wild night out!), and the buyers might

'The seller could draw the deposit and could spend the whole amount on whatever they chose (perhaps a wild night out)'

have very great difficulty in ever recovering the money from them. The sellers' solicitors on the other hand are unlikely to be happy holding the deposit as stakeholder as this will not allow the sellers to make use of the deposit in their own purchase. The compromise effected by the Standard Conditions is not without risk to the buyers but is probably sensible. In a chain of conveyancing transactions it is not sensible for everyone to have to borrow the full amount of the deposit on their purchase when a substantial deposit has been paid on their sale. The Standard Conditions allow the sellers to use the deposit but only for the deposit on their purchase and only on the basis that insofar as it is not used on a purchase by the person from whom they are buying it must be held by that person's solicitor as stakeholder. To put it simply the deposits can be used in the chain but the solicitor at the top of the chain whose client is selling a house but not buying, must hold it as stakeholder. There is a slight risk to the buyers in that if something goes wrong it may be difficult to trace the money further up the chain but at least it will be recoverable rather than converted into a night on the town.

Insurance

Insurance has traditionally been of concern to buyers as the open contract rule is that the risk passes with the property on exchange of contracts rather than completion. The effect of this is that the buyers who do not insure could find themselves having to buy, at full contract price, a burnt-out shell of a property. The Standard Conditions change this situation and are more acceptable to the buyers. The Standard Conditions state that the property is at the sellers' risk until completion and that if at completion the property is unusable then the buyers can rescind the contract. The buyers could be almost entirely happy with this condition if it required the sellers to insure the property but it does not. Instead it expressly relieves the sellers of any obligation to insure. If the buyers want the property to be adequately insured between exchange and completion then they must either insist on a special condition that the sellers insure and produce evidence of the policy, or the buyers must themselves insure the property from exchange in which case the contract must include a special condition for the purchase price to be reduced by any amount that the buyers are unable to recover because of the existence of a policy of the sellers.

In addition to simply checking the terms of the contract the buyers' solicitors must remember to keep their clients fully advised about the terms and in particular any terms which appear unusual or onerous. Certain matters, as we have seen, may be negotiable; others which are part of the property already may not be open to change and it is simply a question of the buyers accepting the terms or deciding not to proceed with the proposed purchase of that particular property. If there are any matters which are capable of being negotiated and which the solicitors or the buyers are unhappy about then the solicitors should attempt to agree amendments to the draft contract.

Common examination problem areas

1 In order to be able to answer any question on drafting or approving the contract you must be familiar with the open contract rules and with the provisions of the Standard Conditions. The Standard Conditions look daunting but remember you are unlikely to be required to repeat them verbatim. You must know the *effect* of the conditions and when you will need to alter or exclude them by means of a special condition. Don't leave the learning of the provisions of the Standard Conditions until the last minute. Familiarise yourself with each condition as you come across it in your study.

2 When you come across an exam question which asks you to draft a contract or to approve a contract remember:

(a) If you are asked to draft the contract this is a task done by the sellers' solicitors and so must be looked at from the sellers' point of view. If you are asked to consider a contract which has been sent for approval you will be looking at it from the buyers' point of view.

(b)   Be able to explain the problem which gives rise to the need for any special conditions.

(c)   Be able to explain what the best contractual provision would be from your clients' point of view *and* what the best would be from the other parties' point of view *and* what form a reasonable compromise might take.

SEVEN

PRE-CONTRACT ENQUIRIES AND SEARCHES AND EXCHANGE OF CONTRACTS

Pre-contract enquiries and searches

We have seen from looking at the open contract rule, how limited the sellers' duty of disclosure can be. Although the Standard Conditions place a wider duty on the sellers, nevertheless there are matters which the sellers are not bound to tell the buyers and about which the buyers must make their own searches and enquiries. Standard Condition 3.1.1 says that the property is sold free from encumbrances other than:

(a) matters disclosed in the contract and
(b) adverse interests existing at the time of the contract.

Therefore the buyers' solicitors must make their own enquiries about any adverse interests which exist at the time of the contract. It will be no use the buyers complaining about the existence of such an interest after exchange of contracts. The time will have passed for such enquiries and the buyers will have to accept the position. It is true that Standard Condition 3.1.3 places a duty on the sellers to disclose all adverse interests of which they knew before the contract, but the buyers will still be at risk from adverse interest about which the sellers did not know.

The Standard Conditions define adverse interests as:

(a) public requirements,
(b) legal easements benefiting the owners or occupiers of other property,
(c) entries on public registers other than HM Land Register or the Land Charges Register,
(d) overriding interests (where the title is registered).

This list of adverse interests form the basis for most of the enquiries and searches which are undertaken before the contract is made.

It is also important to realise the importance of making enquiries additional to those of the sellers themselves. Whilst a fraudulent, negligent or even innocent misstatement by the sellers may give the buyers a right of action against the sellers, nevertheless the buyers may still be forced to accept the property subject to the third-party interest which was misrepresented by the sellers. Even the ability to sue the sellers may be fraught with the usual complications of any litigation, not least the fact that by the time action is taken or judgment obtained the sellers may be worth nothing and so winning the case against the sellers may be an empty victory.

As a student learning these searches it is very easy to get the right general idea about searches but simply fail to be specific enough to score reasonable marks. The solution I find is to ask myself in respect of each search: Do I know the three W's: What, Where and Why?

There are certain searches and enquiries which will be undertaken in every case. Others will only be appropriate where the facts of the particular transaction suggest they are needed. The following are the searches, enquiries and inspections which will be required in every case.

Local land charges search

This search must be made in every case and whether or not the title to the land is registered or unregistered. Registers of local land charges are kept by district councils, metropolitan councils and London borough councils.

The search can be done personally or by application on a standard form. The advantage of the more formal application over the personal search is that it provides a certificate of search which, amongst other things, will protect a solicitor from liability in the case of an error in the certificate and will provide compensation for buyers where the search fails to reveal an existing charge. The search does not confer any type of priority period and so will become out of date as soon as it is issued. Solicitors should therefore be wary of relying on a search that is out of date. (The Local Search Validation Scheme may be used to help alleviate this problem. See further chapter 18.)

The types of matters which will be revealed by a search of this register are: planning matters, compulsory purchase orders, matters regarding buildings which are listed as being of historic interest, tree preservation orders and financial charges made by the local authority (e.g., a charge levied by the local authority for making up what used to be a private road and a local authority's buy-back option on an ex council house).

Additional enquiries of the local authority

These enquiries are often ignored by students who seem to believe that reference to the local authority search will somehow make it clear to the examiner that they understand that additional enquiries must be sent too. It won't, and you will lose marks if you take this approach.

The enquiries are made of the same authority as the search and again there is a standard form. In practice the two are submitted together.

To be able to deal adequately with a question in this area there really is no substitute for sitting down with a copy of the form and working out what the questions are saying and whether you would be hoping for a positive or negative answer to that question.

Below is an attempt to extract from some of the enquiries an idea of the more common problem areas. The list is not comprehensive and does not cover all the enquiries on the standard form.

Enquiry 3 concerns the roadway on to which the property fronts. The question is concerned to establish whether the roadway is adopted by the local authority (if not the solicitors for the buyers should be sure to remember to check the deeds to ensure that there is a right of way over the road), and whether the frontagers are likely to incur any charge either before and/or in the event of adoption. Enquiry 3.3.1 will be of particular importance to new properties. When a new property is bought very often the roads will not yet have been made up. It is usual for the builders to enter into an agreement with the council that if the builder makes the road up initially the council will then adopt the road and thereafter maintain it at public expense. The agreement (often referred to as a 'section 38 agreement') should be accompanied by a bond to cover the cost of the initial making up of the road if the builder should fail to do it (enquiry 3.3.2).

Enquiry 2 concerns the drainage from the property and whether it drains into a public sewer. As with the roads, if the sewer is not a public one the buyers' solicitors should be sure to check the deeds to see that there is an adequate easement of drainage benefiting the property. Again, as with roads where the property is newly built, it is usual for the builders to enter into an agreement to construct a sewer whereafter the water company will take it over and maintain it. As with the roads this should be supported by a bond. (These are often referred to as a 'section 18 agreement and bond'.)

Enquiry 4 is mainly concerned with whether there are any plans for new subways, flyovers or roads within 200 metres of the property.

Enquiries 5 and 6 ask whether there are any notices or proceedings in respect of various statutory provisions. The answer one is usuallly hoping for is that there is none.

Enquiries 7 to 13 largely deal with planning permission and other related matters.

Enquiries 15 and 16 relate to whether the property is in a smoke control area and whether the property is included in the Register of Contaminated Land.

There are in total 16 questions in this part of the additional enquiries. There are in addition 17 optional questions which will only be answered if you specifically request it. These extra enquiries will only be necessary if they are relevant to the particular property your client is buying, for example, if you are concerned as to whether the property is crossed by a public footpath or bridleway.

Enquiries of the sellers

These enquiries will cover all matters concerning the property which cannot be discovered from the title deeds or copies of the register and matters which the seller is not bound to disclose. There is a standard form which is commonly used which asks about such matters as whether there have been any disputes relating to the property, and about the ownership and maintenance of fences (a matter about which the documents of title are all too often silent).

The standard form also asks about the existence of various guarantees including the guarantees offered under the NHBC scheme. In the case of property which is under 10 years old the protection of this scheme or a similar insurance will be regarded as essential by many buyers and most mortgagees. The benefit of the scheme is that it guarantees the work of the builder against the large number of defects in the first two years and against major defects in the first 10 years after the house is built. The form also asks about the existence of guarantees such as dry rot or woodworm treatment guarantees.

The form looks at matters such as the routes of services to the property, whether there are any shared facilities such as a driveway and the existence of any easements. Also included are questions concerning whether there have been any breaches of covenant and whether there has been any development at the property which required planning permission (see further chapter 16).

The form is a useful place to start but it is important to ensure that any additional matters relevant to the property which your clients are proposing to buy are made the subject of specific enquiries. For example, if the property is next to or near a river the buyer may be concerned to know about the incidence of flooding and whether that might affect the buyer's ability to obtain property insurance. Care should be taken not only to think carefully about what matters to raise but also what not to raise. Certain matters which do not relate to the property should not be dealt with via this medium (e.g., an enquiry about the catchment area for local schools) but are better dealt with by the buyers' own enquiries rather than those made between the parties' solicitors. Beware also of asking unnecessary and irrelevant questions and ones to which you have already been told the answer!

Once the buyers have raised these enquiries of the sellers what use can they make of them? It is important to remember that the task of the sellers' solicitors in helping the sellers to complete the form of enquiries will be to ensure that the sellers do not, wittingly or unwittingly, make a misstatement of fact which could amount to misrepresentation (i.e., which induced the buyers to enter into the contract). The answers which the buyers can therefore expect to these enquiries may be very vague and often refer to the state of the sellers' belief about the matter (e.g., an answer may say 'Not so far as the sellers are aware'), or worse still the answer may simply say 'The buyers must rely on their own inspection'. Wherever the replies are vague or unhelpful the buyers' solicitors must be sure to point out to the buyers the problems of relying on the answers and should also undertake any additional searches and enquiries and inspections which may be needed.

Inspection of the property

In a conveyancing transaction the property should be inspected both before exchange of contracts and before completion.

The first matter which the buyers should be checking is the physical state of the property, since in this respect the sellers are under no duty of disclosure. If the standard conditions are being used, Standard Condition 3.1.5 states that the buyers accept the property in the physical state it is in when the contract is made (unless the sellers are in fact building or converting it). This is a quite clear indication to the buyers that they should have the property surveyed. If the buyers decide to instruct a surveyor they should be sure before they enter into the contract for the survey that everyone is clear about what exactly is expected of the survey and what matters it is expected to cover (e.g., whether it is to be a full structural survey and whether it is to cover the need to treat timbers for woodworm). If the buyers are obtaining a mortgage, the mortgagee will usually undertake a survey of the property. Often buyers will rely on this survey rather than undertake one of their own at considerable expense. In most cases this will be a reasonable approach to take as recent cases have decided that not only may the surveyor be liable to the buyers as well as the mortgagee for any error in the report, but also in most ordinary domestic conveyances any attempt to exclude liability by an exclusion clause will not be 'fair and reasonable' under the Unfair Contract Terms Act 1977. Care should be taken, however, in that the limits of the decisions are not entirely clear. It may be, for example, that where the buyer is obtaining a very small percentage of the purchase price by way of mortgage the court may take the view that the buyer and the building society must have been aware that the extent of the survey would effectively be limited to investigating the adequacy of the security.

The second matter which should be considered so far as a physical inspection of the property is concerned is the possibility that there may be defects in title. Although the buyers' solicitors will have asked certain questions of the sellers in the enquiries before contract it must be remembered that what the buyers want is to buy a property free from any unacceptable defects in title. For example, they do not want to buy a property and discover that someone had an equitable interest in the property which then binds them as the owners of the property. It is true that, if the Standard Conditions are being used and the sellers have failed to disclose an adverse interest of which they knew then they may be liable for breach of contract. Similarly if they have given an incorrect reply to one of the enquiries before contract then they may be liable for misrepresentation. Damages (if the sellers can pay them) may be some consolation to the buyers but wouldn't it have been better to avoid the problem in the first place? Also you must remember that even under the Standard Conditions, which go somewhat further than the open contract rule, the sellers are only bound to disclose adverse interests *of which they knew*.

What type of things are you looking for when you inspect the property? First of all you will be looking for evidence of any easements affecting the property. For example, if there is a gate in the fence between the property your clients are hoping to buy and the property next door, what is it for? It may be the physical evidence of a legal right of way which the owners of the property next door have over the property your clients are hoping to buy. In unregistered title a legal right of way may be binding on the buyers even though they know nothing about it. In registered title also a legal easement may be binding on the buyers even though it did not appear on the register as it may be an overridding interest under the Land Registration Act 1925, s. 70(1)(a).

Secondly there is the question of occupiers of the property. The buyers must set out to discover:

(a)   Who, other than the sellers, is in occupation.
(b)   What rights, if any, that person has.

The position of the buyers in relation to such occupiers depends on whether the title to the property is registered or unregistered.

In unregistered title the buyers are concerned with the doctrine of notice. Equitable interests which affect the property are either registrable or non-registrable under the Land Charges Act 1972. If they are registrable, they cannot bind the buyers unless they are registered at the Central Land Charges Department at Plymouth, in which case the buyers will be able to discover them (and object to them if they have not been disclosed) when they do the pre-completion search (see chapter 9). If they are not registrable then the doctrine of notice applies. This means that the buyers will buy the property free of the interest if they can prove that they are bona fide purchasers for value of the legal estate without notice of the equitable interest. The most important element of this from a conveyancer's point of view is the question of notice. Broadly speaking the buyers will have notice of the interest if:

(a)   they knew about it, or
(b)   their agent (e.g., solicitor) knew about it, or
(c)   they or their agent *ought* to have known about it.

The importance of inspecting the property is to be found in this last element. The buyers are under a duty to make such enquiries and inspections as a prudent buyer acting under professional advice would. It is well established that inspection of the property is one of the things which a prudent buyer must do. If the buyers fail to inspect the property then they will be deemed to know about anything they would have discovered if they had inspected the property.

Similarly, this idea of deeming the buyers to know about something ('constructive notice') requires the buyers to follow up on anything that looks suspicious or hints at the existence of an interest. For example, if the buyers have been told that the seller's mother lives with the seller in the property, enquiries should be made of her about whether she has any interest. If the buyers fail to make any enquiries then they will be deemed to know about any interest she has and will take subject to that interest. In relation to the inspection of the property what does this require of the buyers? It requires them not simply to rely on the replies given by the seller but also to inspect the property and to see if there is any evidence of anyone living at the property and if so to make follow-up enquiries to find out if they have any interest in it. A failure either to inspect or follow up any evidence discovered on inspection may result in the buyers taking the property subject to the interests of the occupier.

In registered title there are certain rights which will be of particular concern to the buyers, e.g., 'the rights of every person in actual occupation of the land or in receipt of rents and profits thereof, save where enquiry is made of such person and the rights are not disclosed' (Land Registration Act 1925, s. 70(1)(g).

It is a common mistake for students to assume that the doctrine of notice and the rule in s. 70(1)(g) are the same. They are similar but they are not the same and indeed the position of the buyers where the title is registered is considerably more precarious than in unregistered title. There are two major differences between the two ideas:

(a)   The rule in registered title includes protection not just for occupiers but also the rights of those 'in receipt of rents and profits'. In other words the rights of a landlord.

(b)   The rule in registered title does not limit the protection of the buyers to situations where there is evidence of occupation by someone other than the seller. The test is whether the person is in actual occupation (given its ordinary meaning) of the land. Unlike in unregistered title it is immaterial that there is no way that the buyers could have discovered the occupation. If Grandma lives with the seller and has provided money for the double glazing, but is spending a month in Benidorm when you inspect, you may be bound by her rights nonetheless.

Finally we must consider what you would do if you did discover, as a result of your inspection of the property, that there was some defect in title. First of course you should make full enquiries about it. Secondly discuss it with your clients. What can be done about it depends on the type of interest you have discovered.

If the interest is an equitable interest arising under a trust (e.g., where the occupier contributed to the original purchase price of the property) then the problem is not insoluble. The interest of that occupier, whether the title is registered or unregistered, can be overreached. In other words as long as *all* the legal owners are parties to the receipt for the proceeds of sale (contained in the purchase deed) *and* so long as there are *at least two of them* (or one that is a trust corporation) then the interest of the occupier will be turned into an interest in the proceeds of sale rather than the property. This will mean that the buyers can take the property free of the interest. If there is only one seller (not being a trust corporation) then overreaching can be made to operate by another trustee being appointed (usually by the seller) to act with him or her to receive the sale proceeds.

If your inspection of the property reveals any other interest then the problem may not be so easily solved. The sellers may be able to negotiate a release of the interest. If they cannot then it is simply a question of the buyers deciding whether they want to go ahead and buy that property at that price. If not they may either try to negotiate a reduced purchase price or alternatively not proceed with the proposed purchase at all.

Other searches and enquiries

The searches and enquiries which we have just looked at must be undertaken in all cases. There are other searches which should be undertaken if the particular transaction requires it. These searches include:

(a)   Search of the public index map. This search is made at the District Land Registry. The public index map will reveal whether title to a property is already registered and if not whether there are any cautions against first registration. A search should be undertaken in every case involving as-yet unregistered title.

(b)   Commons registration search. Determining when a commons registration search is necessary is not quite so easy. It is a matter of common sense for the solicitor concerned. This search will reveal amongst other things the registration of common land or rights of common over land which is not actually common land. If any registrations are revealed there will be certain public and local rights which affect the property and will prevent the property being built upon. Even if it is not proposed to build upon the property there may be rights which are quite simply not acceptable to your buyer clients. The search should be undertaken whenever the land has not been built upon before. It is also sensible to undertake it where the title documents indicate that the land has previously belonged to the lord of the manor (indicating the possibility of a special form of common land).

(c)   British Coal search. Whether this is necessary depends on the area in which the property is situated. There is a directory which will enable solicitors to determine whether the property is in an area where such a search is necessary. The search is undertaken by submitting a standard form to the British Coal office. The object of the search is to find out whether there is any current mining which may affect the property or whether there has been any in the past or whether any is planned in the future. The risk of subsidence affecting the property can then be considered.

(d)   Central Land Charges Registry search (unregistered title). Sometimes a Central Land Charges search should be undertaken before exchange of contracts (for example, if the contract specifically provided that the buyers should buy subject to any matters revealed by a search of the

Central Land Charges Registry). In theory it is not usually strictly necessary at this stage as:

(i)   The sellers under the open contract rule and under the Standard Conditions are under a duty to disclose a land charge. If the sellers fail to disclose a land charge which the buyers then discover in their pre-completion search of the Land Charges Registry then the buyers may be able to claim damages (possibly completing at a reduced price) and may be able to claim rescission of the contract.

(ii)   Although the Law of Property Act 1925, s. 198, provides that registration of a land charge is 'deemed actual notice' (in other words buyers are regarded as knowing about it whether they actually did or not), nevertheless s. 24 prevents this from prejudicing a buyer at the pre-contract stage. The effect of the two provisions is that if the buyers discover, between exchange of contracts and completion, that there is a land charge affecting the property which the sellers did not disclose, the sellers cannot rely on s. 198 to say that the buyers are deemed to know about it anyway. If, however, the buyers discover a land charge after completion then the situation is different. After exchange of contracts the buyers are no longer protected by s. 24. If they fail to make the appropriate Land Charges Registry search between exchange and completion then s. 198 deems them to have notice of any registered charge and they purchase subject to that interest.

Despite these rules it may save time and expense if you know about any charges at this stage rather than having to sort the problem out immediately before completion.

(e)   Central Land Charges bankruptcy only search. This would be done before completion against the buyers where there is to be a mortgage. What about the client you have never seen before and about whom you are a little suspicious? You can save an awful lot of time if you discover the client is bankrupt *before* you start.

Exchange of contracts

Preparing for exchange of contracts

It is the buyers' solicitors' responsibility to ensure that all the necessary and relevant searches, enquiries and inspections have been undertaken. Anything which is revealed must be followed up by the buyers' solicitors making further enquiries where necessary, and they must in any event discuss their findings with the buyers. Once the buyers' solicitors have approved the draft contract and are entirely happy with the pre-contract searches, enquiries and inspections then they return one copy of the contract to the sellers' solicitors. Both the sellers' and the buyers' solicitors should obtain the signatures of their clients to their respective copies of the approved contract in readiness for exchange of contracts which will be the time when the sellers and buyers first enter into a legally binding relationship.

Exchange of contracts

If you are acting for buyers who are only buying a property and do not have another property to sell then the problem of exchange of contracts is not a particularly thorny one. It is nevertheless important to appreciate how an exchange of contracts is effected as until that moment it is highly unlikely that either the sellers or the buyers will have any rights against the other. The question of such things as breach of contract and misrepresentation can only become an issue once the contract has actually come into existence.

If you are acting for clients who are selling one property and buying another then there are two additional issues to consider:

(a) *Synchronisation of completion of the sale and purchase.* You must usually make sure that your clients sell their existing property on the same day as they buy their new property (i.e., check that the completion date inserted in your clients' contract for sale is the same date as that in your clients' contract to purchase). What is more, the time of day for completion must be checked. The final time for completion of the sale must be a reasonable time in advance of the final time for completion of the purchase so as to ensure that your clients receive the sale moneys before they have to pay for the property which they are buying and do not find themselves liable for damages for late completion on their purchase when they have no redress against the person who is buying from them. The only times when it is acceptable not to have the sale and purchase synchronised is when the implications have been discussed with your clients and they are in agreement. If the clients wish to complete their sale before their purchase they must be able to find alternative accommodation between the two completions. If they wish to complete the purchase before the sale they must for the interim period be able to finance the purchase independently of any money they expect to receive from their sale.

(b) *Synchronisation of exchange itself.* It is usually important that you do not commit your clients to selling their house without being sure that the sellers of the house they are buying will actually enter into the contract, and similarly they do not want to commit themselves to buying a house until they are sure that the buyers who are interested in their own property will go through with it. There are different procedural methods for exchanging contracts and establishing when the contract comes into existence. There are also some procedural refinements which attempt to minimise or eradicate the risk between effecting an exchange on say your clients' sale and having time to effect the exchange on your clients' purchase.

Methods of exchange

Personal exchange   This method involves the solicitors for both parties quite simply meeting and swapping their clients' signed copies of the contract. Although at one time this method was quite common it is not only very time consuming but also totally inappropriate unless the solicitors acting for the buyers and the sellers are in close proximity to each other. In addition if there is a chain of transctions involved then all the solicitors for all the buyers and sellers would have to meet together in one place to avoid the risk of failing to synchronise the exchanges.

Postal exchange   It is possible to effect exchange of contracts by post. The procedure is that one party's solicitors (let us say the buyers) would send their clients' signed part of the contract to the sellers' solicitor. The contract is then made in accordance with the postal rule when the solicitors for the sellers put their client's part of the contract in the post. There are risks if this method is used in a chain as illustrated in figure 7.1.

Figure 7.1

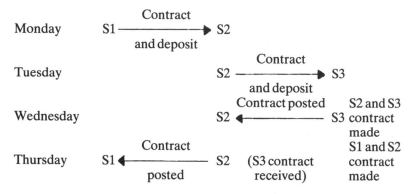

The risk might be almost completely overcome by S3 undertaking to advise S2 the moment exchange was effected on the contract between their clients (i.e., the moment S3's clients' part of the contract was put in the post).

Telephonic exchange   Often it is necessary to try to exchange contracts in a much shorter space of time than the traditional methods of personal or postal exchange would allow. It is possible for contracts to be exchanged by telephone. If two solicitors agree, over the telephone, to treat the parts of the contract as exchanged then in law it will be regarded as an exchange of contracts rather than a simple oral agreement. From the time when exchange takes place each solicitor will hold his or her clients' signed part of the contract not on behalf of the client but on behalf of the solicitor for the other party.

The Law Society has developed three methods of telephonic exchange of contract (formulas A, B and C) and solicitors should adopt one of these methods. Once your clients have authorised exchange at all this will be sufficient authorisation to use either of formula A or B. However, formula C can be used only with the express authority of your clients.

Formula A applies where one party's solicitors have sent their clients' signed part of the contract to the other party's solicitors. One party's solicitors are therefore holding both parties' signed copies of the contract. During the telephone conversation between the solicitors:

(a)   They agree a completion date.
(b)   The solicitor holding both parts of the contract confirms that he or she holds both copies signed by the respective clients and that they are identical.
(c)   The solicitor holding both copies confirms that he or she will forthwith insert the agreed completion date in both parts.
(d)   Both solicitors then agree that exchange shall take place at that moment.
(e)   The solicitor holding both parts confirms that from the moment he or she holds the copy signed by his or her clients to the order of the other solicitor and undertakes to send his or her clients' signed part of the contract (and deposit if the solicitor holding both copies is the buyers' solicitor) to the other that day by first-class post or document exchange.

Formula B is similar to formula A but is for use where each solicitor holds his or her own clients' signed copy of the contract. During the conversation between the solicitors:

(a)   They agree a completion date.
(b)   Each solicitor confirms that he or she holds his or her clients' signed part of the contract in the agreed form and will forthwith insert the agreed completion date.
(c)   Both solicitors agree that exchange shall take place from that moment.
(d)   Each solicitor undertakes to hold his or her clients' signed copy of the contract to the other's order and to send it, that day, to the other by first-class post or document exchange.
(e)   The buyers' solicitors also undertakes to send the deposit with the copy of the contract signed by his or her clients.

In the case of both formula A and formula B the solicitors who are parties to the telephonic exchange must make a file note of the conversation. The information which must be included in the file note is:

(a)   The *date* and *time* of exchange.
(b)   The agreed *completion date*.

(c)   The *identities* of the parties to the conversation.

There are still some possible risks with using either of these formulae. First they do not in any way help with the problem of synchronising your clients' sale and purchase in a chain transaction (unless the solicitors for all the parties were on the phone together at the same time). There may also be problems particularly with formula B in that, for example, the copies of the contract may in fact not be identical and the exchange therefore ineffective.

The *formula C* method of exchange is designed to overcome the risk in a chain transaction and to avoid that dangerous period, however short it may be, when you may have committed your clients to their sale without having a binding contract for their purchase or vice versa. As mentioned earlier your clients' written authority should be obtained before this method is used.

If formula C is used then there are two parts to it. It is used where each solicitor holds his or her own clients' copy of each contract.

Part I involves the parties confirming that they hold their clients' signed copy of the contract and agreeing:

(a)   The completion date.
(b)   To whom the deposit should be paid (either the sellers' solicitor in that transaction or another solicitor further up the chain if preferred).
(c)   The latest time for exchange that day.

Each solicitor then undertakes that he or she will continue to hold his or her clients' part of the contract until the final time for exchange has passed (e.g., he or she will not either give it back to the clients or tear it up at their request: if the client does request it the solicitor will be prevented from complying with the request by the undertaking).

They also undertake that if the sellers' solicitor requests the buyers' solicitor to exchange at any time before the latest time for exchange they will comply with part II of the formula (see below).

The buyers' solicitor also undertakes that there will be a named person available at the office until the latest time for exchange in order to activate part II of the formula.

Part II involves a phone call from the sellers' solicitor later that day requesting that part II be activated and that contracts are treated as exchanged. The buyers' solicitor cannot refuse to activate part II and exchange contracts so long as the request from the sellers' solicitor comes before the latest time for exchange as the buyers' solicitor has agreed to do so by undertaking.

The basic principle is that the exchange takes place in two stages which, by the use of undertakings, removes the risk of you completing on your clients' purchase only to find that since you last spoke to the solicitor for the other party in your clients' sale, his or her client has given instructions not to proceed with exchange. It is perhaps best illustrated by imagining a chain situation. The example below shows how it can be used in a relatively short chain involving only four people.

Mr A is selling the Mansion to Ms B.
Ms B is selling the Semi to Mr C.
Mr C is selling the Hovel to Ms D.

Mr A is therefore selling only.
Ms B is buying the Mansion and selling the Semi.
Mr C is buying the Semi and selling the Hovel.
Ms D is buying only.

Imagine a series of telephone calls as follows:

(a)   11 a.m. C's solicitor telephones D's solicitor and agrees formula C part I with the latest time for exchange being 4 p.m.

(D is now bound to exchange at C's request at any time before 4 p.m. There is no risk to D as D is only entering into one contract and so there are not two contracts which require to be synchronised.)

(b)   11.30 a.m. C's solicitor telephones B's solicitor and agrees formula C part I with the latest time for exchange being 3.30 p.m.

(C is now bound to exchange on the purchase of the Semi at B's request at any time up to 3.30 p.m. but there is no risk to C in this as C can oblige D to exchange on the sale of the Hovel at any time up to 4 p.m.)

(c)   12 noon. B's solicitor telephones A's solicitor and agrees exchange of contracts by formula B. Contracts relating to the Mansion are exchanged.

(There is no need to use formula C. It is the top of the chain and there is no need to have a time delay between the two parts. A is not at risk because he is selling only and therefore there is no need to synchronise anything. B is not at risk because C is bound to exchange at her request any time up to 3.30 p.m.)

(d)   12.30 p.m. B's solicitor telephones C's solicitor and activates part II. Contracts relating to the Semi are exchanged.

(B now has contracts exchanged on both her purchase and her sale. C has exchanged contracts only on his sale but is not at risk because he can require D to activate Part II and exchange contract at any time up to 4 p.m.)

(e)   1 p.m. C's solicitor telephones D's solicitor and activates part II. Contracts relating to the Hovel are exchanged.

By the time the fifth phone call takes place all the contracts are exchanged and without any of the parties who are both buying and selling ever being at risk of committing themselves to one contract without being able to ensure that the other was also successfuly exchanged.

Formula C also provides a convenient means of ensuring that any deposits which are paid do not get held up in travelling through the chain. The formula includes an undertaking by the buyer's solicitor on exchange of contracts that he or she will pay or procure the payment of the deposit to the seller's solicitor or someone further up the chain whom the seller's solicitor requests. Suppose in the same example the prices of the properties were:

The Mansion: £200,000.
The Semi: £100,000.
The Hovel: £50,000.

D is paying a deposit of £5,000 on the Hovel. C will no doubt want to use that as part of the £10,000 deposit paid to B in respect of the Semi. B will no doubt want to use the £10,000 received on the sale of the semi towards the £20,000 deposit on the Mansion. In effect *all* the deposit money paid will ultimately end up at the top of the chain with A. Formula C allows this to be achieved much more directly. During the phone calls regarding exchange the deposit will have been mentioned in the following terms:

(a)   11 a.m. C would request D to pay the deposit, in the event of part II being activated, directly to B's solicitor.
(He would not at this stage request the payment to A as he probably does not yet know of the existence of A.)
(b)   11.30 a.m. B would request C to pay the deposit, in the event of part II being activated, to A's solicitor.
(c)   12 noon. On exchange with A, B should undertake to pay or procure the payment of £20,000 deposit to A's solicitor. B would then send £10,000 to A's solicitor.
(d)   12.30 p.m. On exchange with B, C would undertake to pay or procure the payment of £10,000 to A's solicitor. C would then send £5,000 directly to A's solicitor.
(e)   1 p.m. On exchange of contracts with D, C would amend the request regarding payment of the deposit and ask for it to be paid to A's solicitor rather than B's solicitor. D would then send £5,000 directly to A's solicitor.

Next day A's solicitor should receive £20,000 made up of £10,000 from B, £5,000 from C and £5,000 from D.

EIGHT

DEDUCING AND INVESTIGATING TITLE

Objectives and terminology

This chapter is probably the heaviest going of all. It is certainly the longest. It is essential that you take this chapter very steadily and one step at a time. Don't leave a section until you are sure you understand what it was getting at. At the end of each section test yourself by seeing if you can reproduce the main points and, above all, whenever you are feeling bleary eyed, take a break.

Before dealing with the detail of deducing and investigating title it is perhaps useful to look at the stage you have reached in the transaction and the purpose of what you are about to do. Investigating title is a task undertaken by the buyers' solicitors. The modern practice is to investigate title before exchange of contracts although traditionally (and still in a number of cases today) it was undertaken between exchange of contracts and completion. The timing of it though really makes little difference to the objective. The sellers have promised (or will promise if contracts are yet to be exchanged), to sell the property to the buyers. The sellers have, in the contract, told the buyers the extent of the property that they own and are willing to sell and should have pointed out any rights which any third parties may have over the property. (This must of course be looked at in the light of the sellers' contractual duty of disclosure and the buyers' responsibility to undertake certain searches, enquiries and inspections prior to exchange of contracts, see chapter 7.)

Before the buyers actually hand over the purchase money they will want to check:

(a)   That the sellers can actualy sell the property as they have promised in the contract, and that all the documentation is in order.

(b)   That there are no third parties who have interests in the property other than have been disclosed in the contract.

Investigation of title involves the buyers' solicitors in three main tasks:

(a)   Inspecting the documentary evidence of title.

(b)   Undertaking pre-completion searches at the Central Land Charges Registry in the case of unregistered title and the District Land Registry in the case of registered title.

(c)   Inspecting the property itself to check whether there are any occupiers and if so what rights they have and whether there are any signs which may indicate the existence of easements which do not appear on the documents of title.

The terminology involved in the investigation of title sometimes causes unnecessary problems. The basic procedure behind investigation of the title by inspection of the documents of title is simple:

(a)   The sellers' solicitors will produce for the buyers' solicitors copies of the documents which they say will prove that the sellers can sell the property as they promised in the contract (the sellers' solicitors 'deduce title').

(b)   The buyers' solicitors, having received the copies of the documents will check through to see that everything is in order (the buyers' solicitors 'investigate title').

(c)   The buyers' solicitors, having checked through the documents, then ask the sellers' solicitors to rectify anything which they think is unsatisfactory in the documents which they have been shown or to provide evidence of anything which is not in the documents but which ought to be (the buyers' solicitors 'raise requisitions on title').

(d)   The sellers' solicitors then reply to those points (the sellers' solicitors 'reply to requisitions on title').

(e)   The sellers' solicitors at, or before, completion provide the buyers' solicitors with the original documents to check against the copies with which they have already been provided ('verification of title').

Whilst some of the underlying principles in registered and unregistered title are similar, the procedure, the terminology and the solutions to problems vary widely between the two systems and they should always be dealt with separately. If you are one of those students who has little difficulty in studying the two systems at once then fine. If you are, as most of us are, less fortunate then keep the two systems separate in your study. Once you have got to grips with what is going on you can allow yourself to see the similarities of principle. Above all, though, before you start an exam question, be sure to establish in your mind which system you are dealing with.

You should also bear in mind that whilst solicitors often use a standard form of requisitions on title this form has two shortcomings. First some matters dealt with do not relate to title at all and there may be no obligation on the sellers to respond. Secondly by no means all matters are covered and usually additional requisitions must be considered and raised.

Deducing title

The sellers' obligation in deducing title is to show that they can actually convey what they have promised in the contract and free of any third-party rights other than those disclosed in the contract. It is common for the documentary evidence of title to be delivered to the buyers' solicitors before exchange of contracts. Under the open contract rule evidence of title must be delivered to the buyers' solicitors within a reasonable time after exchange of contracts. The Standard Conditions require the evidence to be delivered immediately after the contract is made (Standard Condition 4.1.1).

Unregistered title

The contract will specify a document as the root of title. This is usually the earliest document which the seller is obliged to produce. The seller must then provide the buyer with an abstract or epitome (see glossary) showing that document and every document since then which shows how the estate has devolved. The only documents which do not need to be shown are:

(a)   Documents concerning an equitable interest which has been overreached.

(b)   Leases which have expired by effluxion of time (but one which has come to an end by surrender must be shown).

(c)   Equitable mortgages which will be discharged on or before completion.

(d)   Documents of record such as searches made against previous estate owners and death certificates. (Although these are often provided to the buyers as a matter of courtesy and where the death certificate is not shown the date and place of death must be stated.)

Registered title

Section 110(1) of the Land Registration Act 1925 requires the sellers to provide copies of the entries on the register and of the filed plan. (If the Standard Conditions are being used, Standard Condition 4.2.1 requires them to be office copies.)

Section 110(2) of the Land Registration Act 1925 provides that, in the absence of any contrary provision in the contract, the seller should also provide evidence (if there is any) of matters as to which the register is not conclusive, such as overriding interests.

Investigating title: Unregistered title

Documentation

Once the relevant documents have been delivered by the sellers' solicitor to the buyers' solicitors it is then the buyers' solicitors' task to check through them. The buyers' solicitors are checking to see that the documents which have been supplied are technically in order and whether there is anything missing which ought to have been included.

In an examination and in practice it is vital to take a clear and logical approach to checking the documents of title and to take notes as you go through them. As the buyers' solicitors you would first check whether there is a good root of title and an unbroken chain of legal title. You will also check that all documents have been correctly stamped.

A good root of title   The contract will tell you what root of title is being offered. One of the matters which must be considered in approving the draft contract is that the length of title should be at least 15 years. There are serious risks to the buyers if they accept less. In addition to the age of the root you must also check that the root you are given is a good root in that it:

(a)   deals with the whole legal and equitable interest (so, for example, a post-1925 will could not be a good root as it only takes effect in equity),
(b)   contains an adequate description of the land,
(c)   contains nothing which casts doubt on the title (so, for example, a document which included a statement revealing, expressly or by implication that the seller did not have the power to sell the property would not be adequate).

The best root will be a conveyance on sale providing it satisfies the above requirements. A voluntary conveyance (deed of gift) or an assent by personal representatives can also be a good root. The reason why a conveyance on sale is to be preferred is that it is likely that when the buyers bought on that occasion they made the usual searches and enquiries to check the title of the property they were buying. In the case of a gift it is highly unlikely that the donee carried out any searches or enquiries at all. The possibility of a pre-root defect about which the buyers know nothing is therefore considered, in the case of a gift, to be a greater risk.

If, having examined the root of title you are satisfied that it is a good root then the general rule is that you must assume that the title prior to the root is correct and you may not raise any requisitions about any matter prior to the root. However s. 45(1) of the Law of Property Act 1925 contains three exceptions to this rule:

(a)   If an abstracted document refers to the property as sold subject to any matter contained in an earlier document then the buyers are entitled to see that earlier document.

Example. A conveyance dated 2 January 1960 which in all other respects satisfies the definition of a good root but describes the property as: 'All that freehold property known as 37 High Street, Kettleham, Sudshire which property is for the purpose of identification only edged red on a plan annexed to a conveyance dated 3 March 1939 and made between X (1) and Y (2)'.

In this case the buyers, whilst accepting the root, should raise a requisition asking to be provided with a copy of the plan.

Example. A conveyance dated 1 December 1973 which in all other respects satisfies the definition of a good root of title but describes the property as: 'All that freehold property known as 73 Church Lane,

Kettleham, Sudshire subject to the restrictive covenants contained in a conveyance dated 1 December 1898 and made between X (1) and Y (2)'.

In this case the buyers, whilst accepting the root, should raise a requisition asking for a copy of the 1898 conveyance containing the covenants. The 1898 conveyance itself does not become the new root otherwise it would be necessary to check the whole title between 1898 and the present day.

(b)   If any document is executed under a power of attorney then even if the power predates the root the buyers are entitled to see it.

Example. The abstracted documents in a sale by S are a conveyance dated 1 January 1974 and made between X (1) and Y (2) and a conveyance dated 4 April 1980 and made between Y (1) and S (2) but executed on behalf of Y by his attorney A, A being appointed his attorney by a power dated 1 January 1973. The buyers are entitled to raise a requisition asking to see the power and for a copy of it notwithstanding that it is dated a year earlier than the root.

(c)   Any document creating any limitation or trust by reference to which the property is disposed of in an abstracted document.

An unbroken chain of legal title   The documents contained in the epitome or abstract show the history of the ownership of the property. Any story has to have a beginning, a middle and an end. If anything is missed out it will simply be a muddle and will not make sense. If the documents which you are shown establish A as the original owner in the root of title, and your clients are buying from E, then you must establish from the documents what happened in between; for example, that:

A sold to B and then
B sold to C and then
C sold to D and then
D sold to E who is now selling to your clients.

If the documents show that:

A sold to B and then
B sold to C and then
D sold to E who is selling to your clients,

then there must be a document missing.

Another problem you might encounter is that the title shows:

U sold to V and then
V sold to W, X and Y and then
X and Y sold to Z.

People (W in this case) cannot simply disappear from the legal title without explanation. If someone who was a legal owner has disappeared from the title and there is no explanation then there is a missing link. In the case of co-owners like this there are two likely explanations:

(a)   W has died, in which case the legal title passes to X and Y by survivorship. The missing link is therefore W's death certificate.

(b)   W has retired as trustee of the legal estate in which case there ought to be a deed of retirement, which is the missing link. Anything short of a deed will not do. It needs a deed to create or convey a legal estate (Law of Property Act 1925, s. 52(1)).

Simply listing the names of all the parties to the documents in the abstract or epitome will highlight the missing links and will be time well spent when it comes to checking what searches are needed (see below).

Once you are sure that you have all the necessary documents then you must check that those documents are technically in order. This will include checking that they have been properly executed. Where a deed is required, if it was made prior to 31 July 1990 it must have been 'signed, sealed and delivered'. On or after 31 July 1990 the provisions of s. 1 of the Law of Property (Miscellaneous Provisions) Act 1989 apply and require a deed to appear on the face of it that it is intended to be a deed. The requirement for a seal has been removed and the requirement for the signature to be witnessed has been added.

Stamping   It is necessary to check that each document bears the correct stamp as until the document is properly stamped it cannot be produced as evidence of title in court proceedings (nor will it be accepted on application for first registration by the Registrar). It will not therefore be an acceptable link in the title.

Even if the contract purports to exclude the buyers' right to raise requisitions regarding stamping the buyer is still entitled to insist on all instruments being properly stamped (Stamp Act 1891, s. 117).

Stamp duty can be either *ad valorem* or fixed rate and what is needed depends on the type of document and its date.

(a)   *A conveyance on sale.* The current requirements are for *ad valorem* duty at 1 per cent of the total consideration or nil if the consideration does not exceed £30,000 and a certificate of value in the prescribed form is included (see chapter 10 for the prescribed form).

In the past the rates have varied and it is necessary to check the tables of rates for that particular period to ensure the correct amount was paid.

(b)   *A voluntary conveyance or deed of gift.* Prior to 25 March 1985 *ad valorem* duty was payable on the value of the property and the value had to be adjudicated by the Inland Revenue. From 25 March 1985 to 30 April 1987 a 50p fixed duty was payable. From 30 April 1987 no duty is payable and no adjudication is required providing the deed includes a certificate in accordance with the Stamp Duty (Exempt Instruments) Regulations 1987.

(c) *An assent.* This is one of the few exceptions to s. 52(1) of the Law of Property Act 1925, which requires a conveyance of a legal estate to be by deed. If the assent *is* in the form of a deed then, prior to 30 April 1987, a fixed duty of 50p was required. Since 30 April 1987, no duty is payable but the assent must be certified similarly to the voluntary conveyance under the Stamp Duty (Exempt Instruments) Regulations 1987. If the assent is written but not in the form of a deed then no duty or certificate is required.

(d) *Mortgages.* Since 1 August 1971 no stamp duty has been payable on mortgages, deeds of discharge or vacating receipts (prior to 1971 only building society receipts were exempt).

In addition to any stamp duty which may or may not be required it is necessary for a conveyance on sale to bear a 'particulars delivered' stamp ('PD stamp').

Searches   The abstract or epitome with which you have been provided may or may not include Land Charges Registry search certificates against each of the previous owners of the property. There is no obligation on the sellers to provide them but they will often do so as a matter of courtesy. If they have not been provided you should ask for them. If they are then not forthcoming or if they are unsatisfactory then you should undertake them yourself.

Assuming you do receive any searches you should:

(a) Check that you have a search against each owner of the legal estate.

(b) Check that each search is in the correct name. (A misspelling of Denis as Dennis or vice versa will make the search worthless.)

(c) Check that each search is for the correct period of ownership. (If Y owned property from 30 December 1979 to 1 February 1981 then the search must cover 1979 to 1981 otherwise a search covering 1980 and 1981 would not protect against any charge registered on the last day of December 1979.)

(d) Check that completion took place within the priority period. Each search affords the person making it a priority period of 15 working days. If completion takes place between the date of the certificate and the end of the priority period then the buyers would take free of any interest registered in that period. (If a search was made against X, the priority period in respect of which expired on 4 April 1979, then a conveyance by X on 7 April 1979 would be subject to any matter registered against X between 4 and 7 April 1979.)

(e) Once you are sure that the certificate is satisfactory on the above points then check the entries. The buyers will be bound by any subsisting entry that is revealed by the certificate. If you discover that the entry relates to something which has been disclosed in the contract, e.g., restrictive covenants subject to which the proprty is sold, then that is acceptable. Otherwise requisitions should be raised to establish what the charges are, whether they will be removed, and indeed whether they relate to the property which you are buying.

If the title reveals that a company has owned the property then a search of the Companies Registry should be checked (see further chapter 9).

Particular problems in the chain   So far you have checked the general nature of the chain. You have checked for a good root, you have checked that the links in the chain of title are secure, you have checked that each document is properly stamped and you have checked the Land Charges Registry against each of the previous owners. Depending on the nature of the documents and the owners of each particular title the possible requisitions will vary. It is necessary now to look at particular dispositions and some of the problems and defects which may be found if you have such a disposition as part of the title of the property you are buying.

A sale by trustees for sale   A trust for sale may be created expressly or it can be implied in certain situations. For example, where two or more people buy property as co-owners then statute will imply a trust for sale. So if property were conveyed to A and B then A and B would hold the legal estate as trustees on trust for themselves in equity (see table 8.1).

Table 8.1

Legal	*Equitable*
A and B (joint tenants and trustees for sale)	A and B

The legal estate must always be held by the legal owners as joint tenants so if, for example, A should die then B would be the sole legal owner. The equitable interest may be held as joint tenants or tenants in common depending first on the express wording, secondly on the surrounding circumstances and finally on whether, if they were joint tenants at the outset, there has been severance of the joint tenancy since then.

The maximum number of trustees is four and therefore if property were conveyed to five adults A, B, C, D and E then A, B, C and D would hold the legal estate as trustees on trust for sale for themselves and E in equity (see table 8.2).

Table 8.2

Legal	*Equitable*
A, B, C, D (joint tenants and trustees for sale)	A, B, C, D, E

A trust for sale may also be implied where, for example, property is conveyed to X alone but in fact the purchase money has been provided by X and Y, in which case the picture may be as in table 8.3.

Table 8.3

Legal	Equitable
X (as trustee for sale for . . .)	X and Y

Whenever the chain of title includes a sale by trustees for sale there are certain matters that the buyers should consider. First, though, you need to be aware of the matters which do not concern you and about which it would be illegitimate to raise requisitions:

(a)   You need not concern yourself with any direction to postpone the sale.

(b)   You need not concern yourself with any express or implied requirement that the trustees consult with the beneficiaries before the sale (e.g., under the Law of Property Act 1925, s. 26(3)).

(c)   You need not concern yourself whether the trust is still subsisting (e.g., whether it is in fact now a bare trust with an individual absolutely entitled to require the trustees to convey the property to him).

(d)   You need not concern yourself whether the correct people have been appointed trustees. (For example, the original document establishing the trust may provide for Joe Bloggs to decide upon who should be new trustees. The purchaser can presume that Joe Bloggs did in fact decide upon the trustees who have actually been appointed and accept their actual appointment at face value without asking for evidence of his approval.)

The matters which do concern you are:

(a)   *The power of the trustees.* Trustees for sale have the combined powers of the trustees and the tenant for life under the Settled Land Act 1925. These powers include the power to sell property but there are certain dispositions which are not within their powers (e.g., granting an option in excess of 10 years). If the disposition which the trustees are undertaking is not authorised by the Settled Land Act 1925 then confirmation should be sought that the powers of the trustees were extended at the time the trust was created and evidence of the extension of powers provided.

(b)   *Consents.* It is possible for the terms of a trust for sale to provide that the consents of certain people are obtained before the property is sold. Whilst it is the responsibility of the trustees to ensure that *all* such consents are obtained, buyers need only see that two of the consents are obtained and they need never concern themselves about the consent of someone under a disability such as minority or mental disorder.

Example. If the trust requires the consent of X, Y and Z to be obtained, the buyers need raise no requisition if they are provided with evidence of the consents of X and Y. If evidence of the consent of X alone is provided then a requisition should be raised requesting the provision of evidence of the consent of either Y or Z.

(c)   *Over-reaching.* If the buyers pay the purchase money to all the trustees and there are at least two of them (or if there is only one it is a trust corporation) then the interests of the beneficiaries under that trust can safely be ignored as they are overreached and converted into interests in the proceeds of sale of the property. The buyers will not be bound by them and will take the property free of them.

Example, the trust for sale in the title appointed X, Y and Z as trustees for A, B and C in equity (see Table 8.4).

Table 8.4

Legal	Equitable
X, Y and Z (as trustees for sale)	A, B and C

A sale by X, Y and Z to P would overreach the interests of A, B and C (see table 8.5.

Table 8.5

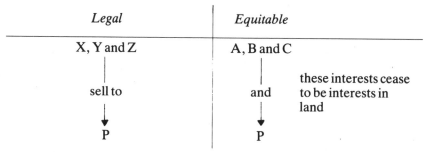

Legal	Equitable	
X, Y and Z	A, B and C	
sell to	and	these interests cease to be interests in land
P	P	

However if, in the same situation, X and Y had died so that Z held as trustee for A, B and C then the position would be as in table 8.6.

Table 8.6

Legal	Equitable
Z	A, B and C

A sale by Z to P would not overreach the interests of A, B and C (see table 8.7).

Table 8.7

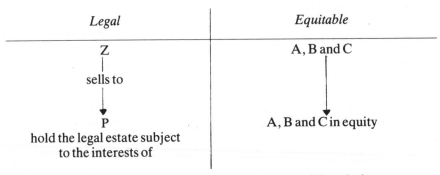

If this type of situation arose then there are two possible solutions:

(a)   First that A, B and C (if they are of sound mind and full age) could join in the conveyance to P to release their equitable interests in which case P would take the property free of them.

(b)   Secondly, if Z appointed another trustee to act in the sale so that Z and T (the new trustee) together conveyed the property to P then that would overreach the interests of A, B and C as in the earlier example.

The second solution is the most common. First because the buyers (P) are entitled to insist on this method rather than the first method if they so wish and also because it will overreach the interests of anybody else other than A, B and C who might also, unbeknown to the buyers have an equitable interest under the trust.

If the situation arose earlier in the title which you are investigating then either of these solutions would be acceptable but you need the documentary evidence of them. It is part of the title to the property. If your clients are in fact buying directly from a sole trustee then you should require the appointment of a second trustee either in the conveyance or earlier by a separate deed which will form part of the title. In either event your requisitions should state clearly what the problem is and ask the seller to confirm that the situation will be remedied by the appointment of a second trustee.

Sale by a surviving co-owner   This is closely related to the previous situation of a sale by trustees for sale. If co-owners buy property then, whether or not the conveyance to them contains an express trust for sale, statute will imply one. Whilst the co-owners must be joint tenants at law they may be either joint tenants or tenants in common in equity.

Example. A and B were co-owners and it is established that, on the death of B, they were tenants in common in equity (see table 8.8).

Table 8.8

Legal	Equitable	Legal	Equitable
A and B hold as joint tenants and trustees for sale for . . .	A and B as tenants in common in equity	A hold as trustee on trust for sale for	A and B's estate in equity

Before B's death   After B's death

The solution here is the same as we have just seen for the sale by a trustee for sale, i.e., either

(a)   appoint a second trustee to overreach the equitable interest of B's estate, or

(b)   have the beneficiary under B's estate join in the conveyance to release his or her equitable interest.

However, if it can be established that A and B were joint tenants when they first bought the property, and there is no evidence of severance of the joint tenancy thereafter then the buyer is faced with a different problem. If, in fact, there had been no severance then on B's death A should become the sole legal and equitable owner by virtue of survivorship (see table 8.9).

Table 8.9

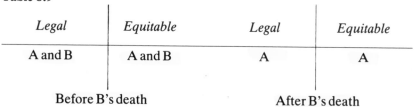

Legal	Equitable	Legal	Equitable
A and B	A and B	A	A

Before B's death   After B's death

Hence only B's death certificate should be necessary to complete the title (to explain B's absence from the later conveyance). However, there may have been severance of which the buyers may have no knowledge. It is usual on severance of the joint tenancy (e.g., by service of a written notice by one of the joint tenants on the other) to endorse a memorandum of severance on the original conveyance to them as joint tenants and if this has been done the buyers will be able to see the evidence of severance. However, even if no memorandum is endorsed the severance will nevertheless be effective. How then can buyers be sure that the situation they are looking at is that in table 8.9 and not that in table 8.8? The answer is that the buyers are given some protection by the Law of Property (Joint Tenants) Act 1964, the effect of which is that the buyers can assume that the survivor is solely and beneficially entitled to the property providing:

(a)   The conveyance by the survivor is made in his or her capacity as beneficial owner or contains a statement (for example, in the recitals) that the survivor is solely and beneficially entitled to the property.

(b)   No memorandum of severance has been endorsed on the original conveyance to the co-owners.

(c)   No bankruptcy petition or receiving order has been registered against either of the joint tenants (bankruptcy would itself automatically have severed the joint tenancy).

So, in investigating the title, if you should come across a sale by the survivor of joint tenants you should:

(a)   Check they were joint tenants at the time of the original conveyance to them.

(b)   Check that the conveyance to the co-owners is not endorsed with a memorandum of severance.

(c)   Check or undertake a land charges search against the co-owners to ensure (amongst other things) that no bankruptcy proceedings are revealed.

(d)   Check that the conveyance by the survivor did (or, if your clients are buying directly from the survivor, will) contain the necessary statement that the survivor is solely and beneficially entitled to the property.

If the result of any of these checks is unsatisfactory then the buyers should protect themselves by requiring the appointment of a second trustee. If a second trustee was not, but should because of severance have been, appointed at the time, then one way of remedying the title would be to obtain a disclaimer of interest from the deceased co-owner's estate.

Sale by personal representatives   If a joint owner of the legal estate of a property dies then the legal estate will pass by survivorship to his or her co-owner. The personal representatives (executors or administrators) of the deceased will not hold the legal title of the property at all. However, if the deceased was the sole legal owner of the property then his or her personal representatives will be entitled to the legal estate and the grant of probate or grant of administration will form part of the title to the property.

The personal representatives have all the powers of trustees for sale and can either sell the property or pass the legal title to a beneficiary who is entitled to it under the will of the deceased or under the intestacy rules. If the property is sold then the personal representatives will execute a conveyance. If instead they give the property to one of the beneficiaries of the estate then they will execute an assent. A conveyance must always be in the form of a deed. An assent is one of the very few exceptions to the rule that it needs a deed to convey a legal estate in that it may either be in the form of a deed or simply in writing. Whichever form of document is used all the personal representatives must execute it. However, if there is only one personal representative then that personal representative can, unlike a sole trustee, overreach the interests of the beneficiaries under the will or intestacy. It is therefore acceptable to have a conveyance or assent in the title executed by only one personal representative if he or she was the only person to whom a grant was issued and not one of a number of such persons.

There are two problems which are peculiar to the situation of a sale by personal representatives whether your buyers are buying directly from the personal representatives or whether there is a disposition by personal representatives in the earlier title.

In the case of a sale by personal representatives, the buyers would be concerned that the personal representatives had not, by an earlier conveyance or assent, passed the property to someone else. If there was an earlier sale to someone, and the buyers could not have known about it, whilst they have a right to sue the personal representatives they will have no right to the land. Similarly if the earlier disposition was an assent but then the assentee sold the legal estate for valuable consideration. However, where the earlier disposition was an assent and there has been no subsequent sale for valuable consideration then the later buyers will, notwithstanding the earlier assent, take the legal estate free of the assent in certain circumstances. This protection is provided by s. 36(6) of the Administration of Estates Act 1925, the effect of which is that the later buyers will take the legal estate if they:

(a)   Obtain a statement in writing from the personal representatives that they have not made any previous conveyance or assent of the legal estate.

(b)   Check that there is no memorandum of a previous assent or conveyance endorsed on the original grant of probate or administration.

Example. C and D are executors of, and have obtained a grant of probate in respect of, X's estate which includes Cherry Trees.

(i)   C and D assent to the vesting of Cherry Trees in B. C and D then purport by way of sale to convey Cherry Trees to P. Providing P has checked there is no memorandum of the original assent to B endorsed on the original grant of probate and if the conveyance to P includes a s. 36(6) statement then P takes the legal estate notwithstanding the earlier assent to B.

(ii)   C and D convey Cherry Trees by way of sale to B. C and D then purport to convey Cherry Trees by way of sale to P. B keeps the legal estate even if the conveyance to P included a s. 36(6) statement and there was no memorandum of the conveyance to B on the original grant of probate.

(iii)   C and D assent to the vesting of Cherry Trees in B. B then passes the legal estate by a conveyance on sale to F. Thereafter C and D purport to convey Cherry Trees to P. F keeps the legal estate even if the conveyance to P included a s. 36(6) statement and there was no memorandum of the assent endorsed on the original grant of probate.

The second problem peculiar to a disposition by personal representatives is where there is an assent by personal representatives. The effect of the Administration of Estates Act 1925, s. 36(7), is that providing there is no memorandum of a previous conveyance or assent endorsed on the original grant of probate or administration then, in the absence of evidence to the contrary, the buyers are entitled to assume that the assent was made to the correct person. It is not therefore usually necessary to check the will of the deceased when investigating the title. However, if the title does in any way suggest that the wrong person was given the property then the buyers must continue to make full enquiries.

When there is a grant of probate or administration involved in a title it is usual to check for certain things and to raise requisitions if the information is not available from the abstract or epitome or if the information which is available is unsatisfactory. For example:

(a)   Check that the grant of probate or administration had no memorandum of an earlier disposition endorsed on it (one of the precautions required by the Administration of Estates Act 1925, s. 36(6) and (7)).

(b)   Check that the conveyance by the personal representatives did (or will if your clients are buying from them) contain a statement in accordance with s. 36(6).

(c)   Check that a memorandum of the disposition by the personal representatives has been endorsed on the original grant of probate or administration (or will be if your clients are buying directly from them). The person in whose favour the conveyance or assent is being made is entitled to insist on this. (Even in the case of a buyer for valuable consideration, where such a memorandum will make no difference to the buyer under s. 36(6), it should nevertheless be done as a matter of good conveyancing practice.)

(d)   Check that the original grant of probate or administration will be available for inspection on completion. You need to check the accuracy of the information requested in (a) to (c) above and also to check the accuracy of the copy you have been given and to mark it as examined with the original. Also it forms part of your title as it explains and proves the devolution of the legal title. However, the original will not be handed over to you as the personal representatives will need to keep it to prove their title to other parts of the deceased's estate.

(e)   Check that an acknowledgement for production of the original grant has been given (or will be given if you are buying directly from the personal representatives). The grant forms part of the legal title to the property. Therefore anybody who buys from your clients will also wish to see the original, and this acknowledgement obliges the personal representatives to make it available.

One additional problem can be encountered when buying property where at some stage in the title the same person has been the personal representative and the person entitled under the will or intestacy to the property.

Example. Y has been appointed sole executor of X's estate and has also been given the Manor House in X's will.

It is possible under these circumstances for Y to sell the property in his or her capacity as personal representative or as beneficial owner. If Y sells as personal representative then the last document in the title would be the grant of probate. If, however, Y sells as beneficial owner then his or her title must include not only the grant of probate but also an assent by Y as executor to Y as beneficial owner (see figure 8.1).

Figure 8.1

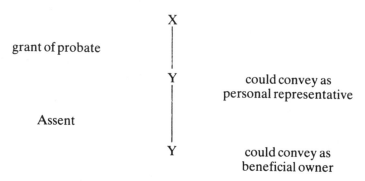

Sale of settled land   A strict settlement is created by two deeds: a trust instrument, which is usually a private document which does not form part of the title which the buyers are entitled to see, and a vesting deed. The vesting deed will, where there is a tenant for life, give the legal estate of the property to the tenant for life. If there is no tenant for life then the legal title will be given to the statutory owners (usually the trustees of the settlement). The vesting deed does form part of the title to the property.

If the tenant for life dies then there are two possibilities:

(a)   If the settlement continues then the trustees of the settlement will obtain a special grant of representation and will then execute another vesting instrument to give the property to the next tenant for life. Both of these documents will form part of the title to the property.

(b)   If the settlement comes to an end on the death of the tenant for life then the tenant for life's own personal representatives will take the property and vest it in the person entitled to it. The grant of probate or of administration in the tenant for life's own estate will form part of the title to the property as will the conveyance to the ultimate beneficiary of the settlement.

It is possible that a tenant for life might, during the course of the settlement, wish to sell the property. The tenant for life has the power to do this but must comply with certain requirements (for example a tenant for life must obtain the best consideration for the property that can reasonably be obtained). The tenant for life also has certain other powers set out in the Settled Land Act 1925 and evidence of any extension of these statutory powers will be found in the vesting deed. (The statutory powers cannot be restricted, only extended.)

The position of buyers from a tenant for life is relatively straightforward:

(a) *Documentation.* The buyers do not need to see the trust instrument. The vesting deed will tell you who is the tenant for life, who are the trustees and what (if any) extra powers the tenant for life has. If any new trustees have been appointed since the vesting deed then the buyers will need to see, not a deed of appointment, but simply a declaration saying who the new trustees are.

(b) *Protection of the buyer.* Although the Settled Land Act 1925 includes various requirements as to the way in which the tenant for life exercises his or her powers, these provisions will not concern buyers in good faith from the tenant for life who are conclusively deemed to have complied with them (e.g., a purchaser in good faith is conclusively deemed to have given the best price for the property).

(c) *Overreaching.* Overreaching will operate in a sale by a tenant for life providing the purchase money is paid to all the trustees, there being at least two of them (or only one then that one is a trust corporation). This means that if the trustees are parties to the conveyance in order to receive the purchase money then any equitable interests under the strict settlement can be safely ignored by the buyers.

Sale by fiduciary owners   If the title reveals that, at some stage in the past, there has been a sale or other disposition by legal owners in a fiduciary position (e.g., trustees or personal representatives) to themselves, or one of them, then care should be taken. Such a disposition would be voidable at the request of the beneficiaries unless it was authorised. Authorisation could be found in the trust instrument, or be provided by the consent of the court to the disposition, or by the consent of the beneficiaries (providing they are of full age and of sound mind).

Example. If the title shows that X, Y and Z held property as executors and on trust for P and Q and goes on to show that X, Y and Z sold the property to Z, P and Q could later challenge the sale to Z (see table 8.10).

Table 8.10

Legal	Equitable
X, Y and Z	P and Q
sell to	
Z	

This will not be a danger if there is also evidence in the title that:

(a)   the transaction was authorised by the will, or
(b)   the consent of the court has been obtained, or
(c)   P and Q were of full age and sound mind and consented to the sale

Buyers buying from Z should not accept the title unless such evidence is provided. If the transaction was voidable the title could be rectified by P and Q joining in the conveyance to B to confirm the original conveyance to Z.

The buyers should take care because if they can see from the title that someone in a fiduciary position has immediately acquired the property in his or her personal capacity then the buyers will be deemed to have notice of any rights of the beneficiaries.

Deeds of gift   Care should be taken if, when investigating the title, you discover a deed of gift as part of the title. The Insolvency Act 1986 and the Matrimonial Causes Act 1973 both provide for gifts and sales at undervalue to be set aside if made with the intention of putting assets beyond the reach of creditors or frustrating a claim for financial provision on divorce respectively.

Perhaps the biggest threat is the Insolvency Act 1986 which provides that a deed of gift (or transaction at undervalue) is voidable by a trustee in bankruptcy should the donor become bankrupt within two years of the gift. (The time-limit is five years if the donor was insolvent at the time of the gift.) There is protection for a purchaser in good faith without knowledge of the 'relevant circumstances', but if the deed is of gift rather than a conveyance at undervalue, the very existence of the deed of gift in the abstract or epitome will give notice of the 'relevant circumstances'. The buyers should therefore, in theory, refuse to complete if there is a deed of gift within the past five years. Even if the deed of gift is longer ago than that the buyers should ensure that a bankruptcy search for the period of ownership plus five years is undertaken and is satisfactory.

A practical solution if the deed of gift was made between two and five years ago and the searches are clear might be to obtain a statutory declaration from the donor that he or she was solvent at the time of the gift. Whilst this is certainly not a foolproof guarantee it is thought unlikely that a trustee in bankruptcy would attack the buyers who had taken such a precaution.

Sale by attorneys   A power of attorney makes it possible for the donee of the power to carry out certain acts on behalf of the donor. For example, if X is the sole legal and beneficial owner of property and she is going away and wishes Y to deal with the sale of it, she need not convey the property to Y so that Y can sell it. She may instead give Y the power to sell on her (X's) behalf. If you are buying property from an attorney, or if there is a sale by an attorney earlier in the title you will want to check:

(a)   That the power covers the particular transaction.
(b)   That the power has or had not been revoked.

Scope of a power of attorney   If the donor of the power is the sole legal owner of the property then the following types of power could be used:

(a)   A specific power. This spells out exactly what the donee is entitled to do (for example, execute a particular conveyance on sale).

(b)   A general power. This entitles the donee to do most things which the donor could have done and will include the right to sell or lease the property.

(c)   An enduring power of attorney. This form has the advantage that it will not become revoked by the donor's mental incapacity (although the powers of the donee are suspended for a period after incapacity).

The contents of each of the forms, and the formalities required for their execution, vary depending on the type of power and the circumstances.

If the legal owner is a trustee then only a specific power can be used and even then only for a period not exceeding 12 months and not to a sole co-trustee. A trustee cannot give a blanket authority to someone else to carry out his or her duties. Remember that a person may be a trustee not only because of an express appointment but also in every case where land is held on an express or statutory trust for sale.

Table 8.11

Legal	*Equitable*
X and Y hold the legal estate as trustees on trust for themselves in	X and Y equity

In the example in table 8.11, if Y wanted to appoint an attorney then:

(a)   It could not be a general power but must be a specific one.
(b)   The power can only be for a period of 12 months.
(c)   The donee of the power cannot be X.

The only alternative which would allow X to be the attorney for Y would be to use an enduring power of attorney.

A purchaser is entitled to see a copy of any power of attorney affecting the title and should ensure it is a copy which has been marked as examined with the original by a solicitor. The purchaser from an attorney or with a disposition by an attorney in the title should therefore check that:

(a)   The power is an appropriate one and gave authority for that particular transaction.

(b)   The power has been properly executed.

Revocation of a power of attorney   Unless a power is irrevocable (for example, when combined with a mortgage) it can usually be revoked expressly by the donor. It is revoked automatically by the donor's death, incapacity or bankruptcy.

Buyers from an attorney will be concerned to know whether the power has been revoked. Buyers are, however, afforded some protection by s. 5(2) of the Powers of Attorney Act 1971, the effect of which is that a buyer without knowledge of the revocation will get good title to the property notwithstanding the revocation. Care must be taken, though, as knowledge of an event giving rise to the revocation (e.g., death) will have the same effect as knowledge of the revocation itself.

Example. If B buys property from S as attorney for Y. B cannot rely on the protection of s. 5(2) if she knew of the incapacity of Y even if she did not know that the incapacity automatically revoked the power.

A buyer who buys property where there is a sale by an attorney earlier in the title will therefore be concerned about the state of the earlier buyers' knowledge.

Example. If P buys property from X as attorney for Y, and later P contracts to sell to B, it is relevant to B and those who may buy the property from him in the future whether or not P had any knowledge of revocation or an event giving rise to revocation.

The Powers of Attorney Act 1971, s. 5(4), gives protection if the buyer is a purchaser in good faith and for valuable consideration. In favour of the buyer it is conclusively presumed that the first buyer did not know of the revocation or an event giving rise to revocation if either:

(a)   The sale to the original purchaser was made within 12 months of the date when the power came into operation, or

(b)   If the sale is after 12 months from the date of the power, the original purchaser made a statutory declaration before or within three months of completion of the sale by him or her that he or she did not know of any revocation or an event giving rise to revocation at the time when he or she bought.

So take in the example above where X acts as attorney for Y and sells to P and P later sells to B, on the sale *to P*, P will be protected if he did not know of the revocation by Y or an event giving rise to automatic revocation. P's solicitor should check this with P. On the sale *to B*, B will be protected if either the creation of the power by X and the sale from Y to P were within 12 months of each other *or*, before or within three months of the sale *from P to B*, P makes the necessary statutory declaration. B's solicitor (and the solicitors for any later buyer) should check the dates are appropriate or that the necessary statutory declaration is included as part of the title.

Similar but considerably more complicated provisions apply in relation to an enduring power of attorney (see Enduring Powers of Attorney Act 1985) and different provisions apply in relation to dispositions by an attorney prior to 1 October 1971 (see Law of Property Act 1925).

Mortgages   Whenever you see a mortgage in the abstract or epitome you need to check that it is no longer subsisting. This means that you need to look for one of two things, either a discharge of the mortgage or a sale by the mortgagee.

Existence and form of a receipt   If there is neither a receipt nor a sale by a mortgagee then the mortgage is still subsisting and a requisition will need to be raised asking that it be discharged before completion or that the sellers' solicitors undertake to discharge it on completion and forward the receipted charge to you. It is not sufficient that you are told that the money has been repaid. There should always be a formal written receipt. There are two forms of formal receipt, one prescribed by the Law of Property Act 1925, s. 115 and sch. 3, and in the case of building societies a form prescribed by the Building Societies Act 1986, s. 13(7) and sch. 4.

Effect of a receipt   Even if there is a receipt, care should be taken to check it is in an appropriate prescribed form as required by statute. If the receipt is in the Law of Property Act 1925; s. 115, form then there is an additional problem to consider. Statute provides that if it appears that the mortgage has been paid off by someone who is not the person immediately entitled to redeem the mortgage then the receipt operates not to redeem the mortgage but to transfer it.

So, for example, if X owns Greenwood Farm and it is subject to a mortgage in favour of B Bank Ltd then X is entitled to redeem the mortgage. If X, on 1 May 1988, sells the farm to Y subject to the mortgage then Y is the person entitled to redeem it after 1 May 1988. If on 2 May 1988 X were to pay off the mortgage then paying it off would operate to make X the mortgagee in place of B Bank Ltd (see figure 8.2).

Figure 8.2

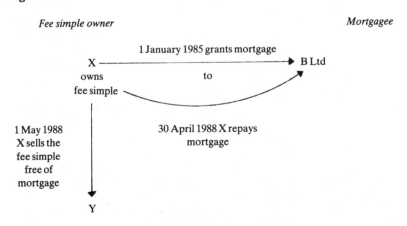

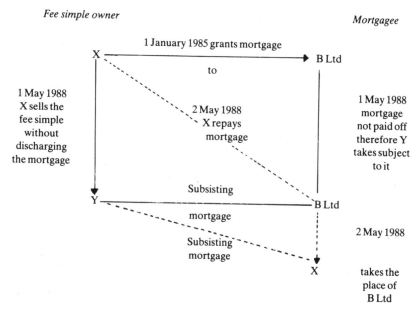

There are exceptions where, even if X did repay the mortgage after Y became the owner of the fee simple, it would not operate to transfer the mortgage to X, namely:

(a)   Where X had, in the conveyance, sold the property 'free from encumbrances' he would then be estopped from claiming that Y must repay the mortgage to him.

(b)   Where it was expressly provided that the payment should not operate as a transfer of the mortgage to X.

There are also provisions that apply so that the payment does not operate as a transfer of the mortgage where payment is made by trustees or where there are subsequent mortgages.

The effect of these provisions is that the buyers' solicitors should be careful not only to check the existence of the receipt but also, in the case of non Building Societies Act receipts, to check who repaid it and when, and whether in fact the repayment did discharge the mortgage or simply transferred it. If the effect of the receipt was to transfer the mortgage it should be treated as an existing mortgage requiring to be paid off at completion.

Sale by a mortgagee   A legal mortgage which does not expressly exclude the power of sale will give the mortgagee a right to sell the property. If the mortgagee sells there is no need for the mortgage to be receipted as the sale by the mortgagee will be free of that mortgage. If there is a sale in the title by a legal mortgagee then the buyers' solicitors should check:

(a)   Whether the power of sale has arisen. Usually mortgages contain a legal redemption date (often six months after the mortgage was granted). This is not in practice the date on which the money is expected to be repaid as the mortgage may continue for many years. However, it is the date after which it is possible for the mortgagee to sell the property as it then has the *power* to do so. This power will not in practice be exercisable, nor usually be exercised, until the mortgagor defaults in some way (see Law of Property Act 1925, s. 103). The buyers, in any event, need not enquire whether it was in fact exercisable, only whether it had arisen. The buyers should therefore seek confirmation from the mortgage deed that the legal date for redemption had passed by the time of the sale.

(b)   Whether there are any earlier mortgages. A sale by a mortgagee will pass the property to the buyers free of any later mortgages. There is therefore no need for later mortgages to be discharged and receipted. However, any earlier mortgages must be treated in the same way as on an ordinary sale, that is, they must be discharged and receipted.

Example. Z owns Quarry House and enters into the following transactions:

(i)   A legal mortgage to E dated 1 January 1985.
(ii)   A legal mortgage to F dated 1 January 1986.
(iii)   A legal mortgage to G dated 1 January 1987.

If F then sells the property the buyers would be concerned to check:

(i)   That the legal date for redemption of F's mortgage had passed before the sale.
(ii)   That the mortgage to E had been properly discharged.

The buyers would not, however, have to see a discharge of the mortgage to F (as the sale by F would pass the property free of it) nor to G (as the sale by F would overreach it).

Sales by charities   The Charities Act 1960 requires the consent of the Charity Commissioners or the court where either 'permanent endowment' property or property which at any time has been occupied by the charity has been sold. Enquiries should be made as to whether the property was permanent endowment property and if so the consent obtained. In the case of property occupied by the charity there is protection for the purchaser in good faith for money or money's worth even if consent is not obtained.

Sales by companies   For sales by companies prior to the coming into force of the Companies Act 1989, s. 108, there was some protection provided for a purchaser in good faith from the company even if the sale was beyond the powers of the company. There were, however, problems with this in that the sale had to have been 'decided upon by the directors'. It was very difficult for a purchaser, particularly later in the title to establish this. It was therefore advisable always to check the memorandum of association of the company to see that the transaction was within the company's powers. If no copy of the memorandum was available one could be obtained from the Companies Registry.

In the case of a sale after the coming into force of s. 108 of the 1989 Act (4 February 1991) there would seem to be little problem for a bona fide purchaser whatever the objects and powers of the company.

Marriages and Deaths   Marriage and death may form part of the title to a property. We saw earlier how if one of joint owners died the evidence of death would be needed to prove the entitlement of the survivor to convey the property. Similarly if a marriage results in a woman changing her name then the certificate will be required to explain why, for example, there is a conveyance to Joseph Smith and Tracy King in 1985 and a conveyance from Joseph Smith and Tracy Smith in 1987.

Marriage and death certificates are both documents of public record and there is no obligation on the seller to provide copies but only to provide the buyers with sufficient detail for them to obtain a copy from the Registry of Birth, Deaths and Marriages. Nevertheless if the sellers have the certificates or copies it is usual and courteous to provide them as part of the documents of title.

Sale of part   If X and Y own a house with a large garden and decide to sell off part of the garden as a building plot, they will execute a conveyance of that plot which they will hand over to the buyers. However, X and Y will need to keep the earlier deeds to prove their title to the house and part of the garden which they have retained.

Example. X and Y's title consists of

(a)   A conveyance on sale dated 2 January 1974 and made between R (1) and S (2).

(b)   A conveyance on sale dated 2 January 1981 and made between S (1) and T (2).

(c)   A conveyance on sale dated 4 April 1985 and made between T (1) and X and Y (2).

All these deeds relate to the whole of the property and therefore on sale to B and C, X and Y will need to keep them. X and Y will execute a conveyance of part to B and C and hand it over to them.

B and C now have two problems, first they want to feel comfortable that X and Y, who appear from the title deeds still to own the whole property, will not attempt to resell the plot which they have bought. This can be avoided by B and C ensuring before completion that X and Y agree to endorse a memorandum of the sale on the 1985 conveyance. The second problem is that B and C's title to the property consists of all four deeds. If they want to sell their plot they must show all these deeds to the Land Registry. It should therefore be ensured, when buying part of a property, that the sellers give an acknowledgement for production (and usually also for safe-keeping) of the earlier documents. If a sale of part is earlier in your title you should check this was given by the sellers at the time. If it was not it should be obtained or, at the very least, the buyers provided with examined and marked copies of those earlier documents.

Pre-completion searches and inspection of the property

These form part of the buyers' solicitors' tasks on investigation of title. They are dealt with in detail in chapter 9.

Investigating title: Registered title

In registered title the task of investigating title and raising requisitions is usually substantially simpler than in unregistered title. Instead of a root of title and all the documents affecting the title between then and the present day, the buyers are given copies of the Land Register entries. The objectives of investigating title and raising requisitions are still the same:

(a)   To see that the sellers can sell what they are, in the contract, promising to sell.
(b)   To check whether there are any third-party rights other than those disclosed in the contract.

The method of investigating title, though, is slightly different. The buyers are still required to inspect the documentary evidence of title, it is just that in registered title the evidence of title is the register. It is not usually necessary to check any earlier transactions. (You may occasionally need to look at earlier deeds which contain covenants or easements referred to in the register because the register does not always set these out in full.) Whether any additional evidence is required will depend on the circumstances.

The buyers are still required to undertake a pre-completion search but this time it must be at the District Land Registry against the title number and not at the Central Land Charges Registry against the previous owners of the legal estate.

Inspection of the property is still required in registered title as in unregistered title. The purpose of the inspection at this stage is to look for evidence of any overriding interests which have not been disclosed in the contract.

Documentation

The copies of the register should be checked very carefully.

(a)   The property register and filed plan should be checked to see that the physical description, the extent of the property and the rights benefiting it accord with the contract and the buyers' understanding of what they are buying. It is possible, for example, that the property register made no mention of a right of way of which the buyers had been told they would get the benefit, in which case additional documentary evidence (for example, a statutory declaration as to long user) would be requested.

(b) The proprietorship register. There are three main things to check here. First whether the estate is freehold or leasehold. Secondly the class of title. If, for example, the contract refers simply to the title being registered but mentions no class then it is implied that the title is absolute. It would be unsatisfactory to find that in fact the title was qualified. Thirdly, who are the registered proprietors and can they sell the property? If the sellers are shown as registered proprietors and there is nothing telling you of any limitation on their power to dispose of the property then there is no problem. If, though, either the sellers do not appear on the proprietorship register or they do appear but with somebody else as well and/or there is some mention of their inability to sell the property then further enquiries need to be made and requisitions raised. As with unregistered title the nature of the enquiry and requisition depends on the particular circumstances and some of the possibilities will be discussed later.

(c) The charges register. This must be checked carefully to see that the third-party rights shown there accord with the contract and are acceptable to the buyers and to see that the sellers discharge any mortgage on completion of the sale.

Particular problems in registered title

Sale by trustees for sale As we saw in unregistered title, a sale by trustees for sale will overreach the equitable interests of the beneficiaries under that trust so long as all of the trustees receive the sale moneys and there are at least two of them or one which is a trust corporation. Unless the trustees hold the legal estate on trust for themselves as joint tenants in equity there will usually be a restriction on the register preventing the sole survivor of them from transferring the property. The terms of the restrictions tell the buyers what they must do in order to take free of the equitable interests under that trust. For example, if a restriction says that no disposition is to be registered without the consent of Z then the buyers know to raise a requisition requiring evidence of Z's consent.

So long as the restrictions are complied with, usually all other provisions of the trust are irrelevant to the buyers. However, unless the buyers also ensure that overreaching operates, notwithstanding that there may be no restriction on the register or caution on the charges register, the buyer might take subject to the interest of a beneficiary who is in actual occupation. (The categories of overriding interest were discussed earlier in chapter 4.)

At this stage, suffice to say that if a beneficiary under a constructive trust is in actual occupation and no enquiry is made of the beneficiary about his or her interest and overreaching does not operate then the results can be catastrophic.

Table 8.12

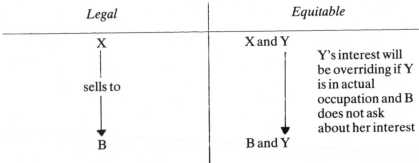

Legal	Equitable
X	X and Y
↓ sells to	Y's interest will be overriding if Y is in actual occupation and B does not ask about her interest
B	B and Y

In table 8.12, X is the sole registered proprietor. The registrar knows nothing of the trust and therefore there is no restriction on the proprietorship register. Y had not protected her interest by registering a caution. Despite there being no mention of Y's interest expressly or by implication on the register, nevertheless Y had an interest. If Y is in actual occupation it may be an overriding interest and B, the buyer, will only take free of Y's interest if overreaching operates, i.e., X appoints another trustee (see table 8.13).

Table 8.13

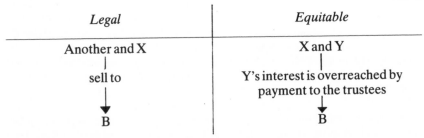

Legal	Equitable
Another and X	X and Y
↓ sell to	Y's interest is overreached by payment to the trustees
B	B

Sale by a surviving co-owner The Law of Property (Joint Tenants) Act 1964 does not apply to registered title.

If no restriction appears on the register and the seller can prove the death of his or her registered co-proprietor (e.g., by providing the death certificate) then the buyers are entitled to assume that they were joint tenants in equity and that therefore the survivor is solely entitled to deal with the property. This is subject, of course, to the possibility of there being anyone who could establish an overriding interest under the Land Registration Act 1925, s. 70(1)(g).

Sales by personal representatives Unlike unregistered title, buyers of a registered estate do not need to concern themselves with the possibility of an earlier disposition by the personal representatives nor whether the personal representatives have assented the property to the correct person. The register is regarded as conclusive in this respect.

When a sole or sole surviving registered proprietor dies the legal estate will pass to the personal representatives. (Remember if there are surviving joint proprietors the legal estate will pass by survivorship to them.) The personal representatives can deal with the property in one of two ways. Either they can apply to be registered as the proprietors of the property and for the deceased to be removed as registered proprietor (in which case there will be no problem, the sellers and the registered proprietors will be the same people), or they may transfer the property to the buyers, without first being registered as proprietors, and provide the buyers with a certified copy of the grant of probate or administration which will accompany the buyers' application for registration.

Sale of settled land   If land, the title to which is registered, is the subject of a strict settlement then the tenant for life will be registered as the proprietor. There will be a restriction entered on the register naming the trustees and telling the buyers that the purchase money must be paid to the trustees. The procedure, therefore, is that if the transaction is within the tenant for life's powers, the buyers comply with the restriction, and the trustees are joined in the transfer to give a receipt for the purchase moneys. The buyer will take free of any equitable interests under the settlement.

Sale by donees   In unregistered title we saw that there could be a problem for buyers who discovered a deed of gift within five years of the purchase by them. The situation with registered title is much clearer. There will be no indication on the register whether there has been a deed of gift in the past. The buyers will normally therefore be able to claim to be purchasers in good faith without notice of the relevant circumstances and will be protected from attack by a trustee in bankruptcy.

Sale under a power of attorney   Buyers from an attorney must make the same check about the scope of the power and about the state of their own knowledge regarding revocation as in unregistered title. They will also need to provide, on their application for registration, a certified copy of the power and, if the sale takes place more than 12 months after the power came into force, statutory declarations made by them that they had no knowledge of revocation of the power nor any event giving rise to revocation.

Mortgages

Undischarged mortgages   Each mortgage will appear on the charges register. If the property is to be sold free of them they must be discharged. The buyers must ask the sellers to confirm that each mortgage will be paid off on or before completion. The sellers should also be required to provide the application for discharge receipted by the mortgagee (a receipted form 53, a form prescribed by the Land Registration Rules 1925), and a charge certificate in respect of each charge. There are no problems with the Law of Property Act 1925, s. 115, equivalent to those encountered in unregistered title. If the sellers are unable to provide the receipts on completion a satisfactory undertaking to obtain and forward them should be required.

Sale by a mortgagee   The principles where the buyers are buying from a mortgagee, including the need to check whether the power of sale has arisen, are the same as in unregistered title. So too are the effects, in respect of other mortgages, of a sale by a mortgagee. If a mortgagee has priority over the sellers' own mortgage then the buyers must insist that the prior mortgage be discharged as above.

Sale by charities   Where a charity is selling property the trustees of the charity will be the registered proprietors. If the consent of the Charity Commissioners is required a restriction will tell the buyers what they must do in order to be protected.

Sales by companies   If the powers of a company to acquire or dispose of land are limited in any way this should be discovered on application by the company for registration as proprietor. In the event of the powers being limited in any way the registrar will place a restriction on the proprietorship register. If no restriction appears on the register the buyers may assume that the transaction is within the powers of the company.

Marriages and deaths   If the legal ownership is changed by the death or the marriage or a joint proprietor then an application for registration by buyers accompanied by a certified copy of the death certificate or marriage certificate will be accepted by the Land Registrar as sufficient proof of the event.

Sale of part   If the sellers are only selling part of the land included in their title the land certificate must be deposited at the Land Registry so that it can be amended to show that part of the land has been removed from the title. The buyers should therefore ask the sellers to confirm that the certificate has been placed on deposit and that the buyers will be provided with the deposit number.

Pre-completion searches and inspection of the property

As with unregistered title it must not be forgotten that part of the buyers' solicitors' job in investigating title is not only to deal with the documentary evidence but also to carry out pre-completion searches and an inspection of the property. These are both dealt with in more detail in chapter 9.

Procedural problems in raising requisitions

If you have been given the opportunity to raise requisitions prior to exchange of contracts then there is no real problem with the time-limits. The parties are still at negotiation stage and the buyers can simply refuse to enter into a contract unless and until they get satisfactory replies to their requisitions. However, if requisitions are being raised between exchange of contracts and completion, time-limits apply and a failure to observe these limits may leave the buyers with no right to a remedy to a defect in title or leave either party liable to damages for breach of contract.

Open contract rules simply require that the requisitions are raised within a reasonable time of delivery of the abstract or copy documents.

Where the Standard Conditions are being used Standard Condition 4.1.1 sets out the time-limits and states that the buyers lose their right to raise requisitions or to make observations on the sellers' replies if they do not comply with the time-limits. The time-limits are as follows:

(a)   Raising requisitions: must be done within six working days of exchange of contracts or delivery of the sellers' evidence of title.
(b)   Replying to requisitions: the sellers have four working days from receipt of the requisitions to reply (but, of course, if the buyers were out of time in raising the requisitions there is no obligation at all to reply).
(c)   Making observations: the buyers can make any observations they think necessary on the replies within three working days of receiving the replies. So if the buyers are unhappy with a reply they must say so within this time-limit.

Where the sellers initially provide incomplete evidence of title, Standard Condition 4.5.1 permits the buyers to raise requisitions relating to that evidence within six working days of delivery of the further evidence of title.

Example. If S delivers an epitome of title but omits one document B must raise requisitions on the evidence supplied within six working days and would request a copy of the omitted document. B would then have a further six working days from receiving the missing document to raise any further requisitions resulting from that document.

Under open contract rules it is possible that the buyers can prejudice their right to raise requisitions by indicating acceptance of the title by submitting a draft purchase deed for approval or by going into possession of the property before completion. The Standard Conditions specifically provide that neither of these actions affect the buyers' right to raise requisitions.

Common examination problem areas

Investigation of title is perhaps the area which students traditionally find most difficult. One reason for this is that there are often a number of documents to read through rather than a simple narrative followed by questions. The second reason is that, in this area in particular, all the learning in the world will not help you if you cannot interpret and apply it to the particular facts.

1 *Reading through.* To avoid you having to read the documents through several times to examine different aspects of the title, try to make the most economical use of your time by establishing the facts and making notes under various headings as you go through them. For example if you look at the sample notes for an imaginary title shown in table 8.14, a glance down columns 3 and 4 will enable you to establish any missing links. For example, between 3 May 1980 and 4 July 1985, what has happened to E? There is a missing document. Probably there is either a deed conveying the property from D and E to D or a death certificate of E.

A glance down column 5 will enable you to deal concisely with any requisitions regarding stamping. Column 6 will show you which searches you need, and any requisitions you need to raise in respect of any entry revealed by searches you have been given. Column 7 allows you to make brief notes about particular areas of concern relating to the document. It may be that something later in the title puts your mind at rest with regard to the point, but at least you have a careful note of the potential problem areas and will know what requisitions to raise.

2 *Raising the requisitions.* There are no set rules about the phraseology of requisitions. There are traditional styles but at the end of the day the important thing to ask yourself is: in the light of this problem what do I want the seller to do? If your requisition makes this clear to the person who will read it then it is effective. If your requisition leaves the sellers with the reaction, 'So what?' or 'Really!' then it is not.

So, for example, if you have observed from your copy of a conveyance on sale that there is no particulars delivered stamp, an inadequate requisition could say: 'The conveyance dated 2 March 1989 and made between X (1) and Y (2) has no PD stamp'.

The reply comes back, 'Noted', and you are no further on. An adequate example of a requisition under those circumstances would be: 'Please confirm that the original of the conveyance dated 2 March 1989 and made between X (1) and Y (2) does in fact bear a particulars delivered stamp or that one will be endorsed before completion'.

Never start a requisition with the phrase, 'We presume that . . .'. It usually receives (and deserves) the reply, 'Your presumption is noted'.

3 *Explaining the requisitions.* If a question asks you to state and explain the requisitions you will raise then it is very easy to get carried away in a general waffle around the problem. It may help, if the question permits, for you to divide your page down the middle and put your requisition in one column and your explanation in the other. Disciplining oneself in this way seems to have the effect of focusing the mind on what the examiner wants to know.

Remember also the task of the examiner. It is a difficult one. Imagine an exam question which shows in the title an assent by personal representatives and asks what requisitions you would raise and why. Two students each spot that there is no evidence of a memorandum of the assent endorsed on the original grant of probate. Both students answer:

Table 8.14 Sample notes

1	2	3	4	5	6	7
Date	Document	Seller	Buyer	Stamping	Search against seller	Other notes
1.2.61	Conveyance on sale	A	B	Ad valorem but PD missing. OK.	Yes. Valid and clear.	None.
2.4.79	Conveyance on sale of part	B	C	OK.	No.	New restrictive covenants imposed including not to alter property. Pre-contract information tells us sun lounge added. Prima facie breach. Not disclosed in contract. Is it enforceable? No acknowledgement for production of earlier deeds. Breach of restrictive covenant as above.
3.5.80	Conveyance on sale	C	D and E	OK.	Yes. Valid D(ii) registered against C. No.	Registered, therefore binding. Insurance? Release? Discharge?
3.5.80	Mortgage	D and E	XY Ltd	NA.	No.	Receipt needed or sale by mortgagee otherwise needs to be discharged before completion.
4.7.85	Receipt	—	XY Ltd	NA. No ad valorem. No certificate of value.	No. Yes. Valid and clear search against E.	Receipt OK. No requisition needed.
4.7.85	Conveyance on sale (by surviving co-owner?)	D	F			Disappearance of E? Death certificate? Joint tenants in 3.5.80? Yes. D selling as beneficial owner? Yes. Is there a clear bankruptcy search? Is there any memo of severance on conveyance 4.7.85?

I would raise a requisition asking the seller to confirm that there is a memorandum of the assent (dated etc.) endorsed on the original grant of probate.

But neither student says why. To the examiner, what difference is there between the student who knows of the potential problem with s. 36(6) of the Administration of Estates Act 1925 and the student who thinks it is simply a matter of convenience and good conveyancing practice? The answer is none. The only thing the examiner can mark is what is on the paper. All the correct thought processes in your head or shown on a piece of rough paper will not help to distinguish you from the weak student. Only what actually appears in your script counts.

4   *In the face of adversity.* Occasionally most students will find themselves sitting in an exam not knowing what to do. Sometimes it is because they have panicked, sometimes because they do not know the answer. Either way, if it happens to you, you can lose nothing and may either calm yourself or work out a possible solution by breaking the situation down into basic facts and concepts. Don't be afraid of putting the written scenario into a simple diagrammatic form. For example, the question says:

John lives with Kay and two years ago they moved into 87 High Street which was bought with money provided by them both. John is the only registered proprietor and a year ago granted a legal mortgage to M Bank Ltd in return for a loan. M Bank Ltd is selling to you under their power of sale.
    What problem do you envisage in the mortgagees' title?

A simple diagrammatic form of this question is shown in table 8.15.

Table 8.15

1	*Legal*	*Equitable*
		J and K
2	*Legal*	*Equitable*
	J (holds as trustee for J and K)	J and K
3	*Legal*	*Equitable*
	J | mortgage to ↓ M ⋮ possible sale to ⋮ ↓ US	J and K ? K's interest? Is it overriding? Is it overreached?

The very fact of having put the facts on to a diagram will have helped to sort out your thoughts.

In short, when dealing with titles makes sure you:

(a) Do not panic.
(b) Establish the *facts*.
(c) Keep a clear division between legal and equitable interests.
(d) Take your answer one logical step at a time.

NINE

PRE-COMPLETION SEARCHES AND INSPECTIONS

The stage which you have reached so far in your transaction, assuming that you are acting for the buyers, is that you undertook pre-contract searches and enquiries and checked the contract through with your clients. Being satisfied with those you then exchanged contracts and at that stage your clients had entered into a legally binding contract. When the investigation of title takes place will depend on the terms of the contract. If the contract is silent then the buyers can investigate the sellers' title after exchange of contracts. Part of this process of checking that the sellers can actually sell what they have promised to sell will involve carrying out searches to check for undisclosed third-party interests.

As we saw when we were looking at investigation of title, it is possible for the contract to include a term that the sellers will provide evidence of the title to the property before exchange of contracts and that after exchange the buyers shall raise no further objection or requisition in respect of the title. If there is a condition like this in the draft contract then care should be taken to ensure that, before contracts are exchanged, not only is the title checked but also the condition is amended to allow for the buyers to make and object to any untoward entry on the pre-completion searches (at the Land Registry in the case of registered title and the Land Charges Registry in the case of unregistered title).

Problems with the terminology and timing

One source of confusion found by students is the different names of the different registers. The main confusion lies in the difference between:

(a) The local land charges registry.
(b) The Central Land Charges Registry.
(c) The Land Registry or District Land Registry.

Before you even start to think about searches you must keep these separate in your mind.

(a) The local land charges register is a register of local matters which is kept by the local district council and which must be searched before exchange of contracts irrespective of whether the title is registered or unregistered.

(b)   The Central Land Charges Registry is, with one exception, only relevant to transactions involving unregistered title.

(c)   The Land Registry holds the register where details of all registered titles are kept.

Another source of confusion to many students is why certain searches are undertaken before exchange and others before completion. In its simplest terms the problem is one of taking into account the obligations of the sellers under the contract and the protection afforded to the buyers by the searches. We have already seen that, if the Standard Conditions are being used, the sellers agree in the contract to sell the property free from encumbrances other than matters mentioned in the agreement and adverse interests (Standard Condition 3.1.1). We have already seen that the implications of this for the buyers are that all matters which come within the definition of 'adverse interests' must be checked before exchange of contracts. So, before exchange of contracts, you have checked, amongst other things:

(a)   The register of local land charges.
(b)   The register of rights of common (if appropriate).
(c)   The property itself for signs of any third-party interests.

However, in the definition of 'adverse interests' (Standard Condition 3.1.2), the entries on the register at the Land Registry and the Central Land Charges Registry are specifically excluded. The implications of this are that, in the absence of any special condition in the contract, the sellers agree to sell the property free from encumbrances revealed by a search of the Land Registry or Land Charges Registry. The sellers must disclose such entries in the contract or must risk being in breach of contract when they are discovered between exchange of contracts and completion.

The Standard Conditions therefore tell us why there is no *need* for the buyers to check these registers before exchange of contracts but why is it actually *necessary* to leave it to this late stage to do the searches? The answer is that the searches *could* be done before exchange but they would have to be repeated before completion. The search will provide the buyers with a 'priority period'. The buyers will only be protected if they complete the transaction (or, in the case of registered title, complete and apply for registration of the transaction) within the priority period. Only in such a case will the buyers take free of any entries which another person attempted to put on the register during the priority period.

Pre-completion searches in unregistered title

Searches in the Central Land Charges Register

Before completion of the purchase of a property whose title is unregistered the buyers' solicitors must ensure that they have checked a search against the name of each owner of the legal estate in the title. The reason why this must be done is because the entry of a charge on the register will bind a buyer who is deemed to have actual notice of it whether or not the buyer did, in fact, check the register (Law of Property Act 1925, s. 198). Your first practical step should be to make a list of all the names of the owners of the legal estate since and including the root of title. Usually the sellers will provide the buyers with searches against all the estate owners prior to the sellers. There is, however, no obligation on the sellers to provide these. It is simply done as usual practice and as a matter of courtesy. If you are provided with any searches then you should have checked these to make sure that they are satisfactory. What you are looking for is a search which states that it reveals 'No subsisting entries'.

Even if your search says this, there are still other matters which you must check to ensure that the search is adequate protection for the buyers. You must check:

(a)   The name. Is the name *exactly* the same as the name shown on the deeds. A search against Jane Jones will not protect the buyer if the name in the deeds is Jayne Jones.

(b)   The Period. Each search certificate will state the period for which the search was undertaken in respect of each name. The period searched should be the *full* years of ownership. A search against Joseph Jackson which was for the period 1980 to 1984 will not be adequate protection for the buyer if the title deeds reveal that Joseph Jackson owned the property even for as little as one day in 1979.

(c)   The priority period. Each search certificate includes in the top right-hand corner a date on which priority will end. This period of protection will protect the buyer only if completion takes place within the period. The deeds should therefore be checked to ensure that the conveyance from the particular estate owner took place before the end of that period.

If any of these checks are not satisfactory then the search must be repeated. A search against the sellers themselves will not usually (unless the National Protocol is being used, see chapter 18) be provided by the sellers' solicitors. The buyer must undertake this.

Timing of the search   The search must be done within 15 working days of completion. If it is done any earlier the priority period will have run out before completion takes place and for the buyer to be adequately protected a second search would have to be made before completion.

The entries revealed by the search   Usually you will be looking for a search that reveals 'No subsisting entries'. If there are any entries revealed then there are two possibilities. The first is that the entry relates to something which the sellers have disclosed in the contract and so the buyer will not need to raise any objection to it.

Example. The contract between Alice Bates (the seller) and Brian Collins (the buyer) states that the property is sold subject to the matters contained in a conveyance dated 2 April 1961 and made between Samuel Smith (1) and Alice Bates (2). On inspection the conveyance reveals various restrictive covenants which affect the property. The search against Alice Bates reveals a D(ii) land charge. (The D(ii) is the way in which restrictive covenants are protected.) Brian has already contracted to buy the property subject to the restrictive covenants contained in the 1961 conveyance. The only thing that needs to be done in respect of this search is to check that the entry revealed does in fact relate to *those* restrictive covenants.

The second possibility is that the search reveals entries which were not revealed in the contract. The first thing that you need to be able to do is to identify what type of interest the charge represents.

Land charges   The entries on this part of the register are split into six classes some of which are subdivided. What can be done when a search reveals an entry depends on the terms of the contract and the nature of the entry. (For example, purely financial charges can usually be removed on payment of money by the sellers.)

Classes A and B are both financial charges which arise directly or indirectly from statutory provisions. Neither of them are commonly encountered in practice but if they do appear the buyers must know that they will take the property subject to a financial charge unless the third party who owns the charge is repaid and the entry discharged.

Class C has four subdivisions:

Class C(i) is a legal mortgage which is not protected by deposit of title deeds (a puisne mortgage). Usually that will mean that it is a second legal mortgage. (The first mortgagee in unregistered title will usually take deposit of the title deeds. If it does so this is regarded as adequate protection for the mortgagee as the fact that the mortgage deeds are not available would alert any informed buyer to the fact that there might be some charge on the property. In practice the mortgagee will not release the title deeds to the sellers' solicitors without an undertaking to hold the deeds to the mortgagee's order or repay the amount outstanding on the mortgage.)

If a C(i) entry is revealed it is possible (but highly unlikely) that the property is, in the contract, expressed to be sold subject to the charge. If this were the case then the buyers would simply have to check that the charge revealed in the search and the charge referred to in the contract were one and the same. If no reference is made to it in the contract then the sellers will be in breach of contract if they cannot or will not remove the charge. The sellers' solicitors should therefore be asked to confirm that the mortgage will be repaid and the entry removed.

Class C(ii) is a financial charge which may be imposed by someone who is not the absolute owner of the property but has paid death duties, capital transfer tax or inheritance tax on the property. As with the other financial charges, unless the property is sold subject to the charge the sellers must be asked to ensure that it is discharged on completion or that an undertaking to do so is obtained from the sellers' solicitors.

Class C(iii) is a general equitable charge. Any third-party right which is equitable (not one of the five legal interests in the Law of Property Act 1925, s. 1(2)), which cannot be fitted into one of the other categories of land charge, and which is not specifically excluded from falling within this category can be registered in this class. Rights which are specifically excluded from being capable of being registered in this class include:

(1)   a charge protected by deposit of title deeds, and
(2)   the interest of a beneficial owner under a strict settlement or a trust for sale.

If the search certificate were to reveal an entry in this class then the sellers should be asked to secure its discharge before completion or for their solicitors to give an appropriate undertaking to discharge it.

Class C(iv). To be registrable as a class C(iv) land charge the interest must be an 'estate contract'. An estate contract is a contract to create or convey a legal estate. This definition will cover not only an ordinary contract by the sellers to sell their property to buyers but also an option to purchase and a right of pre-emption. It will also include a contract to grant a lease, an option to renew a lease and a contract to create a legal mortgage.

If the search certificate reveals an entry in this class then enquiries should be made to discover who entered it. If the entry was put on the register by the sellers (at the time they were buying the property) then the sellers can agree to provide a signed application for removal of the charge on completion. If however, the charge was not registered by the sellers then the situation is more problematic. Again, in theory, it is possible that the contract may expressly provide for the property to be sold subject to the charge. If this is not the case then the buyers must ensure that the sellers arrange for the removal of the charge before completion. This is unlikely to be as simple as in the case of other charges. For example, a class C(i) charge is a mortgage. One of the fundamental principles of a mortgage is that the borrower should be able to repay the loan and thereby remove the incumbrance from the property. There is no such principle in the case of an estate contract. The property is subject to the third-party right and the owners of the property cannot insist on the charge being removed. They may be able to negotiate with the owner of the charge to remove it but if the owner of the charge is unwilling to do so there is nothing that the owner of the property can do about it. If the sellers are unable to remove the charge then the best advice to the buyers must be to refuse to go through with the contract. If the buyers were to go ahead with the purchase subject to this particular type of incumbrance they could in the future find themselves forced to sell the property to the owner of the charge under the terms agreed with the previous owner.

Class D has three subdivisions:

Class D(i) is a charge which will be imposed by the Inland Revenue for unpaid death duties, capital transfer tax or inheritance tax. It is very uncommon in practice but the solution to the problem if such an entry were revealed is, as for the other financial charges, relatively simple. The contract should be checked to see whether the property was to be sold subject to the charge. If it was not then the sellers' solicitors should be required to arrange for the discharge for the entry before completion or to give a suitable undertaking to remove it. The Inland Revenue's interest is in the outstanding tax being paid, and provided the sellers pay the full amount they can have no grounds for refusing to remove the charge.

Class D(ii) charges are very commonly encountered. A class D(ii) charge is used to protect restrictive covenants in unregistered title created after 1925. The effect of such an entry against a previous estate owner is that the interest can be directly enforced against the current owner of the property at the time. For example, the chain of title shows the following:

A sold the property to B in 1951
B sold the property to C in 1983
C sold the property to D in 1985
D sold the property to E in 1987
and now E is selling to your client F.

If B entered into restrictive covenants in the 1951 conveyance (e.g., not to use the property for business purposes) and A registered a class D(ii) land charge against B before the sale of the property to C in 1983 then A could, assuming he still retains some adjoining land, enforce that covenant *directly* against F when F buys the property. Any plan by F to use the property as a doctor's surgery could, even if the relevant planning permissions were obtained, be frustrated by A taking action to enforce the covenant against F.

When we looked at the problems surrounding restrictive covenants in chapter 6 we looked at the problems of being offered property subject to restrictive covenants which the buyers did not like or which had been breached in the past. Being able to tackle the problem before exchange of contracts assumes that the buyers have been told about the covenants either directly (e.g., by a condition in the contract that the buyers shall buy the property subject to certain specified covenants) or indirectly (e.g., a condition which says that the buyers shall purchase the property 'subject to all matters contained, mentioned or referred to in the documents of title' and the documents of title contain the covenants or at least reference to them). If the sellers have made no direct or indirect reference in the contract to the sale being subject to such covenants then the sellers will be in breach of contract if a D(ii) entry is revealed and the sellers cannot secure its discharge. If the purchase of the property is to proceed at all the buyers must either accept the covenant or require the sellers to secure the removal of the charge. As with the estate contract the removal of the charge is almost entirely dependent on the willingness of the covenantee (A in our example) to release the covenant. It is possible for an application to be made to the

Lands Tribunal to discharge the covenant. The grounds for such an application can be found in the Law of Property Act 1925, and include the fact that the covenant is obsolescent by virtue of a change in the character of the neighbourhood. Because of the length of time an application takes and the uncertainty of its outcome, this is hardly a suitable course for the sellers to rely on if they are in breach of contract for non-disclosure and as a result liable to pay substantial damages.

As this category of land charge only includes restrictive covenants made after 1925 mention should be made here of the status of covenants made before 1926. These cannot be entered on the register but will be binding if the buyers had notice of them. Notice may be actual, constructive or imputed because the buyers' agent has actual or constructive notice.

Class D(iii) comprises equitable easements. Equitable easements tend to be those which have been granted in writing rather than formally granted in a deed or are for a term not equivalent to a fee simple or a term of years (for example, an easement for life). Legal easements are not registrable on the Land Charges Register and will be binding on the buyers of unregistered land whether or not they had notice of them. In this context it must be remembered that not only the easements which you can read in deeds will be legal but also those which you cannot actually see such as rights granted under the Law of Property Act 1925, s. 62, or under the rules of implied grant or indeed easements acquired by prescription.

Class E comprises certain annuities created before 1926 which are rarely encountered in practice.

Class F. An entry in class F will protect a spouse's statutory right of occupation under the Matrimonial Homes Act 1983 and it is quite commonly encountered. It may be registered by the other spouse, in respect of the matrimonial home, wherever the legal estate is in the sole name of one spouse. It can be registered whether or not the spouse who does not hold the legal estate owns, or has acquired by agreement, an equitable interest in the proceeds of sale.

The existence of this right on a search will mean that the buyers will buy the property subject to the other spouse's right to live there. If the seller has contracted to give vacant possession of the property on completion then there is a term implied into the contract by the Matrimonial Homes Act 1983, s. 4, that the seller will secure the release of the charge by completion. This term will be satisfied by the seller's solicitors providing the buyers with an application for removal of the charge signed by the spouse who registered the charge. If the seller is unable to secure the removal of the charge then the buyers may withdraw from the contract and claim damages. The charge will only become ineffective and capable of being removed from the register on death, agreement, divorce or court order. The seller may encounter some problem in persuading his or her spouse to remove the charge. If the other spouse is prepared to do so at all the seller will most likely need to make some financial provision in consideration for the signing of the application.

Other registers maintained at the Central Land Charges Registry

In addition to the register of land charges there are also four other registers which are kept here. The *register of pending actions* will reveal any proceedings commenced during the past five years which relate to the land and which have been registered. The type of entries found here might relate to a simple dispute about the boundaries of a piece of land, or an application by a spouse for a property adjustment order ancillary to divorce. Also included in this register are bankruptcy proceedings. The *register of writs and orders* includes court orders which have been made affecting land. Many of these will be the conclusion of matters which were originally, before the hearing of the matter, registered as pending actions. The *register of deeds of arrangement* records agreements which have been reached between debtors and creditors in order to avoid bankruptcy, and whereby the debtor gives control of the land to the creditors. The *register of annuities* is simply a continuing record of matters registered before 1926. No new entries can be put on this register and to find a subsisting registration affecting a property is rare.

What do you do if a search reveals an entry?

What practical steps would you take on first discovering an entry? The first and most obvious steps is to raise a requisition regarding the entry. It is also possible to apply to the Land Charges Registry for an office copy of the entry which will give the details of the charge which were not revealed by the very simple entry on the search certificate (which gives little more than the type of charge and the date it was registered). There are four main possibilities:

(a)   It may be discovered that the entry relates to a matter which was disclosed in the contract and which the property was sold 'subject to'. In this case the buyers having established this can do nothing further. They are already committed, by the contract, to buying the property subject to that charge.

(b)   Since the registration of land charges is by reference to the name of the estate owner and not the land it is possible that the search may reveal some entries which do not affect the land which is the subject of the contract but affect other land owned by the person whose name has been searched. The buyers' solicitors should of course raise a requisition regarding the entries. If the reply from the sellers is that the entries do not affect the property which is the subject of the current transaction then the buyers should ask the sellers' solicitors to confirm that they will, on completion, certify the entries on the official search certificate as not applying to the property. Office copies can also be obtained from the Land Charges Registry to confirm this.

(c)   The sellers may be able to provide the buyers with full details of the charges and secure their release at completion. The sellers' solicitors must be required to confirm that they will secure the release before completion or undertake to do so on completion.

(d)   The sellers may be unable to secure the removal of the charge in which case the sellers may be liable for non-disclosure and breach of contract (see chapter 14) which will usually entitle the buyers to withdraw from the contract and/or claim damages.

How is the search carried out and what is the protection afforded by the official search certificate?

The usual method of doing a land charges search (which will in fact be a search of all five registers) is postal application on a prescribed form (form K15). The application may also be sent by fax. It is also possible to request a search by telephone. If there are no more than four entries against each particular name the result may be read out over the phone. However, it is only the written certificate which can be relied upon, not the details provided verbally.

The official search certificate is conclusive in favour of a 'purchaser', which by definition includes a mortgagee or a lessee. The purchasers will not be bound by any registered charge which is omitted from the certificate (provided of course the details on the search *application* were correct). The purchasers' solicitors are also protected by the certificate.

The search certificate will also give the purchasers a priority period of 15 working days within which completion must take place for the purchasers to take the property free of any charges which may be entered on the register between the date of the search and completion.

Searches in the Companies Register

Whenever a company has owned property in the past it will be necessary either to check or, if none is provided by the sellers, undertake a search of the Companies Register. After 1969 any fixed charge will be revealed by a search against the name of the company at the Central Land Charges Register. However, if land was sold before 1970 then a search of the Companies Register would have to be checked to ensure that there were no fixed charges.

Floating charges, which usually attach to a class of property rather than named properties, will not take effect and bind the buyers of any particular property unless and until the floating charge crystallises. The buyers who see that a company is selling the property or has owned it in the past must do a search of the Companies Register to check whether there are any floating charges potentially affecting the property. These would not be revealed by a search of the Land Charges Register. If the search reveals a floating charge the buyers must obtain a 'certificate of non-crystallisation' from the owner of the charge. The certificate can take the form of a certificate or a simple letter but it must state that the charge has not yet crystallised. If the charge has crystallised then the property is subject to it and in order for the buyers to take free of the charge the sellers must be required to procure the release of the charge before completion or their solicitors provide a suitable undertaking to do so.

A companies search is undertaken by instructing a firm of law agents to undertake a personal search of the register and to report their findings.

Further search of the local land charges registry

It is unusual to undertake a second search of the local land charges registry unless a considerable time has elapsed since the date of the first search. Even then the occasions when it will be done are usually limited to situations where the buyers' mortgagee insists on a more up-to-date search before the loan is made. There is little point undertaking another search after exchange of contracts, however old the pre-contract one is, as the result will not usually affect the rights and obligations of the buyers and sellers. The buyers will have undertaken a search before exchange of contracts. The search is immediately out of date but insurance against any further matter being put on to the register between the date of the search and exchange of contracts may be obtained using the Law Society's search validation scheme (see further chapter 18). Any matter which is entered on the register after exchange of contracts will bind the buyers and afford them no right of redress against the sellers.

Inspection of the property

Inspection of the property is not strictly speaking a search but as it must be done before completion and because the reason for doing it (to check for third-party rights including easements which would bind the buyers) is the same as for the searches it is appropriate to include it here. The only really safe course is for an inspection of the property to be undertaken before exchange and *in addition* before completion of the transaction.

The interests which are being looked for are interests which may be revealed by inspecting the property but which cannot be protected by registration as a land charge and so will not appear on the search of the land charges registry. In practice the most common thing to look for at this stage is to see whether there is evidence of anyone other than the seller being in occupation and if there is to find out whether they have any equitable interest in the property.

If you do discover evidence of anyone else being in occupation of the property then further enquiries must be made to find out who it is and what, if any, interest they have. If your enquiries were to reveal someone who had an equitable interest in the property then one of two methods could be used to overcome the problem:

(a)   The person with the equitable interest could be asked to join in the conveyance to release that interest in the property.

(b)   The seller could, by deed, appoint a second trustee to sell the property and to receive the purchase moneys. The effect of this would be to overreach the equitable interest of the third party and to turn it into an interest in the proceeds of sale. The third party would then have a right to bring action against the trustees to obtain a proportion of the proceeds of sale but would have no rights in respect of the property.

The latter method is considered by many to be preferable as the appointment of the second trustee and the payment of the purchase money to all the trustees being at least two in number (or a trust corporation) has the effect of overreaching any other possible equitable interests arising under a trust.

Example. Adam is the legal owner of the property and is selling the property to Desmond. Adam's girlfriend Betina and his mother Catrina live with him. His mother contributed towards the initial purchase price of the property and his girlfriend paid for some substantial improvements and so it is possible (subject to evidence about agreements between them) that each of them might have an equitable interest in the property. If both Betina and Catrina have an equitable interest the situation is as in table 9.1.

Table 9.1

Legal	Equitable
A	A, B and C

Assume that evidence of occupation of both Betina and Catrina was discoverable (i.e., the buyers would have constructive notice of their interests). If Betina's interest is discovered and she is asked to join in the conveyance to release her interest the effect after completion would be as in Table 9.2.

Table 9.2

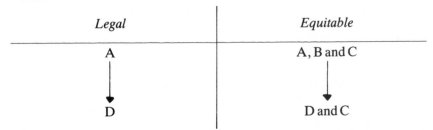

Legal	Equitable
A	A, B and C
↓	↓
D	D and C

If instead Betina (or someone else) had been appointed as a second trustee to overreach the interest the effect after completion would be as in table 9.3.

Table 9.3

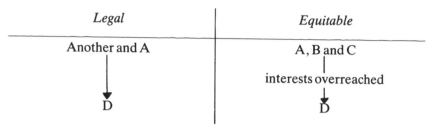

Legal	Equitable
Another and A	A, B and C
↓	↓
	interests overreached
	↓
D	D

The effect of failing to make an inspection of the property or of failing to take either of the above precautions in the event of discovering an interest could be that, although the buyers may be able to bring action against the seller for breach of contract, they may nevertheless find themselves the owners of a property in which a third party has not only an equitable interest but also a right to occupy the property.

Pre-completion searches in registered title

Search at the District Land Registry

When your clients are buying registered land, title will usually be deduced to you by means of office copy entries and an office copy of the filed plan. The office copies are an official copy of the register made and issued by the Land Registry. The purpose of the search is to check whether there has been any other entry on the register since the date of the office copies. (The date of the office copies will be stamped on them.) If title was deduced by means of photocopies of the land certificate or charge certificate then the object of the search would be to find out whether there had been any other entry on the register since the date the certificate was last brought up to date with the register. (This date can be found stamped on the inside front cover of the land certificate or charge certificate and can be ascertained by raising a requisition of the sellers' solicitors asking them to confirm the date.)

The search is done by means of a standard form: form 94A where the whole of the registered title is being sold, form 94B where only part of the title is being sold. The search may be made by post or telephone but a reply given over the telephone does not offer the protection to the buyers which is offered by the official search certificate.

There are two aspects to the protection afforded to a purchaser by the official search certificate. In theory the certificate will show all the entries made on the register from the date stated on the search (the date of the office copies or the date the land certificate or charge certificate was last examined with the register). If any entries are not disclosed the buyers will still take subject to them but may obtain compensation if they suffer loss as a result of the error. The second aspect of the protection is that the search certificate will give the buyers a priority period. If the purchase is completed within this period, and an application made for registration of the buyers as the registered proprietors then the buyers will take free of any matter registered after the date of the search but before the registration of the buyers as the registered proprietors. The period of priority is 30 working days from the date of the search.

As with unregistered title, the response that you are hoping for on the official certificate of search is that no further entry has been revealed. What do you do if the search does reveal a new entry on the register? As with unregistered title, what can be done about the entry depends on the nature of the third-party interest which is being protected. The first thing to do is, of course, to make further enquiries to find out just what the entry protects and who has made it. If it is to protect a financial charge then it is usually a relatively simple matter of the buyers' solicitors asking the sellers' solicitors to discharge it before completion or give an undertaking to do so. If the matter revealed is, for example, a notice protecting a non-owning spouse's statutory right of occupation under the Matrimonial Homes Act 1983 then the situation is different. As we saw with unregistered title, if the seller has agreed to sell with vacant possession then there is a term implied into the contract that the seller will secure the removal of the charge. The seller's ability to do this depends on the cooperation of his or her spouse and if the seller is unable to obtain this cooperation then the buyers will be entitled to withdraw from the contract and claim damages for the breach of contract.

Search in the Central Land Charges Register

If the buyers are buying absolute freehold or absolute leasehold title there is no need to do a search in the Central Land Charges Registry in respect of any previous owners of the property. In the case of other classes of title there may be a need to do a search. For example, if your clients are buying good leasehold title and the freehold is unregistered then if the freehold title is being deduced you should search against all the freehold owners in the title in just the same way as you would have done had your client been buying the unregistered freehold (see further chapter 17).

Search of the Companies Register

In the case of registered title there is usually no need to undertake a search of the Companies Register. Matters affecting the property should be revealed on the Land Register. A companies search is still recommended by some authorities as a safeguard because although the Land Register is usually conclusive it is nevertheless subject to rectification by the registrar under certain circumstances where there has been a mistake or omission.

Search in the local land charges registry

Exactly the same principle applies to registered title as to unregistered title. It is possible for the mortgagee to require a new search to be undertaken between exchange and completion. From the point of view of the contractual obligations between the sellers and the buyers there is no point in doing another search as the buyers will, in any event, be obliged to buy the property subject to any matter revealed.

Inspection of the property

The buyers of registered land take the property subject to overriding interests (which will not appear on the register) whatever the estate and whatever the class of title they are buying. The Land Registration Act 1925, s. 70(1)(g) protects the 'rights of every person in actual occupation of the land or in receipt of rents and profits thereof save where enquiry is made of such person and the rights are not disclosed'.

The rule is similar to that in unregistered title but from the point of view of the buyers it is actually much more worrying.

In unregistered title the buyers are looking for evidence of occupation by someone other than the seller. In registered title even if there is no 'evidence', if the third party can prove:

(a)   an interest in the property,
(b)   the fact of 'actual occupation' (actual occupation is given its ordinary meaning on the facts), and
(c)   no enquiry was made,

then the buyers will take subject to that interest. Although an inspection of the property must have been done before exchange of contracts it must be repeated shortly before completion as the time at which the third party must establish the existence of the overriding interest is at completion and not exchange of contracts.

As with unregistered title the most common risk here is of the third party who has an equitable interest as an equitable owner of the property. If the land registrar knew of the situation then a restriction would have been entered on the proprietorship register. The registrar would not, however, know about a contribution by a third party to the purchase price or to the improvement of the property if no one told him. A spouse's statutory right of occupation under the Matrimonial Homes Act 1983 cannot be an overriding interest but must, by statutes, be protected by the entry of a notice on the register.)

The buyers should, of course, make an enquiry of the seller about whether there is anyone else living at the property. An untrue reply to this question might render the seller liable to the buyers for damages but the buyers might still find themselves owning a property in which a third party has an equitable interest and which the third party has a right to occupy.

The solution, if you do find that someone other than the seller is in occupation of the property, is to ask that person for a statement of the interest held in the property. If there is no response then there can be no overriding interest. If an interest is disclosed then, as with unregistered title, the third party can be asked to join in the transfer to release the equitable interest. Alternatively the interest, albeit that it would on the sale by the seller alone be overriding, can be overreached by the appointment of a second trustee to act with the seller and to receive the sale moneys.

Common examination problem areas

Examination questions in this area can take many forms and require not only an understanding of the procedures but also an ability to interpret the information contained in a search certificate and to suggest possible solutions.

Take, for example, an examination question which tells you that the Central Land Charges Registry search reveals a class F and a class C(i) land charge registered against the seller.

(a)   You must first of all be aware that unless completion takes place within 15 working days of the search a new search will have to be undertaken.

(b)   Next you must deal with the actual entries. Remember that part of the answer must be to explain the problem itself to the examiner. An outline of an answer might look something like this:

Class F
(i)   Spouse's statutory right of occupation under the Matrimonial Homes Act 1983.
(ii)   Protects interest of non-owning spouse.
(iii)   Has seller agreed to sell with vacant possession?
(iv)   If yes, s. 4 of the Matrimonial Homes Act 1983 implies that seller will secure cancellation.
(v)   Requirement to cancel satisfied by handing over application for cancellation signed by non-owing spouse.
(vi)   Seller must arrange or is liable for breach of contract (damages and rescission?).
(vii)   Only other possibility is that charge is no longer valid in which case need evidence of death, divorce, or court order.
(viii)   Raise requisition asking seller's solicitors to confirm application for cancellation will be handed over on completion or otherwise provide evidence that the charge is no longer subsisting.

Class C(i)
(i)   Reveals a puisne mortgage.
(ii)   Is property expressly sold subject to it?
(iii)   Sellers under duty to disclose and must secure removal or be in breach of contract.

(iv) Raise requisition asking sellers' solicitors to confirm charge will be repaid and charge cancelled before completion or that an undertaking by the sellers' solicitors to do so will be handed over on completion.

TEN

DRAFTING THE PURCHASE DEED

What is the purchase deed?

It is important, at this stage, not to lose sight of what has happened and is happening in the transaction. So far the sellers' solicitors have drafted the contract which was then approved by the buyers' solicitors. Once both parties were agreed on the details of the contract, contracts were exchanged. At that moment the parties entered into a legally binding commitment to the sale and purchase of the property. The buyers' solicitors have also, either before or after exchange of contracts, had the opportunity to check that the sellers are actually capable of performing the contract (this is the investigation of title). Now it is necessary to prepare a deed which will actually put into effect the promises made by both parties to the contract.

What form does the purchase deed take?

There are three basic types of form which may be used when selling freehold land. In the case of unregistered title which is due for first registration one can choose between a 'conveyance' or a 'rule 72 transfer'. In registered title, a prescribed form of 'transfer' must be used.

Who drafts the purchase deed?

It is usually the buyers' solicitors' responsibility to draft the purchase deed. In certain circumstances, for example, where the property is a part of a new housing estate, the sellers' solicitors may provide a standard draft which will ensure uniformity in the terms for the purchase deed of each plot. If the buyers' solicitors draft the purchase deed then they must send two copies of the draft to the sellers' solicitors for approval. The sellers' solicitors will then check the draft and when it is approved they will return one copy to the buyers' solicitors. It is then the job of the buyers' solicitors to prepare the actual deed in the final form (this is referred to as 'engrossing the purchase deed').

Basic principles of drafting the purchase deed

There are certain simple ideas which you should understand before attempting to draft the deed. The most important of these is to appreciate exactly what it is that you are doing. You are putting into effect an agreement which already exists between the parties (the contract). The contract must therefore be your main guide to the contents of the purchase deed. Neither party can, at this stage, start introducing new terms into the agreement. Most of the clauses of the purchase deed will therefore be putting into effect the promises made by the parties in either the special or standard conditions of the contract. There are a very few matters only which may not be included in the contract but may nevertheless appear in the purchase deed and these matters usually arise as a result of operation of law.

Another thing to remember is the difference between drafting a purchase deed in practice and for an examination. In an examination you may be asked either to comment on particular precedents or a particular draft deed or you may be expected to draft the deed yourself. In practice no one is ever expected to sit down and draft a purchase deed off the top of his or her head. Precedents are widely available and used. It is nevertheless necessary for the practitioner to have gone through the principles of drafting in order to understand how precedents work, when a precedent may be inappropriate, and how to adapt or modify a precedent to the particular case. The task of the student somehow seems much more difficult than that of the practitioner. You will not find it quite so frightening if you remember that the examiner will not be looking for word-perfect repetition of the precedents but rather for an answer which shows quite clearly that the candidate understands the basic principles and can, in simple straightforward language, produce something which does the job. Expert legal jargon will not usually be required.

Contents of a conveyance

In the left-hand column of table 10.1 you will find a draft of a basic conveyance and in the right-hand column is an explanation of the function. The form of draft is a very simple one which is not recommended as a precedent but rather as the type of thing that, with a little study, you might be able to draft in an examination under the constraints of time and nerves!

Table 10.1

THIS DEED OF CONVEYANCE

Commencement. This serves two functions:

(a)   it introduces the deed,
(b)   the express reference to it being a deed will help to ensure that the requirements concerning execution are satisfied (see below).

is made on 12 June 1990

Date.

BETWEEN Mary Jones of 14 New Street Bruddersfield (hereinafter called 'the Seller') and Jane Gill and Simon Gill both of 2 Cedar Close Bruddersfield (hereinafter called 'the Buyers')

Parties. This section identifies the parties. In most transactions the only parties will be the seller(s) and the buyer(s). However, there may be cases where another party may have to be included, e.g.:

(a)   Sale by tenant for life; as the trustees are required to join in the conveyance in order to give a valid receipt for purchase money they must be parties to the conveyance.
(b)   Sale of part of the seller's property where the whole is subject to a mortgage; the mortgagee may be joined as a party to the conveyance in order to release the part sold from the mortgage

WHEREAS the Seller has agreed to sell the property hereinafter described to the Buyers for the sum of £28,000

Recitals. These are not essential but can be used, for example, to explain the circumstances surrounding the sale or as a convenient place to include any statement to be made by the seller such as a declaration by personal representatives that they have not made any previous assent or conveyance of the property (Administration of Estates Act 1925, s. 36(6)).

NOW THIS DEED WITNESSES as follows

Testatum. This simply introduces the operative part of the deed after the recitals.

1   In consideration of the sum of twenty-eight thousand pounds (£28,000) paid by the Buyers to the

Consideration and receipts clause. The consideration is required to be stated by the Stamp Act 1891. The amount

Seller (the receipt whereof the
Seller hereby acknowledges)

stated must be the amount excluding
any payment for chattels.

The most important effect of the
receipts clause is that it acts as authority
for the buyers to pay the purchaser
money to the seller's solicitors rather
than having to insist on the seller
attending at completion to receive
the money personally.

the Seller as beneficial owner
hereby conveys to the Buyers

*Statement or seller's capacity and
operative words.* The capacity in which
the seller sells will tell you what
covenants for title will be implied into
the conveyance. If selling as
beneficial owner there are four
covenants for title implied into the
conveyance:

(a)   The seller has good right to
convey.

(b)   Quiet enjoyment.

(c)   Indemnity in respect of any
undisclosed encumbrances.

(d)   Further assurance.

If the seller is selling as trustee or
personal representative then there is
only one covenant for title: that the
seller has not encumbered the
property.

The operative words are, as the
name suggests, the part of the
conveyance that actually operates to
convey the property.

ALL THAT freehold property
known as 14 New Street
Bruddersfield which is more
particularly delineated and shown
edged red on the plan annexed
hereto (hereinafter called 'the
Property') together with the rights
contained in a conveyance dated
4 April 1977 and made between
R. Price (1) and P. Pest (2)
(hereinafter called 'the
Conveyance').

The parcels clause. This is a
description of the property which
is being sold. There are three elements
to it. You must describe the estate
which is being conveyed ('ALL THAT
freehold property'). You must
describe the physical property in which
the estate exists ('known as'
followed by some accurate
description). The statutory definition
of land includes not only the physical
property but also the rights which

benefit the property. It is obvious then
that any description of land
being conveyed must include any rights
which will pass with it ('together with'
any easements etc. which pass with the
property). Remember that your
description of the property here will be
following the description in the
contract.

2   The Property is sold subject
to the matters contained in the
Conveyance so far as they affect the
Property.

Burdens affecting the property. So far
you have described the property itself
and the rights which go with the
property. Now you must describe the
rights which the property is subject to.
Having already described the property
and the conveyance in full, and having
made it clear how you will refer to them
later in the document, the abbreviated
form of reference used in this clause is
acceptable.

3   The Buyers jointly and severally
covenant with the Seller for the
benefit of the Seller and her estate
that the Buyers and their successors
in title will observe and perform the
restrictions covenants and
conditions contained in the
Conveyance and indemnify the
Seller and her estates against all
claims costs or demands
arising in respect of any failure to
observe or perform them or any of
them.

Indemnity covenant. When the
property was sold in 1977 the buyer at
that time entered into certain
covenants. On reselling the property,
the 1977 buyer would want to have
some way of recovering from subsequent
owners any damages that the 1977 buyer
is required to pay for breach of the
covenants. Each subsequent buyer
should therefore be required to enter
into a covenant to reimburse the person
from whom the buyer is buying so that
there is an unbroken sequence of
covenants from the present owner to the
1977 owner.
  Often the special conditions of the
contract will make no mention of this
covenant but Standard Condition
4.6.3 will oblige the buyer to enter
into this covenant in the transfer.

4   The Buyers hereby declare that
they are joint tenants in law and
equity.

*Buyers' declaration concerning
equitable ownership.* It is not possible
to have anything other than a joint
tenancy so far as the legal estate is

concerned. In equity the buyers may be joint tenants or tenants in common. As we saw earlier, if they are joint tenants then on the death of one of them that person's interest will pass automatically to the survivor notwithstanding any provisions of a will. If they are tenants in common in equity then the interest of the deceased co-owner will pass according to the deceased's will or the rules of intestacy.

The buyers must be properly advised not only about the difference between a joint tenancy and a tenancy in common but also about which may be appropriate to their particular circumstances.

It is possible to include here a provision creating an express trust for sale of the property but whenever there is a co-ownership situation a trust for sale is implied by statute anyway.

6 It is hereby certified that this transaction does not form part of a larger transaction or series of transactions in respect of which the amount or value or aggregate amount or value of the consideration exceeds £30,000.

Certificate of Value. The purpose of this clause is to provide the necessary certificate for exemption from payment of stamp duty. The certificate cannot be included even where the value of the transaction does not exceed £30,000 if there are any other related transactions with a total consideration in excess of £30,000.

SIGNED AS A DEED AND DELIVERED by the said Mary Jones in the presence of . . .

Execution and attestation clauses. In order to be an effective deed the requirements of the Law of Property (Miscellaneous Provisions) Act 1989, s. 1, must be complied with. It must appear on the face of the document that it is intended to be a deed.

| SIGNED AS A DEED AND DELIVERED by the said Jane Gill and Simon Gill in the presence of . . . | It must be signed by the party in the presence of a witness who must then also sign. The deed must be delivered (this can be done by the parties' solicitors or expressed to be done by the wording of the attestation clause). |

What variations might there be on the requirements of a conveyance?

There are many possible variations and additions to a basic conveyance depending on the circumstances of the transaction and the terms of the contract. The following paragraphs discuss some of the most common problems.

Sale of part of the sellers' property Here you should consider whether new covenants and easements are needed. New covenants should be dealt with in special conditions in the contract and the purchase deed will simply follow the terms of the contract. In most cases the same is true of new easements, either those matters which are being 'excepted and reserved' to the sellers or those rights which are being 'granted' to the buyers.

However, unless the contract contains a term excluding the rules of implied grant (e.g., the rule in *Wheeldon* v *Burrows* (1879) 12 ChD 31 which we looked at earlier) and also excluding the operation of Standard Condition 3.4.2(b), the purchase deed may be drafted so as to contain rights of which no specific mention was made in the contract but which will pass either by the common law rules or the generalised provisions of the Standard Conditions.

On the sale of part it is also usual to exclude the acquisition by the buyers of any right of light or air. This must be specifically provided for in the contract, but Standard Condition 4.3.2(a) makes such a provision and so it would, when using the Standard Conditions be perfectly in order to include in the purchase deed a declaration that the buyers shall acquire no rights to light or air.

Also you should remember that where the sellers are selling only part of their property then the description of the property cannot be by reference to an earlier document. There should be a clear and accurate plan attached to the conveyance on which the property is shown 'more particularly delineated' (rather than 'for the purpose of identification only'). The matter of the description should have been fully sorted out at the stage of drafting and approving the contract and the purchase deed should only follow the contract. The importance of the wording used when referring to the plan is that if the words 'more particularly delineated' are used then if the words in the parcels clause and the plan are later found to conflict the plan will prevail. If the words 'for identification purposes only' are used the words will prevail over the plan where there is a discrepancy.

Sale of part of the sellers' property or a sale by personal representatives On a sale by personal representatives, the personal representatives will retain the original grant of probate or administration even though it forms part of the buyers' title.

On the sale of part, the seller will retain the original title deeds to the whole of the property and the buyers will only be given the deed of conveyance of the part of the property to them. Nevertheless the buyers will need to have access to those deeds in order to prove title to the property. The purchase deed should therefore include an acknowledgement for production of the deeds (and in some cases an undertaking that they will be kept safely). The Standard Conditions provide for this to be included as indeed, in the absence of any express provision in the contract, do the open contract rules.

Execution by a company or an attorney The appropriate form of execution and attestation clause must be varied when dealing with a company as the statutory provisions require execution to be by two officers of the company. An appropriate form might be:

> Executed as a deed and delivered by C Limited acting by D (director) and S (secretary).

If the deed is to be executed by the seller's attorney then various forms of attestation clause would be appropriate. Essentially this is still an execution by an individual so an appropriate form might be:

> Signed as a deed and delivered by A as attorney for D in the presence of
> . . ..

Use of schedules The use of schedules is really a matter of style rather than substance. Whenever the content of a clause would become unwieldy it may be sensible to refer to a schedule later in the document. For example, on the sale of part of the sellers' property the parties may be entering into a great many covenants. Rather than saying, 'The Buyers hereby covenant to . . .' and then making a long list of them all it may be more sensible to say, 'The buyers hereby covenant to observe and perform the restrictions set out in the schedule hereto'.

Contents of a rule 72 transfer

If the property is due for first registration following the conveyance then either a conveyance or a rule 72 transfer may be used. The provisions and essential contents of the transfer are much the same as the conveyance: it is simply the style and form which differs.

Transfer of registered title

A transfer of registered title may be prepared by completing a printed form which can be obtained from law stationers. Alternatively the buyers' solicitors may draft their own transfer but essentially it will follow the same form. The form is in fact prescribed by the Land Registration Rules 1925 (form 19 for the sale of the whole of a registered title and form 20 for the sale of part of the registered title). In table 10.2, the left-hand column shows the main contents of a basic transfer of the whole of the property.

Table 10.2

County and District: West Yorkshire Leeds	*County and District.* The county and district can be easily ascertained from the office copy entries.
Title number: WYK 77985 Property: 5 Alpine Road Lyneham West Yorkshire	*Title number and Description of the Property.* The title number will be found on the office copies and the description of the property will usually be simply a repetition of the description to be found in the property register.
Date: 1 June 1991	*Date.*
In consideration of thirty-eight thousand pounds (£38,000) the receipt whereof is hereby acknowledged	*Consideration and receipts clause.* This performs the same function as in the conveyance and will provide the buyers' solicitors with authority to hand purchase moneys to the sellers' solicitors rather than to the sellers themselves.
We Alice Rhodes and Robert Rhodes both of 5 Alpine Road, Lyneham (hereinafter called 'the Transferors')	*Sellers' names and addresses.* As in the conveyance you must identify the parties.
as beneficial owners	*Statement of the capacity in which the sellers sell.* The capacity in which the sellers transfer indicates what covenants for title which will be implied into the transfer.
hereby transfer to	*Operative words.*
Charles Woods and Ann Moor both of 2 Farm Lane, Lyneham (hereinafter called 'the Transferees')	*Buyers names and addresses.* As with the conveyance obviously you must identify the parties.

the land comprised in the title
above mentioned

Parcels clause. Unlike drafting a conveyance there is no need for a full description of the property.

The title number of the property has already been mentioned and this will contain a full description of the estate (and class of title), the physical description of the property, the rights that pass with the property and the third-party rights such as restrictive covenants which appear on the register.

Any further reference (unless an indemnity covenant is to be given in which case the wording is very similar to that in a conveyance) is simply superfluous.

The Transferees declare that the survivor cannot give a valid receipt for capital moneys arising on a disposition of the land

Statement concerning equitable co-ownership. In the case of registered title the statement takes the form of a declaration whether the survivor can or cannot give a valid receipt for sale moneys. A declaration that the survivor cannot would lead to the entry by the registrar of a restriction on the proprietorship register effectively warning a purchaser that on the death of one of the joint proprietors the survivor will hold the property as trustee rather than sole beneficial owner. Obviously if the sale is initially to a single buyer then this declaration is unnecessary as the buyer will usually be a sole beneficial owner not a trustee.

Certificate of value. Because the amount of consideration in this particular transaction is above the stamp duty exemption limit, a certificate of value is not appropriate. If it were relevant in another transaction then the form of the certificate is exactly the same as for the conveyance.

Signed as a deed by Alice Rhodes
in the presence of . . .

Execution and attestation. Again the requirements of the Law of Property

(Miscellaneous Provisions) Act 1989, s. 1, must be complied with and the transfer must be signed by all the parties.

Signed as a deed by Robert Rhodes in the presence of . . . This form of execution and attestation clause differs from the suggested in the draft conveyance. For an explanation see chapter 11.

Signed as a deed by Charles Woods in the presence of . . .

Signed as a deed by Ann Woods in the presence of . . ..

Transfer of part of the property comprised in a title number   If the sellers are selling part of the property which is registered with a single title number then there are various additional matters to consider:

(a)   *Description of the property*. Where the whole of the title is being sold the description is easy as it is simply by reference to the title number and the description of the property contained in the property register. When the transfer is in respect only of part of the property the title number should still be referred to but it must be made quite clear that only part of the title is being transferred. The description should describe the property as 'more particularly delineated on the plan annexed hereto' and the accurately drawn plan should be signed by the sellers and the buyers.

(b)   *New covenants*. Any new covenants which the buyers agreed to enter into, in the contract, should be quite clearly set out in the transfer.

(c)   *New easements*. If there are any rights which the sellers are to except or reserve for the benefit of the land they are keeping or if there are any rights which the buyers are to acquire then they should be set out in the transfer. Remember the rules of implied grant and the effect of Standard Condition 4.6.3. Under the rules of implied grant (if they are not excluded by the contract) then, as with unregistered title, even though the purchase deed does not mention them they will pass to the buyer. Easements which cannot necessarily be ascertained by checking written documentation may nevertheless bind a future buyer of the property. In registered title they will be binding by reason of their status as overriding interests under the Land Registration Act 1925, s. 70(1)(a). If it is possible to establish at this stage exactly what rights have been acquired then they should be included in the transfer so that the registrar may include them on the register. If the contract excludes the rules of implied grant then it is in the interests of certainty to include a reference to that exclusion in the transfer.

(d)   *Acknowledgment for production*. This will not normally be appropriate. The register will contain all the pertinent details of anything which affects the property from past transactions. Even though it is a sale of part the buyers have no use for earlier documents as their property will be registered with its own new title based on the obligations shown on the title of the whole property and any new obligations entered into in the transfer.

Common examination problem areas

Being able to tackle a question on drafting a purchase deed is really a question of taking things one step at a time and not panicking. Every case is bound to be different but there are some basic tips which will apply whatever the question:

(a)   Identify the type of document needed. In the case of a sale of freehold you have the choice of a conveyance or a rule 72 transfer for unregistered title. For registered title it *must* be a transfer. Then explain that you understand why that form is appropriate.

(b)   Make yourself a mnemonic to remember the essential elements of each document and write it down. (*Don't* let your answer degenerate into a long but confusing ramble around the clauses as they happen to pop into your memory.)

(c)   Make plain English and common sense your guides in drafting each of the clauses. The examiner is much more likely to appreciate a straightforward answer that is easy to read than an answer where it is quite clear that the candidate does not really understand but has thrown down a few long words or phrases in the hope of impressing the marker. Most students (including myself) have, at some time, tried the latter approach. It does not work and when you become more competent it is simply a source of embarrassment that you once thought the marker might be taken in by it!

(d)   After each clause (unless the question indicates it is not appropriate) write a brief note explaining the purpose of the clause and why you have drafted it in the way you have.

(e)   Perhaps most importantly, when drafting is finished, there seem to be two common mistakes which students make. One is to look to see how much you have written and if it looks enough move on to the next question. The other approach is not even to do that but to move on quickly and try to forget about 'that awful question'. On the whole I do not advocate spending any great length of time reading through answers in an exam; you will not usually have enough time for this luxury. When answering a drafting question, though, I would not regard it as a luxury but an essential. When you have completely finished your draft try to pretend that you are already qualified and you are checking a draft which has been brought to you by a trainee in your firm. A critical reading of your draft, as if for the first time, will often reveal simple grammatical and more serious mistakes which are otherwise difficult for you to spot in the pressure of the exam room.

ELEVEN

PREPARATION FOR COMPLETION

We have looked at what the buyers' and the sellers' solicitors will be doing between exchange of contracts and completion of the transction. We have looked at the procedure surrounding the drafting and engrossing of the purchase deed. We have also looked at the pre-completion searches and inspections which the buyers' solicitors will undertake. This chapter considers the procedural steps involved in getting the matter to completion. For example, we have drafted and engrossed the purchase deed, but what about the mechanics of getting it executed? If the sellers execute it before completion will it operate to give the buyers the legal estate in the house before the money is paid over? If the buyers do not execute it before completion then do they, at the same time as helping load the removal van, really have to go into their solicitors' office to sign the purchase deed on the day of completion? These matters can sometimes seem a complete mystery quite unnecessarily.

Preparation for completion: sellers' solicitors

Execution of documents

So far, the buyers' solicitors have drafted the purchase deed. The sellers' solicitors have approved it and the buyers' solicitors have then engrossed it. What we need to do now is to consider the execution of the purchase deed.

The formalities required for execution of a deed are contained in s. 1 of the Law of Property (Miscellaneous Provisions) Act 1989. There are, in essence, three requirements:

(a)   The document must make it clear on its face that it is intended to be a deed.

The evidence that it is 'intended' to be a deed must come from within the deed itself and not from any outside evidence. With most conveyances this is unlikely to be a problem but the safest course is to include the reference to the document being a deed quite clearly in the attestation clause. Hence the suggested attestation clause in the purchase deed in table 10.1 commences 'Signed as a deed'.

(b)   The deed must be signed in the presence of a witness who attests the signature.

There are two questions to consider here. *Who* must sign it and *how* it must be signed.

Obviously the deed *must* be signed by the seller (or, if there is more than one seller, *all* of them), if the legal estate in the property is to pass from the seller to the buyers. In the case of unregistered title the buyers will only be required to execute the purchase deed if they actually 'do' something in the deed. So if, for example, there are new covenants entered into by the buyers, or if there is an indemnity covenant entered into by the buyers, or if there is a declaration concerning the equitable ownership of the property by the buyers then the buyers must also execute the document. In the case of registered title the Land Registration Rules 1925 actually require the deed to be signed by *all* the parties. If the buyers are required to execute the deed this should be attended to before the deed is executed by the sellers. There is provision in the Law of Property (Miscellaneous Provisions) Act 1989, s. 1(3), for a deed to be signed by someone other than the actual party to it if it is signed by that other person at the party's direction and in his or her presence.

How the deed must be signed is quite straightforward. The parties need only sign their normal signatures and not necessarily their full names. Each signature must, however, be made in the presence of a witness (two witnesses if the deed is executed under s. 1(3)) and the witness must sign to attest the signature.

For the requirements for execution of a deed by a company or an attorney see chapter 10).

(c)   The third element for a deed to be valid is that it must be delivered. Delivery here is used in a specific sense of doing an act which shows an intention to be bound. If all the other formalities have been complied with and the deed is then delivered the deed becomes effective from the time of delivery. So what types of actions will constitute delivery? If the party signs a deed where the attestation clause reads, 'Signed as a deed and delivered in the presence of' this would result in delivery. Alternatively the attestation clause might say nothing of delivery and the deed may be regarded as delivered when the sellers hand the deed to their own solicitors. In either of these cases we have to ask whether, now that the formalities required by the Law of Property (Miscellaneous Provisions) Act 1989, s. 1, have been complied with, the deed has become effective and transferred the legal estate to the buyers? If this were to happen then it seems unfair that because the deed is executed in advance of completion, the buyers get the legal estate to the property before the purchase money is paid over on completion. Because of this the delivery may be regarded as conditional (delivery in escrow). The traditional view is that delivery of the deed by the sellers, which falls short of handing over the deed to the buyers, will be regarded as delivery in escrow and conditional on the payment of the purchase price. However, once even conditional delivery has taken place, the sellers will not be in a position to 'withdraw' the deed. The sellers must instead wait and see whether the condition is fulfilled and if it is then the deed will automatically, and even in the face of the sellers' change of mind, become fully operative.

One way around the problems of conditional delivery is for the attestation clause to make no mention of delivery and for the sellers to hand over to their solicitors both the signed and witnessed deed and an authority allowing the solicitors to deliver the deed on their behalf. In this way the deed may be executed in advance of completion but will not be delivered, even conditionally, until completion takes place.

If there is a plan annexed to the purchase deed then, in the case of registered title, the plan must be signed by the sellers and by or on behalf of the buyers. In the case of unregistered title there is no actual requirement but as a matter of good conveyancing practice a plan should always be signed by the parties.

Financial considerations

When acting for the sellers it is not usually necessary to obtain any money from your clients before completion as the transaction is likely to result in some of the sale proceeds being paid to them. It is, however, still necessary to give careful consideration to the financial situation.

Outstanding mortgages   The sellers' solicitors should check how many mortgages they will be required by the buyers to repay on completion and a statement of the amount required to redeem the mortgage on the completion date should be obtained for each mortgage.

Bridging loans   If your clients were given a bridging loan pending the sale of the property then the bank is likely to have asked you to give an undertaking to pay the net proceeds of sale to it on completion. The terms of this undertaking should be checked and arrangements made to pay the money after completion has taken place and the agreed deductions from the gross sale proceeds have been made.

Apportionments   Standard Condition 6.3.1 provides for the outgoings and income relating to the property to be apportioned on completion. The type of thing which might require apportioning in the case of the sale of freehold property is a flat-rate water charge. If this has been paid by the sellers for a full year and the property is sold halfway through the year then the sellers' solicitors should arrange with the buyers' solicitors for the payment of half the total amount in addition to the purchase price.

Interest   In chapter 14, when we look at the remedies available for breach of contract, you will see that where completion does not take place on the contractual completion date but at a later date then interest may be payable by way of compensation for the breach of contract. If completion has been delayed the sellers' solicitors should discuss the situation with the buyers' solicitors and agree the amount of compensation which, if payable by the sellers will be deducted from the purchase price, and if payable by the buyers will be added to the purchase price.

Statement to clients Once the figures have been agreed the sellers' solicitors should arrange for a financial statement of the whole transaction to be sent to the sellers. This statement is called a 'completion statement'. The statement should set out:

(a)   The amount of costs and VAT payable (in respect of which a bill should be prepared).
(b)   The effect of the apportionment of any outgoings.
(c)   The amounts payable to redeem each mortgage on the property.
(d)   The amount of any disbursements paid by the solicitors.
(e)   The balance due to the sellers.

Other matters to prepare before completion

A note should be prepared of matters to be dealt with on completion. For example, consider the whereabouts of the keys to the property, the whereabouts of any deeds which the buyers will want to inspect on completion (e.g., a grant of representation), the need to make any endorsements (e.g., a memorandum of the sale to be endorsed on the grant at completion).

Preparation of undertakings On completion the buyers' solicitors will require the sellers' solicitors to provide either evidence of the discharge of each mortgage affecting the property or an undertaking in respect of each mortgage to discharge it and to forward the evidence of discharge to the buyers' solicitors. These undertakings should be in writing and may be prepared in readiness for completion (see further chapter 12).

Agreeing place and manner of completion The buyers' and sellers' solicitors must agree between them where and how completion will take place.

Particular matters to be considered on the sale of part of the sellers' property

Registered title If the title to property of which only part is being sold is registered, the land certificate relates to the whole of the property including the part being retained, so the sellers will not on completion be prepared to hand over their land certificate to the buyers. The buyers, though, will need to produce the land certificate to the Land Registry. The solution is for the sellers land certificate to be put on deposit at the Land Registry in advance of completion. The sellers' solicitors will then be given a deposit number which they will give the buyers on completion and to which the buyers should refer in applying to register the transfer.

Unregistered title   On a sale of part of property which is unregistered action may be required by the sellers' solicitors, in advance of completion, to protect the sellers' position after completion. Assume, for example, that you are acting for the sellers, and the buyers are, in the purchase deed, entering into certain restrictive covenants. The sellers want to be sure that the covenants can be enforced directly against any future buyers of the property. This can only be done if the sellers protect the covenants by registering them as class D(ii) land charges. Failure to register them would mean that they could be enforced against the covenantee but not any later purchasers. The problem is that the buyers might resell the property before the sellers have had a chance to register the land charge. In fact if the buyers are obtaining a mortgage advance to purchase the property then the mortgagee, who is within the statutory definition of a purchaser, will take free of the unregistered restrictive covenants. If the property were then sold by the mortgagee under its power of sale, the purchasers from the mortgagee would take free of the restrictive covenants and they could not be enforced against them. The land charge cannot be registered before the sale because the restrictive covenants do not actually *exist* until the sale when the buyers enter into them in the purchase deed.

The solution to the problem is for the sellers' solicitors to enter a priority notice. The notice must be entered in excess of 15 working days before completion. When any further purchaser does a search of the Land Charges Registry (which they must do *within* 15 days of completion), the priority notice will warn them of the new land charge which is about to be created. If the sellers do then register the charge within 30 working days of entering the priority notice the restrictive covenants will bind *any* purchasers from the covenantee buyers.

Preparation for completion: Buyers' solicitors

Very often solicitors will find themselves acting for the buyers and the mortgagees. If this is the case then you must be sure, in addition to the matters discussed below, to remember the matters which arise out of the mortgage which are discussed in chapter 15.

Execution of documents

The same considerations regarding the formalities required for execution of the purchase deed which we looked at when acting for the sellers apply here. The buyers' solicitors will, following approval of the purchase deed by the sellers' solicitors, have engrossed the purchase deed. If the purchase deed is required to be executed by the buyers then the buyers' solicitors should ensure that this is done before the deed is sent to the sellers' solicitors for signature by the sellers.

Financial considerations

Apportionments   The buyers' solicitors must consider the apportionments which should be made in accordance with Standard Condition 6.3.1 in the same way as the sellers' solicitors.

Interest   If completion has been delayed, the buyers' solicitors should discuss the situation with the sellers' solicitors and agree the amount of compensation which, if payable by the sellers, will be deducted from the purchase price and if payable by the buyers will be added to the purchase price.

Statement to clients   Once the figures have been agreed, the buyers' solicitors should arrange for a financial statement of the whole transaction to be sent to the buyers. This statement is called a 'completion statement'. The statement should set out:

(a)   The total amount needed to purchase the property.
(b)   The amount of costs and VAT payable (in respect of which a bill should be prepared).
(c)   The effect of the apportionment of any outgoings.
(d)   The amount of any disbursements paid or to be paid, by the solicitors (e.g., search fees, Land Registry fees, stamp duty etc.).

From this should be deducted:

(e)   The amount of the mortgage advance (if any) taking into account any retentions or other deductions which the mortgagee is making from the initial advance.

The account should finally state the total amount which the solicitors need to receive from the buyers in order to complete the transaction.

Clearing the cheque   If your clients are providing the purchase moneys by cheque, you should ensure there is time for the cheque to clear before completion. If the Standard Conditions are being used, the buyers' solicitors will require cleared funds on completion (usually a banker's draft or a direct telegraphic transfer to the sellers' solicitors' bank account). Cleared funds should not be paid out of the solicitors' client account unless the funds in the account have themselves cleared.

Other matters to prepare before completion

A note should be prepared of matters to be dealt with on completion. For example, consider what arrangements the buyers want to make with regard to the keys to the property. A note should be made of the documents the buyers' solicitors need to collect on completion (e.g., a list of the deeds and any other documents which the sellers have agreed to provide such as guarantees or copy planning permissions). If the sellers are retaining any deeds then the buyers' solicitors should make a note of which documents must be inspected so that the copies can be marked as examined with the originals.

Undertakings   On completion the buyers' solicitors will require the sellers' solicitors to provide either evidence of the discharge of each mortgage affecting the property or an undertaking, in respect of each mortgage, to discharge it and to forward the evidence of discharge to the buyers' solicitors. The buyers' solicitors should make a list of the undertakings required.

Agreeing place and manner of completion   The buyers' and sellers' solicitors must agree between them where and how completion will take place. In particular, if completion is to take place by post, the buyers' solicitors must ensure that written instructions are sent to the sellers' solicitors before completion (see further chapter 12).

Common examination problem areas

As we saw earlier, it will be quite uncommon for a solicitor to act for both the buyer and the seller in a particular tansaction. Nevertheless, in a conveyancing transaction, unless the clients are first-time buyers, the clients will usually be selling one property and buying another both at the same time. The solicitors will therefore find themselves in the position of solicitor for the sellers in the clients' sale and solicitor for the buyers in the clients' purchase. Usually therefore when you are considering preparation for completion you must be able to think of both positions at once. In this chapter they have been looked at separately to avoid confusion. I advise that, so far as is possible, you continue to think of them separately, for the sake of avoiding confusion in your own mind and in order to produce a clear and comprehensive answer. There are, however, some points where the two roles must come together. For example, when thinking about the completion statement, even if you do two separate statements you must be able to reconcile the overall effect of the two on your clients. In other words, in respect of the two transactions, is money due to or from your clients and how much?

Remember also the warning given at the beginning of the section on the buyers' solicitors' preparation for completion. It is quite common for the buyers' solicitors also to act for the buyers' mortgagee. The special considerations involved when acting for a mortrgagee are dealt with in chapter 15. You must be able to adapt to the particular facts of the question and if necessary include in your answer mention of the pre-completion matters which are referred to in that chapter.

TWELVE

COMPLETION

Timing of completion

The question of the timing of completion should have been dealt with at the stage of drafting and approval of the contract. If your clients are both buying and selling a property and the two transactions need to be synchronised, care should have been taken to ensure:

(a)   that the completion date in respect of both transactions is the same, and

(b)   that the latest time for completion (after which the party who is not ready to complete will technically be in breach of contract) is later for the clients' purchase than for the sale. It is necessary to complete the sale earlier in the day then the purchase because usually the clients will be relying on already having received the proceeds of sale in order to complete the purchase.

Methods of and venue for completion

The venue for completion depends on the facts of the situation. If the Standard Conditions are being used these provide that completion is to take place in England and Wales and either at the office of the sellers' solicitors or at some other place which the sellers reasonably specify. The most likely venue then is the office of the sellers' solicitor. The other usual possibility is the office of the sellers' mortgagee. At the beginning of the transaction we looked at obtaining title deeds from the mortgagee. We saw that the mortgagee was under no obligation to part with possession of the deeds but would usually be prepared to part with the deeds provided the solicitors gave an undertaking to redeem the mortgage or return the title deeds. It is also usual for the mortgagee to agree that the solicitors may act as its agent to receive the moneys required to repay the mortgage. If the mortgagee was not prepared to do this then the title deeds will usually still be in the possession of the mortgagee. Completion must therefore take place at the office of the mortgagee or the mortgagee's solicitors.

There are three possible methods for completion:

(a) *Personal attendance*. The traditional method was by personal attendance by the buyers' solicitors at the office of the sellers' solicitors. This has become increasingly uncommon due to the pressure on the time of solicitors and to the less localised nature of domestic conveyancing.

(b) *Attendance by an agent*. This is simply a variation on personal attendance. Instead of the buyers' solicitors attending the sellers' solicitors' office they appoint another solicitor to attend and to complete the matter on their behalf.

(c) *Postal completion*. The solicitors to the transaction may complete by post if they specifically agree to adopt the Law Society's code for completion by post. The essence of the code is that:

(i) The sellers' solicitors agree to act as agent for the buyers' solicitors without charging any fee.

(ii) The sellers' solicitors undertake that on completion they have the sellers' authority to receive the purchase money and that they are also authorised by the mortgagee (if any) to receive the moneys due to redeem the mortgage.

(iii) The buyers' solicitors must send the sellers' solicitors written instructions about what specific matters should be attended to on completion (e.g., which documents should be examined against the original and certified as such). If the buyers' solicitors fail to send the instructions then the sellers' solicitors are under no obligation to examine or mark any documents.

(iv) On the day of completion the sellers' solicitors ask their bank to let them know when funds are received from the buyers (by automatic transfer). Once they are received, the sellers' solicitors hold the funds to the order of the buyers' solicitors until completion. The sellers' solicitors complete the matter whereafter they hold the title deeds rather than the purchase moneys to the order of the buyers' solicitors.

Procedure on completion

Verification of title

At the stage of deducing title, the sellers' solicitors will have provided the buyers with proof that the sellers can sell the property as promised in the contract. The proof in unregistered title will have taken the form of an epitome or abstract of title rather than sending the buyers' solicitors the original documents of title. At completion the buyers' solicitors must 'verify' the title, that is, they will check to see that each copy document or abstract which has been provided accurately represents the original document. In the case of the sale of the whole property, the buyers' solicitors will be taking the original deeds away after completion so it is simply a question of checking that all the documentation is in order before the purchase moneys are handed over. If the sellers are only selling part of their property then the only original document which the buyers will receive is the purchase deed which passes the legal estate in respect of the part sold. Nevertheless the other documents form part of the title to the buyers' property. The buyers' solicitors must therefore make a 'certified' or 'examined' copy of the original. This will involve not only checking each document in the epitome or abstract against the original of that document but also marking the abstract or copy document with a certificate that it has been examined against the original document. This certificate must be signed and dated by the solicitors.

Where there has been a sale of part of a larger property earlier in the title the sellers themselves will not have the original title deeds. Under the open contract rules, the buyers can insist on the sellers obtaining the originals of the deeds for verification on completion (hence the importance of acknowledgments for production in purchase deeds). Under the Standard Conditions the sellers must produce either the originals or examined copies of the documents of title. Reliance on examined copies is widespread although it is not without risk. There is no guarantee that the solicitor who examined the copy documents in the first place did not make a mistake.

In registered title there is usually no need for verification of title if the buyers have been provided with office copies of the entries on the register. If the buyers were only provided with a photocopy of the land certificate or charge certificate then the photocopy should be checked with the certificate and with the result of the Land Registry search. Verification of documents may be necessary in certain exceptional circumstances, for example, where there is a sale by personal representatives who have not themselves been registered as the proprietors. It would be necessary under those circumstances to check the copy of the grant against the original and to mark it as examined with the original.

Endorsement of memoranda

Where only part of the property is being sold or where the sellers are for some other reason retaining some of the title deeds (e.g., where the seller is an executor the seller will retain the original grant of probate), the buyers should require a memorandum of the sale to be endorsed on the retained document to prevent it being misleading. Standard Condition 4.6.5 obliges the sellers to do this.

The purchase deed

The sellers will on completion hand to the buyers the purchase deed which transfers the legal estate to the buyers. Needless to say, before handing over the purchase money, the buyers' solicitors should check that the deed has been properly executed by the sellers.

The completion date should also be inserted in the purchase deed. Until completion it should have been left blank.

Inspection of receipts

In preparing for completion we looked at the apportionment of outgoings on the property. If there have been any apportionments then, on completion, the buyers' solicitors will want to see the receipt which will prove that the sellers have actually paid the account in respect of which they are claiming to be reimbursed.

What the buyers' solicitors will expect to receive on completion

Keys Arrangements must be made on completion for the buyers to be given the keys to the property. Either the buyers' solicitors may collect them from the sellers' solicitors on completion, or the keys may be held with the selling agent and the sellers' solicitors telephone the agent on completion to

'It is common for clients to be left to make their own arrangements regarding the keys'

authorise the release of the keys to the buyers. It is quite common for clients to be left to make their own arrangements regarding the keys. Although this is common it is not without risk in that it may result in the buyers obtaining possession of the property before completion has actually taken place.

Title documents In all cases the buyers will expect to receive the original of the purchase deed which conveys the legal estate from the sellers to the buyers. If the sellers want to be able to recall what is in the conveyance (which would be particularly important in the case of a sale of part of the sellers' property) then the sellers' solicitors must make a copy of the purchase deed before handing over the original.

In the case of unregistered title the buyers will expect to receive all the original title deeds. However, this may not be possible if, for example:

(a)   the transaction is a sale of part, or
(b)   there has been a sale of part earlier in the title.

In such cases, the buyers will expect to receive, or be given the opportunity to make, examined copies of the originals.

In the case of registered title the buyers will expect to receive either:

(a)   the land certificate or
(b)   a charge certificate in respect of *each* registered charge.

If the transaction is a sale of part then the buyers would expect to be given the deposit number of the land certificate.

In the case of either registered or unregistered title, if the originals of documents which form part of the title will not be handed over on completion, e.g., in the case of a sale by personal representatives or by someone acting under a power of attorney, then an examined copy must be given to the buyers' solicitors or the buyers' solicitors given an opportunity to mark a copy as examined.

Proof of discharge of the sellers' mortgages   The buyers' solicitors must ensure on completion that in respect of *each* of the sellers' mortgages on the property they are sure that the buyers will not buy subject to them. Ideally the buyers' solicitors would like the sellers to hand over proof of the discharge. In unregistered title this takes the form of the legal charge itself endorsed with a receipt of the mortgage (the 'receipted charge') and in registered title in the form of a standard Land Registry form receipted by the mortgagee (the 'receipted form 53').

It is not often possible for these to be provided on completion. Usually the sellers need the purchase moneys before they can afford to repay the mortgages. Some mortgagees may be prepared to execute the receipt or the form 53 before completion and allow the sellers' solicitors to hand it over on completion subject to the sellers' solicitors undertaking to repay the outstanding loan. Not many mortgagees adopt this procedure. It is much more common for the sellers' solicitors, on completion, to provide the buyers' solicitors with an undertaking:

(a)   to redeem the mortgage and
(b)   to forward the receipted charge or the receipted form 53 to the buyers' solicitors as soon as the sellers' solicitors receive it.

There are four things to bear in mind with respect to such undertakings:

(a)   All the general considerations which we have looked at so far in chapter 5 apply to such undertakings.

(b)   The buyers will require an undertaking in respect of *each* mortgage.

(c)   The sellers' solicitors should not undertake 'to discharge all mortgages' but should specify precisely which mortgages they are undertaking to discharge.

(d)   There may be circumstances where the buyers' solicitors should think carefully before accepting such an undertaking. Where the mortgagee is an institutional mortgagee the risk of them accepting the purchase money but failing to receipt the charge or execute the form 53 is minimal. In the case of a private mortgagee, if the receipt were not forthcoming the matter might take some considerable time to sort out. It may be considered preferable to arrange for completion at the office of the mortgagee's solicitors so that the receipt may be obtained immediately.

Where the sellers are selling only part of their property it is unlikely that the sellers' mortgage will actually be discharged. The mortgage is likely to continue over the land that the sellers are retaining. The buyers' solicitors will want to make sure that the part which the buyers are buying is free from the mortgage. This can be done in one of two ways:

(a)   the mortgagee can join in the purhase deed to release the part being sold from the mortgage or

(b)   the mortgagee can execute a deed of release of part of the property from the mortgage or in registered title execute a form 53 in respect of the part being sold. In either case the deed should be accompanied by an accurate plan.

Other documents   There may be other documents which are not strictly documents of title but which the seller has agreed in the contract to hand over. The type of things which the buyer might require in the contract and therefore expect to receive on completion are:

(a)   timber and damp proof guarantees,
(b)   evidence of planning permission,
(c)   certificate of compliance with building regulations,
(d)   NHBC agreement (for details regarding the last three of these see further chapter 16).

Effect of completion

Once completion has taken place the nature of the parties' rights alters. Obviously the sellers are no longer entitled to possession but the buyers are entitled to possession of the property and, in most cases, the documents of title. In addition to this the right of the parties regarding the promises made in the contract will change on completion. The contract is said to 'merge' with the purchase deed. It is not really so much a question of merger as of the contract being superseded by the purchase deed. All the obligations which were contained in the contract and which were covered directly or indirectly by the purchase deed will now cease to be considered at all from the point of view of the parties' 'contractual' obligations. If the buyers are to have any remedy now against the sellers they must rely on suing the seller on the express matters in the purchase deed or on the covenants for title which will be implied into the purchase deed. The covenants for title, as we saw when drafting the purchase deed, will vary depending on the capacity in which the sellers sell.

There are of course certain matters contained in the contract which will not merge with the purchase deed on completion and in respect of which the buyers may continue to be able to sue. Any term which is expressly stated not to be intended to merge will not do so. Nor will certain other terms such as a condition in the contract whereby the sellers agree to give vacant possession on completion. If the buyers complete the transaction and then discover that the sellers have not moved out then the buyers can bring an action for damages arising out of the breach of contract notwithstanding that completion has taken place.

THIRTEEN

AFTER COMPLETION

So far as your clients are concerned the business of buying a new house usually comes to an end on moving day when they finally get the keys to the property. For you the situation is very different. There are numerous matters which have to be attended to after completion in order to perfect the title and protect your clients' interests. What needs to be done differs on whether you are acting for the sellers or the buyers but again you should remember that very often you will be acting for clients who are the sellers in one transaction and the buyers in another.

Acting for the sellers

Keeping your clients informed

As at all stages in a conveyancing transaction you must make it a priority to keep your clients informed about the progress of the sale. Even if arrangements about the keys etc. have been made through an agent do remember to telephone your clients to confirm that all has gone well.

Discharging mortgages

If the property which your clients owned is subject to a mortgage this must be discharged. When we looked at completion we saw that although the buyers' solicitors would prefer the mortgage to be repaid before completion, in practice this is unlikely to be possible as the sellers will need to use the sale moneys to redeem the mortgage. The only acceptable alternative for the buyers' solicitors is to accept an undertaking from the sellers' solicitors, in respect of each mortgage, that the solicitors will repay the mortgage on completion and forward the receipted legal charge (unregistered title) or the receipted form 53 (registered title).

The sellers' solicitors should see to the discharge of the mortgages in strict accordance with the undertakings given on completion. As soon as the receipted charge or form 53 is received this should be forwarded to the buyers' solicitors. If the mortgage was an endowment mortgage, the endowment policy will have been assigned to the mortgagee. On the repayment of the mortgage the sellers' solicitors should ensure that the policy is reassigned to the sellers by the mortgagee and that notice of the reassignment is given to the insurance company. (The procedure for an endowment mortgage is more fully describerd in chapter 15.)

Registration of land charges

On the sale of freehold property, title to which is unregistered, the title will become due for first registration. Nevertheless there may be matters such as restrictive covenants which need to be registered as land charges in the interim period between the buyers acquiring the legal estate and the title being registered. For example, if the sale was of part of a freehold property and the conveyance included restrictive covenants entered into by the buyers these should be registered as class D(ii) land charges. This would of course be done following the entering of a priority notice, a procedure which we looked at in chapter 11.

Dealing with the proceeds of sale

If your clients are both buying and selling a property then you will already have sent a completion statement to them explaining how much would be due to or from them on completion. If you are acting for the sellers and any money is due to them after completion this should be paid directly to them or otherwise according to their express instructions. It may be that your clients have obtained bridging finance in return for which you have given an undertaking with regard to the proceeds of sale. It must be remembered that undertakings are personally and professionally binding. If you do not comply with the exact terms of the undertaking you may find yourself personally liable to pay the amount to the bank and also subject to disciplinary proceedings.

If your client is a mortgagee selling the property in accordance with its power of sale you should remember that there is a statutory order in which the proceeds of sale must be applied. It includes passing the net proceeds of sale, after repayment of the mortgagee's own debt, to any later mortgagee.

Acting for the buyers

Keeping your clients informed

You must remember to confirm with your clients the completion has taken place as planned.

Registration of land charges

If the title to the property is unregistered, you should consider the protection of any land charges created by the purchase deed as you should when acting for the sellers. It is perfectly possible, for example, that the contract and purchase deed provided for both the buyers and the sellers to enter into restrictive covenants. If this is the case then, just as the sellers protected their position by registering a land charge, so must the buyers ensure that the covenants which the sellers entered into are enforceable against anyone who should buy the sellers' retained property.

Discharge of land charges

If the title to the property is unregistered not only should the buyers' solicitors consider whether any new land charges need to be registered but also whether the buyers should see to the removal of any land charges which are no longer appropriate. The buyers cannot of course simply remove any land charge but can remove those which were registered by them. For example, the buyers' solicitors may have registered an estate contract (a C(iv) land charge) in order to protect the buyers' contract. Once the buyers have the legal estate this is no longer necessary and should be removed. Alternatively it is possible that the sellers have, on completion, provided the buyers with an application for cancellation of a land charge signed by the chargee. For example, if a seller contracts to sell the property with vacant possession there is an implied term under the Matrimonial Homes Act 1983, s. 4, that the seller will secure the removal of the spouse's statutory right of occupation registered under the Act. This condition would be discharged by the seller providing the buyers with an application for removal of the charge signed by the spouse. The buyers' solicitors would then make the application to cancel or remove the charge.

Stamping

It is important to remember that the sale of a freehold property is likely to involve two different types of stamp. If both types of stamp are needed you must be able to explain why. If one or both is not needed then you must also be able to explain why.

Ad valorem duty   This duty is payable at the rate of 1 per cent of the total value stated on the conveyance or transfer. The only time this will not be payable is if the consideration stated in the conveyance or transfer does not exceed £30,000 and the conveyance or transfer contains a certificate of value. Note that the duty is payable at 1 per cent on the whole of the consideration, not 1 per cent on the excess over £30,000. For example, where the consideration is £31,000 the amount of *ad valorem* duty payable is £310. Once *ad valorem* duty is paid the deed will be stamped to show the amount of *ad valorem* duty paid.

If property is given away rather than sold then, subject to the inclusion of a prescribed form of certificate in the deed then no duty, fixed rate or *ad valorem*, is payable.

No stamp duty is now payable on mortgages, vacating receipts, or deeds of discharge.

PD stamp PD stands for 'particulars delivered'. Certain documents are required by statute to be produced to the Inland Revenue together with a standard form on which has been set out the details of the transaction. Once this has been done the document will be stamped to show that the particulars have been delivered. (The delivery of these particulars enables the district valuer to build up information on property values to assist in valuations on death, compulsory purchase etc.)

The only transactions involving freehold land which require a particulars delivered stamp are conveyances on sale and transfers on sale.

Procedure for stamping If a document requires *ad valorem* stamp duty and a PD stamp then the document must be submitted to the Inland Revenue. The document must be accompanied by the amount of duty payable and the PD form. If the property is either registered or due for first registration and no *ad valorem* duty is payable then the PD stamp may be dealt with by the Land Registry and the PD form can be submitted to the Land Registry along with the application for registration.

The time-limit for stamping is 30 days from the date of the document. If a deed is not properly stamped it will not be admissible in any court proceedings as evidence of title to the property nor will it be acceptable to the Land Registry as evidence of title. It is possible for a document to be stamped after the time-limit has expired but a financial penalty will be imposed.

Registration

Transfer of registered title If the title to the property is already registered, the dealing in the land must be registered at the Land Registry. Any transfer or mortgage of the property will not give the buyer, donee or mortgagee a legal estate or interest until registration takes place.

In chapter 11 we looked at pre-completion searches. In registered title the buyers must do a search (usually on form 94A). The result of the search will do two things: first it will tell the buyers whether there have been any further entries on the register from the date mentioned in the search. Secondly it will provide the buyers with a priority period within which the buyers must apply for registration of their transfer in order to take free of any entries made after the date of the search. The buyers' solicitors must ensure that an application is made for registration of the transaction within the priority period of the land Registry search (i.e., 30 working days from the date of the search certificate). A failure to do so could result in the buyers taking subject to an unwanted third-party interest or, worse, failing ever to get the legal title to the property.

The application for registration is made on a standard form (Land Registry form A4 for the registration of a dealing in the whole of the registered title).

What are you applying to register?   When you are thinking about post-completion matters it is all too easy to think about an application for registration without thinking what it is that you are applying to register. Often the buyers' solicitors in a normal domestic conveyancing transaction will be making no less than three applications for registration. The application will be:

 (a)   to remove from the register the charges which the seller had charged on the property,
 (b)   to register the sale from the sellers to the buyers,
 (c)   to register the mortgage which the buyers have charged on the property.

In addition to the standard form of application the solicitors must send all the documents relevant to each transaction. The transfer must be sent to support the first application. The charge certificates and the form 53s to support the second and the buyers' mortgage deed (and a copy certified by the buyers' solicitors as being an accurate copy) to support the third.

If the sellers had no mortgage on the property then obviously no form 53s would be needed and the sellers will have handed over the land certificate (or if the sale is of part of the registered title, the deposit number) which will be sent to support the application rather than charge certificates.

The applications must also be accompanied by a fee.

Registration of a previously unregistered title   The property which your clients are buying may be unregistered but due for first registration. Indeed since December 1990 the *sale* of the freehold of any unregistered property will trigger the requirement for first registration. The procedure on application for first registration differs from that on a transfer of registered title.

First, the buyers will get the legal estate in the property on completion. This means that a mortgagee, provided the mortgage deed is in the correct form, will get a legal mortgage on completion. Secondly the time for the lodging of the application for registration of the matter is two months from the date of completion. If the buyers fail to make an application for first registration within that time-limit the buyers will lose their legal title which will automatically revert to the seller. If the time-limit for first registration is missed all may not be lost. The land registrar has it within his power to register the property with absolute title notwithstanding that technically the legal estate has reverted to the sellers and usually there will be no problem in doing this. Nevertheless a failure to apply for first registration within the two-month time-limit is not a mistake to be taken lightly. Once the time-limit is passed the interest of the buyers will be much less secure as it will be equitable only (as will the interest of the buyers' mortgagee).

The application is made on standard form 1B and should be accompanied by the conveyance or rule 72 transfer (and a certified copy) and the buyers' mortgage (and a certified copy). All other deeds and documents relating to the property, including, for example, requisitions on title and the replies to requisitions must also be sent. The application must be accompanied by a list (in triplicate) of the documents accompanying the application, and a fee.

FOURTEEN

REMEDIES

Remedies is a subject which seems to strike fear into the heart of even the most competent of students. As a student myself I hated the area and always prayed that it would not come up in the exam. Only when I began to look at the subject in simple and practical terms and using basic principles did I begin to feel comfortable with it. Remedies for misrepresentation and omissions are examined below on the basis of the buyers' remedies against the sellers. This is not because it is not possible for buyers to make a misrepresentation to the sellers but rather because the more usual action is by the buyers against the sellers. Remedies for breach of contract are examined from both parties' points of view.

Problems requiring remedies

Before you embark on any serious reading in this area let us think about exactly what the problems are likely to be:

(a)   The sellers may have failed to disclose something which the buyers think they should have disclosed. In other words they have kept silent about something. Usually remaining silent about something cannot give rise to an action by the buyers. In order to bring an action in respect of the omission the buyers must show that the sellers were under some duty to disclose the information.

(b)   The sellers may have represented something which the buyers then discover is not true. If the statement was incorporated into the contract then this might lead to the buyers being able to bring action for breach of contract.

(c)   The sellers may have represented something which the buyers then discover is not true. If the statement was not incorporated into the contract then an action for breach of contract will not be available to the buyers and they will have to establish some 'cause of action', other than breach of contract, before they will stand any chance at all of bringing action against the sellers.

(d)   Either party to the contract may have failed to comply with one or more of their obligations under the actual terms of the contract in which case the injured party will usually be able to bring an action for breach of contract.

The second thing to consider after you have considered what 'cause of action' the buyers might have is to ask, in the light of the sellers' behaviour, what is it that the buyers want?

There are three possibilities:

(a)   *Rescission or withdrawal from the contract.* Your clients may want to withdraw from the contract. You will therefore have to look and see whether the remedy of rescission is available for that particular behaviour. You will need to look at the open contract rules to see whether rescission is possible and also look at the terms of the contract between the parties to see whether the parties have agreed to vary the remedies available. Even if it is available in theory it must be remembered that rescission is an equitable remedy and may be refused if, for example, the buyers are considered to have behaved badly and also if the effect of granting rescission would be to injure an innocent third party.

(b)   *Specific performance.* Rather than your clients wanting to withdraw from the contract it may be that the sellers are simply refusing to go ahead with the contract. It may be possible under those circumstances to force the sellers to go through with the contract (ultimately by obtaining an order for specific performance). Again it must be remembered that specific performance is an equitable remedy and that it cannot be demanded as of right but depends on the discretion of the court.

(c)   *Damages.* It may be that as well as an order for rescission or specific performance your clients want monetary compensation for the sellers' behaviour. Alternatively it may be that both parties are prepared to go ahead with the contract but your clients feel that they should be entitled to damages for the way the sellers have behaved.

Having established what general types of behaviour may give rise to a cause of action and what types of remedies might be available now we need to look at more specific examples. The order in which we look at remedies differs slightly from the problem areas which we have looked at because some causes of action could apply to more than one of the factual circumstances.

Misrepresentation

There will be misrepresentation where one party makes a misstatement of fact on which the other party relies and which induces the other party to enter into the contract.

Let us imagine then that you are acting for the buyer of 34 West Lane. Your buyer client tells you that when she looked around the property before the contract was entered into, the seller told her that the property had a mains water supply. She has now discovered this to be untrue, in fact it is a

'The seller told her that the property had a mains water supply. She has now discovered this to be untrue . . .'

spring supply with pipes laid to the house. Consider in relation to this situation:

(a)   The remedies for misrepresentation are available in respect of this statement which the seller made if it induced the buyer to enter into the contract. The statement must therefore have been made before the contract was made.

(b)   The remedies for misrepresentation are only available for misstatements of fact. You must therefore decide whether this statement is fact or opinion. (Consider how your view of the situation might differ if the seller had said nothing about the water supply but had said that 'The neighbours are lovely people'. When your client moved in she discovered that they are quite unfriendly.)

(c)   The remedies for misrepresentation are only available where the statement which the seller made was relied on by the buyer and induced the buyer to enter into the contract. If therefore it could be shown that your client in fact knew of the seller's error before contracts were exchanged, or if it can be shown that the buyer placed no reliance on the supposed fact that the property had a mains water supply, then there will not be a misrepresentation.

Once you have established that there is a misrepresentation then you must consider what remedies will be available to your client. The remedies available for misrepresentation usually depend on the state of mind of the seller when making the misrepresentation. The misrepresentation may be fraudulent, negligent or innocent.

(a) *Fraudulent misrepresentation.* This is where the statement was made either knowing it was false or being reckless as to whether or not it was false. The remedy here would be *both* rescission and a claim for damages.

(b) *Negligent misrepresentation.* This is where the misrepresentation cannot actually be said to be fraudulent but where the seller cannot show reasonable grounds for believing it was true. Here the possible remedies would be rescission *and/or* damages but this would be subject to the power of the court to refuse rescission and award damages alone.

(c) *Innocent misrepresentation.* This is a misrepresentation where the seller has, in making the statement, not been fraudulent or reckless and can prove reasonable grounds for believing the statement to be true, but nevertheless it was untrue. Any claim here would have to be for rescission only. It would only be if the court felt rescission should in all fairness to the buyer have been awarded but there were some special circumstances which prevented it from awarding rescission that the court could make an award of damages in lieu of rescission.

These rules are the ones that will apply if the parties have not attempted to vary their rights and the remedies available. It is common for the contract to contain a term which purports to vary these rights. Standard Condition 7.1 is drafted widely enough to cover not only matters in the contract but also statements made 'in negotiations leading to it'.

The effect of Standard Condition 7.1

Under Standard Condition 7.1.2, the buyer is entitled to compensation for misrepresentation which results in a material difference between the description or value of the property as it was represented and as it actually is.

Under Standard Condition 7.1.3, the injured party is only entitled to rescind the contract if either:

(a) the misrepresentation was fraudulent or reckless, or

(b) where without rescission the injured party would be required to accept something substantially different from what the misrepresentation had led the injured party to expect.

The reasonableness test

Standard Condition 7.1 is a term of the contract which attempts to limit the rights and remedies of the parties. As such it is an 'exclusion clause' and is subject to the reasonableness test under the Unfair Contract Terms Act 1977. This means that the clause will not be valid unless it is reasonable having regard to the circumstances which were, or ought reasonably to have been, known to or in the contemplation of the parties at the time the contract was made. Any special condition which attempted to limit the remedies available to the parties would of course be subject to the same test.

Omission to reveal a fact

Failing to disclose a fact may be actionable on one of two bases. Either it may be a breach of a duty of disclosure or it may be one of the special cases where silence could amount to misrepresentation.

Breach of the sellers' duty of disclosure

The duty of disclosure has been looked at earlier when considering drafting the contract:

(a)   Under the open contract rules the sellers must disclose all defects which are not apparent (latent defects) but are under no duty to disclose those which are apparent (patent defects). The sellers must also disclose, in the case of unregistered title, all matters which are registered at the Central Land Charges Registry.

(b)   Under the Standard Conditions the sellers' duty of disclosure is wider than under the open contract rule in that, subject to the buyers' obligation to inspect the property (Standard Conditions 3.1.4 and 3.1.5), the sellers are under a duty to disclose patent as well as latent defects.

Standard Condition 3.1.1 says that the sellers sell the property *free from encumbrances* other than matters mentioned in the agreement and adverse interests existing when the contract is made.

Standard Condition 3.1.3 puts the sellers under a duty to disclose all adverse interests and anything in writing relating to adverse interests which they knew about before exchange of contracts. Adverse interests include public requirements, legal easements, entries on public registers (other than the Land Registry or Land Charges Department registers) and overriding interests where the title to the land is registered.

The net effect of the conditions is that, in most cases, the sellers can only escape liability for non disclosure if the defect is something which:

(a)   falls within the definition of adverse interests and
(b)   the sellers did not know about at the time of exchange of contracts.

Even if the matter satisfies the two conditions, if the encumbrance is something which prevents the sellers from complying with one of the other terms of the contract (e.g., a condition promising to give vacant possession on completion) then the sellers may still find themselves liable for breach of contract.

If the sellers are liable for non-disclosure then what will be the remedies available to the buyers?

Under the open contract rule if the non-disclosure is substantial (in that it results in the buyers not getting what they contracted to buy) then rescission of the contract and damages may be available. If the non-disclosure is not substantial then the buyers may be obliged to go through with the contract but may negotiate a reduction in purchase price by way of damages.

If the Standard Conditions are used then Standard Condition 7.1 applies to omissions in the same way as to statements made in the course of negotiations. The same considerations of reasonableness will apply to the clause in the case of non-disclosure.

Omission amounting to misrepresentation

Although normally silence will not amount to misrepresentation, there are some very limited circumstances where it may do where, for example, the effect of the silence is to distort some actual representation of fact. In essence to say nothing cannot usually be a misrepresentation but to tell a half-truth, where what you have said is technically true but totally distorted by the omission, could result in liability for misrepresentation.

Breach of contract

Any failure to perform an obligation under the contract may give rise to an action for breach of contract. Below are some of the most common problems encountered in a conveyancing transaction.

Forcing completion on an unwilling party

Faced with the other party to the contract refusing to complete on the agreed completion date there are two courses of action available to the injured party: service of a completion notice or a suit for specific performance.

Service of a completion notice Normally in a domestic conveyancing transaction time will not be of the essence. This means that if one party fails to perform the contract on the agreed date the injured party cannot immediately withdraw from the contract. The service of a completion notice will make time of the essence and will have the effect of encouraging the defaulting party to complete or risk the other party backing out of the contract.

Under the open contract rule a completion notice may be served on the party in default but must allow a reasonable time for completion to take place after service of the notice. Obviously trying to decide what is a reasonable period is fraught with difficulties.

Under Standard Condition 6.6 at any time on or after the completion date the party who is 'ready, able and willing to complete' may serve a notice on the other party requiring completion within 10 working days and making time of the essence.

Often the service of a completion notice will have the desired effect of encouraging the defaulting party to complete within the period of the completion notice. Sometimes it will not work or you may regard the service of a completion notice as pointless because the other party has already declared an intention to refuse to go through with the contract at all. In this case if the injured party wants to withdraw from the contract there can be little problem. However, if the injured party wants to force completion then the appropriate remedy would be to apply for an order for specific performance.

Specific performance   This remedy has the effect of forcing the unwilling party to perform the contract. Although the remedy is widely granted in transactions involving land (on the basis that damages are usually considered inadequate compensation) it must be remembered that it is an equitable remedy and may be refused on equitable grounds including undue delay and even in very exceptional cases hardship to the defaulting party.

Withdrawing from the contract for serious breach of contract   There are certain breaches of contract which are regarded as so serious as to entitle the injured party to withdraw from the contract and treat the contract as discharged by the breach. Examples of such serious breaches include:

(a)   A major misdescription. Misdescription is an inaccurate description of the property contained in the contract. For example, if the property were represented as simply 'registered' title this will be regarded as describing it as 'absolute' title. If the property is subsequently discovered not to be registered with absolute title then this might be regarded as a major misdescription.
The provisions of Standard Condition 7.1 apply, as with misrepresentation and omission, to misdescription.
(b)   Delay in completing when time is of the essence. If either time was of the essence at the outset of the contract, or time has been made of the essence by the service of a completion notice, then failing to complete by the specified date would be a serious breach of contract which would entitle the innocent party to withdraw from the contract.
(c)   The existence of an undisclosed encumbrance. If the sellers are selling the property free from encumbrances other than certain specified ones then the discovery of one which was neither disclosed nor specifically excepted from disclosure by the contract will amount to a breach of that term of the contract.
(d)   Failure to show good title. In contracts where the buyers are not required to investigate title before exchange of contracts then if, after exchange of contracts, the sellers are unable to show the title which they had contracted to show then that may be a breach of contract which is sufficiently serious to allow the party to treat the contract as discharged.

In addition to breaches of contract which are simply regarded as so serious as to justify withdrawal from the contract there may be actual contractual conditions which anticipate withdrawal from the contract or rescission as a remedy for their breach:

(a)   Standard Condition 7.1. We have already looked at this condition in relation to misstatements and omissions prior to the making of the contract. The wording of the condition is also wide enough to cover any 'plan or statement in the contract'. Therefore where the Standard Conditions are used, whether rescission will be available for such matters as misdescription will be covered by that condition.

(b)   Standard Condition 5.1.2. Where the property has, between exchange of contracts and completion, suffered damage then Standard Condition 5.1.2 provides for the buyers to be able to rescind the contract if the property has become 'unusable for its purpose at the date of the contract'. It is also possible for the sellers to rescind under this provision but only if either:

(i)   the property became unusable as result of damage against which the seller could not have insured or

(ii)   it is not legally possible for the seller to make good the damage.

(c)   Standard Condition 4.5.2. Where the sellers are 'unable or, on reasonable grounds unwilling to satisfy any requisition' on title then the sellers may give notice to the buyers to withdraw the requisition and if the buyers refuse, the sellers may rescind the contract. This provision should not be regarded as 'the great escape' for the sellers who suddenly realise that they are unable to perform the contract. Use of the condition is greatly limited by the common law rules which govern when sellers may reasonably take advantage of such a provision. *Inter alia*, the sellers may not use this condition unless they were unaware of the defect at the time the contract was made. What is more the sellers' lack of knowledge must not have been due simply to lack of care.

Damages for breach of contract   Whenever there is a breach of contract and there is no condition to cover the payment of damages then the ordinary contractual rule in *Hadley* v *Baxendale* (1854) 9 Exch 341 should be your starting-point. That is, the injured party can recover:

(a)   loss which arises naturally from the breach, and
(b)   loss which both parties would, at the time the contract was made, have regarded as the probable result of the breach.

Damages if completion never takes place

Buyers' default   If the sellers could have and were willing to give the buyers good title but completion never takes place because the buyers refuse to go through with the contract, the sellers could of course apply for specific performance. The sellers may, however, prefer to keep the property and to sue the buyers for breach of contract. The sellers may forfeit the deposit paid by the buyers. This remedy is particularly useful to the sellers where they do not actually suffer any loss (for example, if the property has in fact risen in value since the contract and the seller makes a clear profit on resale). If the sellers have suffered loss then they may sue for damages on the usual contractual basis including:

(a)   the difference between the contract price and any lower resale price, and
(b)   any expenses on resale.

However, credit must be given for the amount of the forfeit deposit.

Sellers default   If it is the sellers who refuse to go through with the contract then the buyers might, of course, choose to seek an order for specific performance. Alternatively the buyers may prefer to look for another property but sue the sellers for breach of contract. The Standard Conditions provide that sellers who fail to comply with a completion notice must repay the deposit to the buyers. The buyers will be entitled to damages on the usual contractual basis normally including:

(a)   the difference between the contract price and the market price of the property usually assessed at the date of the breach,
(b)   costs incurred in the purchase of a new property, and
(c)   costs of accommodation until the new property is bought.

Damages where completion takes place late   As we saw earlier, unless time is of the essence in the particular contract, a failure by one party to complete on the agreed date will not give the other party any right to withdraw from the contract. Failure to complete by the agreed date is, however, a breach of contract which can give rise to a claim for damages.

The open contract rule is, during the period of delay, to treat the parties as if they had completed on the agreed completion date. The effect of this is that:

(a)   The buyers are entitled to income from the property but must pay the outgoings on the property.
(b)   The sellers must pay a fair rent for their occupation of the property but are entitled to interest on the unpaid purchase money.
(c)   The party who is not responsible for the breach of contract may also claim damages on the usual contractual basis (e.g., the cost of temporary accommodation: *Raineri* v *Miles* [1981] AC 1050).

There are some variations to this 'formula', most of which are designed to prevent the party who is in breach of contract from profiting from the breach. Thus, for example, if the delay is due to the fault of the sellers and if the interest on the purchase money amounts to more than the 'rent' on the property, the buyers may keep the interest rather than the income from the property.

Standard Condition 7.3 provides for compensation for late completion to be paid by the party who is in 'default'. The idea of default is a relative one. It is not simply the period of delay between the contractual completion date and the actual completion date which is taken into account but also any delay in the performance of contractual obligations between exchange and completion. So, for example, if the buyers were to be five days late in completing but the sellers had been two days late in replying to requisitions on title (under Standard Condition 4.1.1) then the buyers would be in default but the net period of delay would be three days and not five. Depending on the circumstances it would be possible for, say, the buyers to delay completing by three days but the sellers to discover that, in fact, due to their delay in respect of obligations between exchange and completion, they owed the buyers compensation rather than the other way around.

The party who is liable to pay compensation must pay interest at the contract rate on the purchase price for the net period of delay or the actual delay in completion, whichever is the shorter. If the buyers are liable to pay compensation then an adjustment is made so that the buyers pay interest on the amount of the purchase price less the deposit (which the sellers already have).

Standard Conditions 7.3.1 and 7.3.2 provide a useful formula for the assessment of an easily calculated amount of compensation for late completion. It is clear, though, from Standard Condition 7.3.3 that, if a party wishes, a claim may also be made for damages for breach of contract on the usual basis. In the event of damages being awarded, the amount payable will be reduced by the amount of compensation paid under the formula in Standard Conditions 7.3.1 and 7.3.2.

Time for pursuing an action for breach of contract

Obviously if an action seeking specific performance is to be brought then the whole nature of the problem is that one party is refusing to complete the transaction. The question therefore of the timing of the action is irrelevant other than that the equitable remedy which it seeks may be refused on the grounds of undue delay.

In certain cases (e.g., where there has been misrepresentation) rescission may be available despite completion having taken place. However, rescission is an equitable remedy which may be refused on the grounds that an innocent third party might be injured by such an order. The risk of an order for rescission being refused on this ground is greatly increased after completion has occurred.

Even where the claim is for damages, care must be taken to ensure that that particular remedy will be available after completion. There are certain matters which may be pursued after completion. (From the practical point of view if the cause of action is known about before completion then it may be most sensible to pursue the matter then when both parties may be in the mood for negotiation in order to see an early conclusion of the transaction.) Actions in respect of misrepresentation can be pursued either before or after completion. An action for non-dislosure must be pursued before completion.

On completion the general rule is that the terms of the contract will merge with the purchase deed. The effect of this is that many of the remedies for breach of contract will be lost and the remedies of the buyer after completion will then depend on whether the seller can be sued on the basis of the covenants for title implied in the purchase deed (see chapter 10). It is possible for the contract specifically to provide that certain terms shall not merge with the purchase deed on completion thus preserving the right to bring an action for breach of contract even after completion. Exceptionally, certain terms of the contract will not merge with the purchase deed even though no express provision is included, e.g., a contractual term whereby the seller agrees to give vacant possession on completion can be sued upon even after completion.

Vendor and purchaser summons

Mention must also be made of the vendor and purchaser summons under the Law of Property Act 1925, s. 49, which is in theory an expeditious means of determining a dispute between sellers and buyers. Its use is very limited. It cannot be used to pursue an action for breach of contract, nor can it be used to determine the validity of a contract. It can be used to settle disputes between the sellers and buyers between exchange and completion. For example, if the buyers were to raise a requisition and the sellers provided a reply which the buyers argued was not adequate, a vendor and purchaser summons could be used to ask the court to adjudicate the point and to decide whether the sellers had provided an adequate reply. The court can make any order it thinks fit, including an order for costs.

Common examination problem areas

How well you tackle an examination question regarding remedies depends very much on how well you keep your head when all about you are losing theirs! Here are a few checks and pointers which may help you to keep a sense of perspective and logic.

(a)   There is obviously the possibility of other remedies being examined, such as rescission where the contract was entered into as a result of undue influence or rectification of the purchase deed where it is discovered that it does not accurately reflect the contract. Don't either forget or ignore basic principles of contract.

(b)   Ask yourself first: What is the cause of action? It is amazing how easy it is in an examination entirely to overlook the fact that neither doing something the other party does not like, nor saying something which is untrue, is of itself actionable.

(c)   In trying to establish what is the cause of action ask yourself: When and where did the matter complained about originate? This will put you on the right track to the right remedy. For example, a misstatement of fact made before the contract which induced the buyers to enter into the contract, unless it was repeated in the contract, could not give rise to an action for breach of contract or misdescription (both of which must arise out of the contract itself).

(d)   Once you have established the possible causes of action then see if your facts actually fit. For example, if the buyers are unhappy about a statement which was made before the contract and was not repeated in the contract then ask: Was it a misstatement of fact which induced the buyers to enter into the contract? Or if the buyers are unhappy about something the sellers have done or failed to do between exchange and completion, check that there is a breach of an actual term of the contract and identify which term.

(e)   Once you have established a possible cause of action and that your facts fit then look at the remedies which will be available to your client. Ask yourself:

(i)   What are the remedies under the open contract rule?
(ii)   Do the terms of the contract attempt to alter or modify those in any way, and if so how?
(iii) Will those terms, if any, survive the reasonableness test?

(f)   Once you have established the remedies which are available in theory consider whether there is anything which might prevent those remedies from being awarded, particularly in the case of the equitable remedies.

FIFTEEN

MORTGAGES

So far mortgages have been dealt with from time to time as one of the procedural matters which need to be considered at various stages in the transaction. We have looked at the procedures which the sellers' solicitors would follow if the property which is being sold is subject to a mortgage or mortgages. We have only briefly looked at the situation if the buyers are obtaining a mortgage on the property which they are buying.

It is somewhat artificial to deal with the topic in this way. Over 90 per cent of domestic conveyancing transactions will involve both the discharge of a mortgage on the sellers' property and the creation of a new mortgage by the buyers. The solicitor who acts for either party must bear in mind the particular problems arising out of the mortgage throughout the transaction, and not simply as an isolated issue at the end. You too, in the exam room, may well be asked to deal not only with the procedural matters but also the problems arising out of mortgages alongside the main transaction. The reason that the detail of this has been left to the end is to give you a chance to feel familiar with the different stages of the transaction generally. Once you have got to grips with that then I hope that you will be able to cope with the additional problems of mortgages more easily and slot them into the overall framework.

There are two additional reasons for considering the process of obtaining a new mortgage as a separate topic. Even where a solicitor is acting for both the buyers and the mortgagee in a transaction you must remember that the solicitor is in fact acting for two quite separate parties in two quite separate transactions. The buyers are buying the property. The mortgagee is making a loan in return for a charge over the property. It is also possible that you may, in practice or in an exam, be asked to act for the mortgagee only.

When can you act for the buyer and for the mortgagee?

When we looked at professional practice matters regarding who a solicitor may act for we saw that there is a prohibition on a solicitor acting for the buyer and seller or for the borrower and lender in a private mortgage. A private mortgage is broadly where the lender is not engaged in the business of giving loans in return for security. There is no prohibition on acting for the lender and borrower in a non-private mortgage, although the overriding rule that a solicitor may not act for two clients or parties where their interests conflict must be remembered and applied. In most cases the interests of the buyers and the mortgagee will be the same. Both want to buy a property with good title, and which, if the need arose, they could resell. It is therefore very common to find one solicitor acting for both the buyers and the mortgagee who is lending part of the money required to buy the house. The situations in which you are likely to find separate solicitors acting for the buyer and the mortgagee are:

(a)   When the buyers are not represented by a solicitor.

(b)   When the mortgagee wishes to engage its own solicitors.

(c)   When the solicitors acting for the buyers are not on the mortgagee's panel of solicitors or are not authorised by the mortgagee to act. (Most solicitors are on the panel of most building societies.)

(d)   When the mortgagee is also the builder or developer.

(e)   When the solicitors for the buyers discover that there is a conflict or a potential conflict of interest between the interests of the buyers and the interests of the mortgagee. Conflicts of interest can arise in the most surprising of ways. It is important always to keep an awareness of the possibility and to look at the facts of the exam question and to see if there is *anything* in there which might hint at the possibility of conflict.

Types of mortgage

There are many institutions in the business of lending money in return for a mortgage over property. The most common ones which you will come across are building societies, banks, finance companies and local authorities. The types of mortgage which can be obtained are also becoming more and more varied. It is essential though, at this stage, at least to appreciate how the different types of mortgage work.

All mortgages work on the basis of a charge over the property, made by the mortgagor (the owner of the property), in return for a loan made by the mortgagee (the bank or building society). These are four types of mortgage which are commonly found.

(a)   *The ordinary repayment mortgage.* The essence of this is that the mortgagee will make a loan which is repayable over a specified period (usually 20 or 25 years). The monthly repayment which is required to pay off the loan and the interest on the loan will be worked out. This figure will vary from time to time as the interest rates change and either increase or decrease the monthly repayments in order to ensure that the whole amount is still paid off over the period (or 'term') of the mortgage. The monthly repayments will, at first, be made up largely of interest but gradually the amount of capital paid off will increase until at the end of the term *all* of the initial loan and interest will have been paid off (see Table 15.1).

Table 15.1

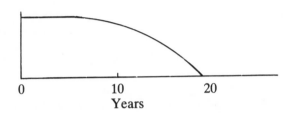

(b) *The endowment mortgage.* This type of mortgage involves the mortgagee making a loan in return for a charge on two pieces of property. It will take a charge on the house *and* on an endowment policy. The mortgagor must, as well as making payments on the mortgage, also pay the premiums on the policy. The policy will provide for repayment of the whole amount of the *capital* of the loan in the event of the death of the mortgagor or the end of the term of the mortgage whichever is the sooner. The mortgage repayments made by the mortgagor will be lower than for an ordinary repayment mortgage as the repayments will consist of interest only. The capital will be paid later from the endowment mortgage (see table 15.2).

Table 15.2

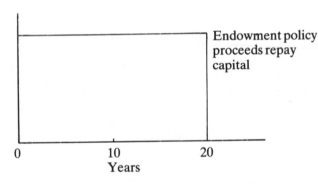

(c) *The fixed-rate mortgage.* It has now become increasingly common for banks and building societies to offer a mortgage where the interest rate is guaranteed for the first two or three years. The advantage of this type of mortgage is that if interest rates should go up the borrowers will be protected against any increase in the mortgage repayments during the agreed period. The disadvantage is that if interest rates should fall the borrowers may find themselves paying at a higher rate than under an ordinary repayment mortgage.

(d) *The repayment mortgage coupled with a mortgage protection policy.* This will simply be an ordinary repayment or fixed-rate mortgage combined with a term life insurance policy. The borrower will still make repayments of both capital and interest over the term of the mortgage. If the borrower survives beyond the end of the term the insurance policy will do nothing but if the borrower should die before the end of the term the policy will pay out sufficient funds to repay the amount outstanding on the mortgage. It is common for mortgagees to make the taking out of such a policy a condition of the mortgage in cases other than where the borrower is single and without dependents.

Mortgage offer and instructions

Once the buyers have made an application for a mortgage advance they will be sent a mortgage offer. The conditions of the offer should be checked carefully with the buyers following which, if everything is satisfactory, the buyers should accept the offer. The mortgagee will then send its instructions to the solicitors (if the solicitors are acting for both buyers and mortgagee). These instructions should also be checked carefully: they are the instructions of a client. All this should be done before exchange of contracts otherwise you may find your buyer clients committed to the purchase of a property but the mortgagee unable or unwilling to finance it.

All the conditions attached to the mortgage offer should be checked carefully. There are, however, certain conditions which are commonly found on mortgage instructions which deserve some explanation:

(a) *Endowment policies*. If the mortgage is to be an endowment mortgage then the instructions will contain details of the endowment policies which need to be assigned to the society. If the policies are already in existence, the mortgagee's solicitor will have to make sure that they are not assigned to anyone else. If the policies are to be new the solicitors must ensure that all is in order and that they are put in force at completion.

(b) *Retentions*. Sometimes the mortgage instructions will state that an amount of the mortgage advance is to be retained until certain works have been carried out. For example a condition might read:

A retention of £2,000 will be made by the Society pending the installation of a full damp-proof course at the property.

First the retention must be explained to the borrowers. The effect is that the amount of the mortgage advance paid on completion will be reduced by £2,000. An extra £2,000 must be found to complete the sale as the mortgagee will not release the money until the work is done nevertheless the sellers will want their full price.

Secondly there are various things which should be considered:

(i) The sellers may be prepared to reduce the purchase price in view of the repairs needed.

(ii) The sellers may be prepared to allow the work to be done before completion. (This is not without risk to the buyers, for example, if the sellers should ultimately refuse to complete.)

(iii) The mortgagee may be prepared to amend its offer and to release the money on completion if the buyers agree to have the work done within six months of completion.

(iv)   The buyers must in any event be advised to obtain estimates for the work. The fact that the retention is for £2,000 is no guarantee that the work will only cost £2,000.

(c)   *Mortgage guarantee premium*. Many offers contain a condition regarding a mortgage guarantee premium. This is a single payment which is usually either added to the total amount of the loan or alternatively deducted from the initial advance. This premium effects insurance which will protect the mortgagee should the buyers default and the mortgagee be unable to recover the full amount of the debt from the sale of the property. It is therefore encountered most often where the mortgage advance is a large percentage of the total purchase price of the property.

Investigation of title

Investigation of the sellers' title will involve much the same considerations as investigation of title on behalf of the buyers. The buyers are concerned to see that the sellers own the property and that it is not subject to any unacceptable third-party interests. The mortgagee is concerned to see the same things. It wants to be sure that if the buyers should default on the repayments and it should become necessary to sell the property, the mortgagee will have a good and saleable title. All the searches which have been undertaken for the buyers are of importance to the mortgagee as well. In the case of registered title, though, the search on form 94A will not automatically protect the mortgagee. If acting for both buyers and mortgagee the solution is to undertake the form 94A search in the name of the mortgagee as this will protect *both* the buyers and the mortgagee.

In addition to checking the sellers' title the mortgagee will also want to check out the borrowers. The mortgagee will already have undertaken an investigation of the buyers' means. The solicitor acting for the mortgagee must also ensure that, in addition to the search which will be undertaken in connection with the purchase, a bankruptcy only search is carried out at the Central Land Charges Registry against each of the buyers. If the search were to reveal any entry at all then the mortgagee could not safely lend the money and be sure of having the first call on the proceeds of sale of the property.

The mortgagee will also be concerned about the possible interests of any third parties which may arise after the purchase. So long as the mortgagee's charge is properly protected after completion of the mortgage there is not usually a threat to the mortgagee if a third party *subsequently* acquires an interest in the property. There is, however, a significant risk if there is any possibility of a third-party interest arising *before* the completion of the mortgage. The problem is most acute where the borrower is already living in the property and is obtaining a second mortgage or is remortgaging the property. Imagine this situation. Harry bought the property two years ago in his sole name. Since then Mary has moved in with him and has paid for substantial improvements to the property. It is possible that this contribution by Mary may give her an equitable interest in the property. If so, the situation would have changed from that shown in table 15.3 to that shown in table 15.4.

Table 15.3

Legal	Equitable
H	H

Table 15.4

Legal	Equitable
H	H and M

If Harry is now remortgaging the property to the Acorn Building Society you must ask yourself what the position of the building society will be in relation to Mary's interest. If Harry defaults on the repayments, will the Acorn Building Society be able to sell the property or will Mary be able to resist the society's application for an order for possession on the basis that she has an equitable third-party right in the property by which the society may be bound (see table 15.5) or it may be free of her interest (see table 15.6).

Table 15.5

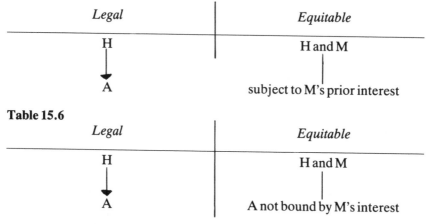

Legal	Equitable
H	H and M
↓	↓
A	subject to M's prior interest

Table 15.6

Legal	Equitable
H	H and M
↓	↓
A	A not bound by M's interest

Which it is will depend on:

(a)   In unregistered title (as Mary's interest is an equitable interest arising under a trust and therefore not registrable as a land charge), whether the society had notice of the interest. The notice could be actual notice, constructive notice (where evidence of the interest could have been or was discovered by inspecting the property), or imputed notice (if the society's solicitor or valuer had actual or constructive notice).

(b)   In registered title, if Mary is in actual occupation of the property and if she was not asked what her interest was so that she will have an overriding interest under the Land Registration Act 1925, s. 70(1)(g), and the Society will be bound by her interest.

The mortgagee's situation is not so problematic in the case of a first mortgage which is being obtained at the same time as the property is being bought. If the borrower is to buy the property in his or her sole name, but the funds are to be provided by the borrower and another then the authorities (e.g., *Abbey National Building Society* v *Cann* [1991] 1 AC 56 and *Paddington Building Society* v *Mendelson* (1985) 50 P & CR 244, CA), suggest:

(a)   That there is in effect no time between the completion of the purchase and the completion of the mortgage. There is therefore no time *before* the creation of the mortgage when the other person can acquire an interest in the property. The other person cannot therefore claim to have an interest which ranks in priority to the Society.

(b)   That if the other person knew that the property could only be bought with the aid of a mortgage, and therefore the other person's interest in the property could only be acquired with the aid of a mortgage, then the other person cannot claim to have an interest which ranks in priority to the society.

It is important to remember when acting for the mortgagee that, however helpful these decisions may be, you should be attempting to ensure that there is no risk of litigation. There are various procedures which should be followed when acting for a mortgagee:

(a)   An inspection of the property should be made to find out whether anyone else is living in the property.
(b)   The borrower should be asked whether anyone else is or will be living at the property and whether anyone else has contributed or is contributing to the property.

If these enquiries reveal anyone who is living at the property and/or may have an interest in the property then there are two possible solutions:

(a)   The third party should, before compleiton, be advised to take independent advice and asked to sign a deed postponing any interest he or she may have to that of the mortgagee.

(b)   The borrower may be asked, before completion of the mortgage, to appoint a second trustee to receive the mortgage money which would overreach the interests of the third party (*City of London Building Society* v *Flegg* [1988] AC 54).

Preparing for completion

The mortgage deed

Usually when the mortgagee's solicitors are sent instructions they will also be sent a bundle of standard documentation including a mortgage deed. The terms of the deed are not usually negotiable but they should be explained to the borrowers before the deed is executed. The matters to which the borrowers' attention should be drawn are:

(a)   *The legal redemption date*. This date is, in theory, the date on which the loan is repayable. It is usually about six months after the date of the mortgage. The requirement to repay the whole loan will be varied by a term agreeing to regular repayments over the term of the mortgage.

In practice the redemption date is merely the date from which the mortgagee's power to sell the property will arise and it will not become exercisable unless and until the borrower breaches the terms of the mortgage in one of the ways specified in the Law of Property Act 1925, s. 103, or in any other way specified in the mortgage.

(b)   *The repayments and the interest rate*. The mortgage deed will specify the interest rate at the time of completion of the mortgage but it must be remembered that this is variable and so too will be the repayments. In the case of an endowment mortgage there will usually be two figures stated for the repayments. The lower one will be the amount payable so long as the endowment policy premiums are paid. The higher figure will be payable if the borrower should fail to pay the premiums on the endowment policy.

(c)   *Tenancies*. Many borrowers, if they have a spare room in the house, have the idea that they will, after completion, take a lodger to help with the finances. The borrower has a statutory right to grant certain leases of the property but this is nearly always specifically excluded in the mortgage deed. It will also usually be provided that a breach of this condition will make the mortgagee's power of sale exercisable.

Preparation and execution of documents

(a)   The mortgage deed must be executed by the borrowers prior to completion. A failure to do this would mean that the mortgagee's money was used for the purchase of property over which it would have no security.

(b)   If the mortgage is an endowment mortgage then the borrowers are effectively offering two things as security, the house and the endowment policy. It is therefore necessary for the borrowers to execute a charge over both the house and the policy. In the case of the house the charge is the 'mortgage deed'. In the case of the policy it is the 'policy mortgage' or the 'assignment of the endowment policy'. Both of these must be prepared and executed before completion. (Some building societies no longer require a formal mortgage of the endowment policy but simply a deposit of the policy document. You should check your mortgage instructions carefully to see which is required.)

(c)   If the mortgage is an endowment mortgage a notice of assignment (in duplicate) must also be prepared in respect of each policy.

(d)   Before completion the mortgagee's solicitors must also prepare a report on title for the mortgagee and send a request for the advance cheque. The report on title will either state that the title is in order or bring to the attention of the mortgagee anything which is unsatisfactory. The request for the advance cheque should state the date of completion.

New policies

If the mortgage involves taking out any new mortgage protection policies or endowment policies the solicitors for the mortgagee should ensure that the policies are put into force immediately prior to completion.

Completion and post-completion

Completion of the mortgage will take place at the same time as completion of the purchase. Once the mortgage moneys are used on the purchase the mortgage deed will become operative.

After completion the solicitors acting for the mortgagee must ensure that the interests of the mortgagee are properly protected. The interests of the buyers and the mortgagee are very closely linked together and, because the mortgagee's title to the property is derived from the buyers' title, any failure to protect and perfect the buyers' title would affect the title of the mortgagee.

(a)   *Stamping.* The mortgage deed does not require to be stamped but the buyers' title must be perfected by ensuring that the purchase deed is stamped with a particulars delivered stamp and, where appropriate, *ad valorem* duty.

(b)   *Registration of the buyers' title.* If the title to the property is either registered or due for first registration then an application must be made. If the buyers' interest is not registered then it will either revert to being (where the title is due for first registration) or remain (where the title is already registered) an equitable interest. If the buyers' title is only equitable so will be the mortgagee's.

(c)   *Protection of the mortgage.* If the title to the property is unregistered the mortgagee can protect its interest by taking deposit of the title deeds along with the mortgage deed. If the mortgagee does not have the first mortgage over the property then this second legal mortgage must be protected by registration as a class C(i) land charge.

If the title is registered or due for first registration then the application to register the buyers' title must be accompanied by an application to register the mortgage in the charges section of the register. Once the registration is complete the mortgagee's solicitors will be sent a charge certificate which the solicitors should check and, having checked it, forward to the mortgagee for safe keeping.

(d) *Protection of the policy mortgage.* The policy documents should themselves be obtained and forwarded to the mortgagee together with the assignments of the policies. Nevertheless, this alone would not be sufficient to ensure that the mortgagee was absolutely safe. It would always be possible for unscrupulous borrowers to sign a declaration that the policy document had been lost and to arrange the surrender of the policy and payment to them of the surrender value. To avoid this, notice of assignment of the life policies should be given to the insurance companies. This will warn them that the policy is no longer the unencumbered property of the policy holder. The notice should be sent in duplicate. Each insurance company will then receipt one copy and return it to the solicitors who will forward it to the mortgagee along with the other documents.

Common examination problem areas

Exam questions concerning mortgages are not usually particularly difficult but they do involve you being able to 'think on your feet' and it is also vital that you do not allow yourself to become confused about your objectives.

1 If the question assumes you are acting for both the buyer and the mortgagee you must remember:

(a) Keep in your mind the possible problem of a conflict of interest arising between your two clients. If a conflict should arise then you must cease to act.

(b) Keep the two transactions separate in your own mind. It is very tempting to think in simplistic terms that the interests of the buyers and the mortgagee are much the same so there is not a lot extra to know. Do not be tempted to do this. Remember that there are matters which you will need to consider when you are acting for the buyers but not when you are acting for the mortgagee and vice versa. The fact that many of the interests of the buyer and the mortgagee are common means only that the purchase and mortgage transactions have a number of common factors, not that they form one transaction.

Remember always to read the question carefully. If the question says, 'What pre-completion searches would you undertake to protect the buyer?' it is a different question from, 'What pre-completion searches would you undertake to protect the mortgagee?' It is true that many of the points will be the same but an answer to the first question would be unlikely to include:

(a)   A bankruptcy only search at the Land Charges Registry against each
of the buyers.

(b)   An additional search of the local land charges registry if there has
been a long time since exchange.

(c)   A form 94A search in the name of the lender in the case of registered
title.

2   Whenever you are acting for the mortgagee remember, What is the
bottom line? What does the mortgagee want out of the transcation? It is that
if the mortgagor fails to keep up the repayment on the mortgage, the
mortgagee wants to be able to sell the property and recoup the debt.

Whenever you are asked to act for a mortgagee be very aware of matters
which may not bother a buyer but could be catastrophic to the mortgagee.
For example, a buyer may not be concerned that his or her cohabitee, or
elderly relative, or adult child, or anyone else at all has, or may acquire, an
equitable interest in the property. If that person is not a party to the
mortgage then the effects on the mortgagee could be to enable that third
party to prevent the sale of the property when the borrower fails to keep up
the payments.

Try to be aware of the type of matters in the narrative of a question which
should give cause for concern:

(a)   The mention of anyone who is or will be living with the borrower.
The other person may not have any interest in the property but enquiries
should be made and, if necessary, steps taken to protect the mortgagee.

(b)   The mention of anyone who may be contributing to the purchase
price of the property. This could give rise to an equitable interest and steps
should be taken to protect the mortgagee.

(c)   The mention of anyone who has contributed to the purchase price or
the improvement of the borrower's existing property. If the borrower is
simply remortgaging the property the mortgagee may find itself bound by
such a person's interest. If the borrower is selling that property and using any
of the proceeds to purchase a new property then that may give the third party
an interest in the new property. Steps should be taken to protect the
mortgagee.

Remember that not only is it part of your job to help to avoid unnecessary
litigation but also, so far as the mortgagee is concerned, to protect its
reputation. Even if you think that someone has an interest in the property
but it will not bind the mortgagee (for example, if it were overreached), ask
the mortgagee what it wishes you to do. Most will say that, notwithstanding
that they will not be bound by the third-party interest, they would prefer that
person to have independent advice at this stage and to sign a deed of
postponement rather than risk the adverse publicity of headlines that read
'Senior citizen loses home because of mortgage no one told her about'.

SIXTEEN

ALTERATIONS TO EXISTING HOUSES, NEW HOUSES, AND BUYING A NEW HOUSE ON A HOUSING ESTATE

In chapter 7 we looked at the searches and enquiries which the buyers would make before exchange of contracts. Included in the enquiries of the sellers were questions regarding whether there has been any development at the property requiring planning permission. There were also matters regarding planning notices which we had to consider when checking the results of the search of the local land charges register and the additional enquiries of the local authority.

Whenever either a new building is proposed or an alteration or extension to an existing building is encountered, you need to know what matters to look out for. Sometimes an examination question may ask you directly to explain the requirements for planning permission etc. At other times there may be something in the facts which should start you thinking about these matters. The information may be included in the narrative of the question or it may be slipped into one of the documents. For example, if the property information form is provided, question 10.1 on the form, which says, 'Has there been any building work on the property in the last four years', might be answered, 'Yes the kitchen extension was built three years ago'. You must remember to consider every piece of information that you are given in the examination and decide what relevance, if any, it has. In order to appreciate the relevance of an answer like the one in the example you need to know something of the limitations on development.

There are four likely situations where you will have to consider the limitations on development:

(a)   You are acting for someone who is building a new property.
(b)   You are acting for someone who is buying a new property.
(c)   You are acting for someone who is buying a property which has, in the past, been altered or extended.
(d)   You are acting for someone who is buying a property with a view to altering or extending it.

Whenever any of these situations arise there are four things which you will need to consider in addition to all the usual pre-contract searches and enquiries: restrictive covenants, easements, building regulations consent and planning permission.

Restrictive covenants

If there are any restrictive covenants affecting the property, find out whether the development would be in breach of any of those covenants. If your clients are buying the new or altered property then the sellers should be asked about these matters in the enquiries before contract. Question 9 on the property information form relates to restrictive covenants.

The way to check for yourself is:

(a) In unregistered title, check the title deeds for the existence of any restrictive covenants and (so long as the current owner is not the original covenantor) check whether they are enforceable either directly by registration as a D(ii) land charge (for covenants created after 1925) or indirectly through an unbroken chain of indemnity covenants.

(b) In registered title, check the register for the existence and enforceability of covenants.

Easements

Again if your clients are buying the property then enquiries must be made of the sellers about the existence of any easements. If there are any third parties who have easements over the property which would be affected by any development then their consent must be obtained.

The existence of easements may be checked from the title deeds in unregistered title and the register in registered title. This check will not, however, necessarily be conclusive. There may be easements which do not actually appear in the typescript of the deeds which are nevertheless legal easements and which exist despite there being no written evidence of them. Easements acquired by implied grant under the rule in *Wheeldon* v *Burrows* (1879) 12 ChD 31 or easements acquired under the Law of Property Act 1925, s. 62, could fall within this category. In unregistered title, even though they do not appear in the deeds and even though the buyers do not know about them, they will bind the buyers of the property. In registered title, even though they do not appear on the register, and even though the buyers do not know about them they will bind the buyers as they are overriding interests within category (a) of the Land Registration Act 1925, s. 70(1). The buyers must simply make as full enquiries and inspections as possible in the hope of discovering their existence.

Building regulations consent

Building regulations arise out of the Public Health Acts and are designed to cover the way in which a building is constructed or altered. The regulations cover such things as the type of materials to be used, the minimum height for a living-room and the amount of ventilation required. A new building or an alteration to an existing building should have a certificate of compliance with building regulations. The certificate is usually issued by the local authority but can in certain circumstances be issued by an approved inspector rather than the local authority itself.

Planning permission

Planning permission consists of various controls which are designed to limit what building takes place at all, what type of building is built, and to what use the building is put.

Planning permission is required when 'development' takes place

Planning permission is in theory required whenever there is 'development' of land. Development is statutorily defined as: 'the carrying out of building, engineering, mining or other operations in, on, over or under land' or 'the making of any material change of use of any buildings or other land'.

The idea of building, engineering works etc. probably does not need too much explanation but it should be noted that certain things which technically fall within the definition of 'development' are specifically excluded from amounting to development. In particular most works which do not materially affect the external appearance of the building will not be development and therefore do not require planning permission (although they may require approval under building regulations).

The making of a material change of use of the property requires a little more explanation. Changing the use of a property may or may not amount to development depending on exactly what the use is changed from and what it is changed to. The Town and Country Planning (Use Classes) Order 1987 specifies 16 classes. Providing the change of use is from a use within one of the specified classes to another use within the same class (e.g., change from a sweet shop to a clothing shop) then the change of use will not be development and will not therefore require planning permission.

Another matter which is specifically referred to as not constituting development is the use of buildings or land, which are within the curtilage of a dwelling-house, for any purpose incidental to the enjoyment of the dwelling house itself. Note, though, that the alteration of a single dwelling into two or more separate dwellings will constitute a material change in use. A particular problem in this area is finding the difference between a single dwelling with a 'granny flat' and a building which actually constitutes two separate dwellings. One of the factors which must be relevant here is the degree of self-containment of each part, although that alone is not likely to be conclusive.

When must an application be made for planning permission?

Whenever there is 'development', planning permission will be required. In certain circumstances although the matter technically falls within the definition of development and although it is not specifically excepted from constituting 'development', nevertheless there is no need actually to make an application for planning permission. This is the case whenever the development falls within development permitted by the Town and Country Planning General Development Order 1988 in which case planning permission is automatically granted by the order.

The most notable things that constitute 'permitted development' under the 1988 General Development Order are:

(a)   Alterations, enlargements or improvements of a dwelling-house. In most circumstances these are permitted provided they are relatively small. If you think that this exception may apply then check the precise limits of the order which amongst other things places specific restrictions on the height and overall size of the development which vary according to the type of property. The type of matters which *may* fall within this type of permitted development are porches and garages if they are wihtin 5 metres of the house.

(b)   The provision or alterations of a building within the curtilage of the dwelling for a purpose incidental to the enjoyment of the property. Again there are precise requirements which must be checked in each case but the type of matter which may be covered is the erection of a garden shed, greenhouse or a garage which is over 5 metres from the house.

(c)   The erection of gates, fences and walls (subject to certain height limits) and the ordinary painting of the exterior of a building.

Although the General Development Order applies to the whole country it is possible for it to be excluded in relation to particular types of development and/or in respect of a particular area. An order suspending the operation of the General Development Order in whole or in part is known as an 'article 4 direction'. Its existence can be discovered from enquiries of the local authority.

Nature of planning permission

An application can be made for planning permission or 'outline planning permission'. An application for planning permission must give full details of the proposed development. Outline planning permission will simply give approval to the principle of erecting a building subject to the local planning authority later approving the actual details. Outline planning permission is particularly useful where someone wants to sell a building plot. The seller can only expect to obtain a low price for the plot unless there is some indication that there will be no objection in principle to building a house there. Nevertheless the seller will not want to go to the expense of having full plans drawn up for a house which may not be what the buyer wants to build.

Once the planning permission is granted it continues to exist for the benefit of that land and is not the personal property of the person who made the application. The planning permission will not continue indefinitely and in the case of 'full' planning permission the development must be begun within five years of the granting of the permission or the permission lapses.

The permission may be made subject to conditions so long as they relate in some reasonable way to the development itself.

Effect of a breach of planning regulations

A breach of planning regulations can occur if either development was carried out without permission or if permission was applied for but a condition attached to the permission has been breached.

A breach of planning controls is remedied by the service of an enforcement notice which must specify the breach, the steps required to remedy the breach and the date on which the notice becomes effective. The date on which the notice becomes effective must be not less than 28 days from the date of the notice. If the local authority is concerned that the development may continue during the period before the enforcement notice takes effect it may, in most cases, serve a stop notice which will prevent any further development of the property during the period between the service of the enforcement notice and the enforcement notice taking effect. Failure to comply with a stop notice is a criminal offence.

If the breach of planning regulations takes the form of a material change of use of the premises without obtaining planning permission then, subject to one exception, there is no time-limit for the service of an enforcement notice.

Where the breach of planning regulations takes the form of building, engineering etc. works or the material change of use of any building *to* a single dwelling-house then an enforcement notice can only be served up to four years from the date of the breach. Thereafter the local authority can take no action in respect of the breach.

Other matters relating to the particular property

The four matters mentioned above are not the only matters which may be relevant but simply the more usual ones. The nature of the particular property may give rise to other considerations. For example, restrictive covenants were looked at above from the point of view of a freehold property. If the property were leasehold then the consent of the landlord may need to be obtained. If the property concerned were a building listed as being of 'special architectural or historic importance' then consent is required for the carrying out of any works (whether or not they would fall within the definition of development) which are likely to affect its character as a building of special interest. The acquisition of a 'listed building' may put the buyers under an obligation to maintain and repair the building.

Additional considerations when buying a new property

When buying a new property, whether or not it is on a housing estate, all the matters of covenants, easements, building regulations consent and planning permission will be relevant. However, when the property is a new one there are some additional matters which need also to be considered.

The National House Building Council's scheme

Where a new house is constructed by a builder who is registered with the National House Building Council, an insurance scheme is available whereby the builder enters into an agreement with the Council. Once the builder has entered into the agreement the effect, so far as the buyers of the property are concerned, is that the builder will be liable to put right any defects arising, within the first two years, from a failure to build the property in an efficient and workmanlike manner. The Council's insurance scheme then provides cover against structural defects for a further eight years. It may be that buyers, having been properly advised about the risks, are prepared to buy a new property without such insurance. It must be remembered, though, that not only will the buyers have difficulty obtaining a mortgage but also any person who wanted to buy the property within the next 10 years would have the same problem. Therefore the resale price of a property which does not have the benefit of insurance under the NHBC scheme or similar insurance is likely to be considerably lower than a property which has the benefit of such cover.

If your clients are proposing to buy a new property you must check that the agreement has been entered into and ask to see evidence of it. If your client is buying a property which is not brand new but was constructed within the last 10 years then details of the agreement should be checked before completion and an assurance obtained that the original documentation will be handed over on completion.

Roads and drains

This matter does not usually present any particular problem on the sale of a single new property. Of course, the buyers' solicitors should check, as with every purchase, whether the roads adjoining the property are adopted (both from the point of view of financial responsibility and whether the buyers will have the benefit of a right of way over the road). They should also check whether the property drains into a public sewer (again both from the point of view of financial responsibility and whether the buyers will have the benefit of the necessary easement of drainage).

Roads   Where the new house is part of a new housing estate then new roads will have been constructed and new drains laid. It is usual for the builder to enter into agreements relating to these. In the case of the roads the buyers' solicitors should check whether the builder has entered into an agreement with the local authority under the Highways Act 1980, s. 38. The basis of the agreement is that the builder will make up the roads on the estate and that thereafter the local authority will adopt the roads and maintain them at public expense. The agreement should be supported by a bond which is of

'The buyers' solicitors should check . . . whether the property drains into a public sewer'

sufficient amount to cover the cost of making up the roads if the builder should default on the agreement.

If the builder has not entered into such an agreement and bond then the buyers' solicitors, in addition to ensuring that the buyers will acquire adequate rights over the roads in the estate, will also have to advise the buyers of the potential liability not only to make up and maintain the road but also to pay a proportion of the cost of making up the roads if the local authority decided in the future to adopt them.

Drains When a property is built on a new estate it is usual for the builder to enter into an agreement with the water company similar to that entered into with the local authority in respect of the roads. The agreement will be that the builder will construct the main drains on the estate whereafter the water company will adopt them and maintain them at its expense. As with the road agreement this agreement should be supported by a bond which will cover the cost of constructing the drains should the builder default.

If the builder has not entered into such an agreement and bond the buyers' solicitors should, in addition to ensuring that the buyers will acquire adequate easements of drainage, advise the buyers of the potential financial liability with regard to maintaining the drains.

Common examination problem areas

Once you have reached the end of this chapter you are probably sighing and wondering how on earth you will remember it all never mind make enough sense of it to answer a question. A straightforward point-by-point check approach may help.

(a)   Remember in each case to consider the four aspects:

(i)   Covenants.
(ii)   Easements.
(iii) Building regulations.
(iv)   Planning permission.

Plus any additional matters which may be relevant like listed buildings consent.

(b)   Remember when dealing with planning permission to take your answer one step at a time:

(i)   Planning permission is needed whenever there is 'development'. Be able to define development and know what matters are specifically excluded from the definition.

(ii)   Is an application for planning permission needed or does it fall within the limits of the General Development Order?

(iii) If it does fall within the limits of the order, does the order actually apply or has there been an article 4 direction?

(iv)   If planning permission was needed and obtained was the development begun within the time-limit?

(v)   If there has been a breach of a condition of planning permission or a failure to obtain planning permission, how can the local authority enforce the planning controls if at all?

SEVENTEEN

PARTICULAR PROBLEMS WITH LEASEHOLD TITLE

If you were to stand outside an examination hall just before a conveyancing exam you would be able to hear at least one student saying, 'I'm all right on freehold but I'll die if leases come up'. What is worse is that you would probably hear a chorus of agreement. Leases seem to frighten students out of all proportion to their difficulty. In fact there is nothing inherently difficult about them. Only one chapter of this book is devoted to leases because, if you have worked steadily through the book so far you will now be beginning to understand something of how a conveyancing transaction works. If you can understand that, all you need to do now is to see what problems you might encounter which are peculiar to leasehold title.

Let us start with basics. What is the essential difference between buying a leasehold property and a freehold property? The answer is really quite simple. What each of them represents is a chunk of time for which the owner can enjoy the property. We do not often think of the freehold in these terms but if you think of what a freehold is, 'the fee simple absolute in possession', we know that the ownership of that property will not end unless and until the current owner dies without having left the property by will and with no relatives to inherit the property under the statutory intestacy rules. Even though the chunk of time for which that property can be owned is unlikely to end, we know the circumstances in which it can end. In the case of the leasehold (the 'term of years absolute in possession'), the essential difference is that the chunk of time is established in the lease. The freehold owner has effectively carved out a chunk of time from the fee simple and handed 'ownership' of the property over to someone else for that time in return (usually) for a rent. If you are buying a leasehold property you are buying a defined length of time of ownership. With freehold property you know the circumstances under which the ownership will end but you have to wait and see when those circumstances will come about. With leasehold property you are given an actual date when the ownership or 'the term of the lease' will end.

Having established the conceptual difference we need now to look at the various stages of the conveyancing transaction and the additional or different factors that must be considered if the property which is the subject of the transction is leasehold. There are two slightly different types of leasehold transaction. The aim of this book is to establish an understanding of the principles of a routine conveyancing transaction. The procedure and problems which relate to the sale of an existing lease are almost identical to the sale of a freehold property and fall within the scope of this book. The creation of a brand new lease involves the consideration of a number of additional matters. Many of these are matters of common sense and the same type of matters as we considered for the sale of part of a freehold property may be relevant. (After all this is in effect a sale of part of the sellers' property, i.e., just part of the time which they own rather than part of the physical property.) Nevertheless there are a substantial number of issues of law to be considered which fall outside the scope of this book.

Assignment of an existing lease

The two systems of conveyancing

Just as there were two systems of title to consider in freehold title so there are two in leasehold title.

Unregistered title   Title to a leasehold property in unregistered title is proved by title deeds. The original lease which contains details of the length and conditions of the ownership must, of course, form part of the title. So will any conveyances (called 'assignments') of the leasehold property itself. The lease will show the exact terms attached to the length of time that you are buying. The assignments will prove that the seller is the current owner and therefore owns the property.

The task of the buyers' solicitors in relation to leasehold property will also involve checking for third-party rights which affect the property. As with freehold title, third-party interests can be dealt with quite easily as:

(a)   Third-party interests which are registrable as land charges at the Central Land Charges Registry at Plymouth.

(b)   Third-party interests which are not registrable as land charges but fall within the class of legal estates or legal interests under the Law of Property Act 1925, s. 1(2).

(c)   Third-party interests which are not registrable as land charges and do not come within the class of legal interests and so must be equitable.

(If these categories do not make sense then it is time for a refresher of the basic principles which we looked at in chapter 4.)

In the case of leasehold property the question of title has an extra dimension. Imagine that your client, Sarah, is thinking of buying a leasehold property from Tom who is the first tenant of the property. You will want to make sure that Tom actually owns the property and so has the power to sell it. This can be checked by looking at the lease itself and seeing that it was granted to Tom. But what if the lease was granted to Tom by Katy who purports to be the freehold owner. If Sarah is going to pay good money for the property would not you, in addition to checking that Tom is the owner of the leasehold property, want to check that Katy really owns the freehold and so had the power to grant the lease in the first place? A failure to check out

Katy's title could lead to real problems if, after Sarah has bought the property Lionel returns from abroad to prove that Katy had the keys to the property without authority and that in fact he rather than Katy is the owner of the freehold. Under those circumstances, although it might be possible to sue Katy it would not be possible to claim any right to stay in the property under the terms of the lease.

Registered title   Similar problems arise in the case of registered title. A lease with over 21 years to run must either on its creation or on its sale be registered with its own title. At the time the lease is registered, the freehold, out of which the lease is carved, may or may not be registered. If the freehold is registered then, if the freehold title is given absolute title, this will be sufficient evidence for the registrar of the freehold title. All the registrar will then require to see on application for first registration of the leasehold title is the lease itself and the assignments of it sufficient to show that the current owner of the lease does actually own it and has the power to sell. If the registrar is satisfied with this then the lease will be registered with 'absolute leasehold title'. This makes the checking of the title relatively simple. The buyers of the lease must check the details of the lease and any entries on the register of the leasehold title. A check must also be made for the existence of any interests which will not appear on the register (i.e., overriding interests under the Land Registration Act 1925, s. 70(1)).

What if the freehold title is not registered? If the person who applies for registration of the lease has checked the landlord's title and obtained certified copies of the documents then, if the registrar is satisfied that the landlord's title is in order, he may give the leasehold property absolute leasehold title despite the fact that the freehold is not registered. If no evidence of the freehold is provided (or the evidence is inadequate) then, even though the registrar may be happy with evidence regarding the lease itself, the title given will be 'good leasehold title'. Whenever you see the property only has good leasehold title it is a warning that the property is subject not only to all the matters mentioned on the register and to any third-party rights which come within the categories of overriding interests, but also any matters which may affect the freehold title but about which you may know nothing.

Taking instructions

If you are acting for the buyers the matter of taking instructions really does not vary at all from freehold title. If you are acting for the sellers you must, of course, follow up your enquiry as to whether the property to be sold is freehold or leasehold with some sensible equiries about the lease. The clients could be asked to complete a standard leasehold questionnaire form with a view to providing answers to the buyers' enquiries before contract:

(a)   The sellers (the current tenants) should be asked to provide the receipt for the last payment of ground rent as the buyer will want to see this in due course.

(b)   Details of such matters as service charge accounts (for at least the last three years) and insurance policies must also be obtained.

(c)   The lease should be checked to see whether the landlord's consent is needed to assign it. If consent is required, the sellers' solicitors should set in motion the obtaining of this consent. Standard Condition 8.3 covers the relationship of the buyers and the sellers. It quite clearly places the obligation on the sellers to apply for and obtain the landlord's consent at their own expense. The buyers are required to provide all necessary information and references which are reasonably required. The Standard Conditions also provide for either party, if they have performed their obligations under the standard condition, to rescind the contract if the landlord's consent is not forthcoming by three working days before completion.

The relationships between the parties to the contract can, of course, be varied by the use of special conditions to override the Standard Conditions. The relationship between the sellers and the landlord is partly regulated by statute and partly by usual practice. The statutory obligations are briefly:

(i)   Landlord and Tenant Act 1927, s. 19(1)(a). If the lease contains a *qualified* covenant against assignment (that is, one which forbids assignment without the landlord's consent), the statute implies a further condition that the landlord will not withhold consent unreasonably. No such condition is implied where the covenant against assignment is *absolute* (that is, where there is no reference to the landlord's consent).

(ii)   Landlord and Tenant Act 1988. This provides that the landlord must, once a written application for consent to assign is received, make a decision within a reasonable time. The landlord must also notify the tenant, within a reasonable time, of the decision and, if consent is refused, of the reasons for the refusal. If the landlord fails to perform the duties imposed by this statute then there may be a liability to pay damages for breach of statutory duty.

When the tenants' solicitors apply for consent to assign, it is usual for them to be asked to give an undertaking to pay the landlord's solicitors' costs incurred in dealing with the matter of consent. Care should be taken if this is asked for and you should consider:

(i)   All the considerations regarding undertakings and their nature that we have looked at so far.

(ii)   Whether the undertaking will oblige the tenant to pay the costs even if consent is refused. Unless the undertaking specifically states to the contrary, this may be implied.

(iii)   The need to specify the maximum amount of the costs.

(iv)   The need to ensure that your clients are asked to provide sufficient funds on account to enable you to perform the undertaking.

Drafting the contract

There are certain matters which are peculiar to leasehold title which should be considered when drafting the contract.

Particulars   In freehold title we looked at drafting the particulars and said that what we were really doing was describing the subject-matter of the sale. The particulars of leasehold property should include the following:

(i)   A statement that the property is leasehold.
(ii)   If the title is registered, the class of the title.
(iii) In unregistered freehold title there would then follow a description of the physical property itself. The same thing needs to be done for the sale of unregistered leasehold property but that alone will not be sufficient. In freehold title, simply describing the property as freehold would tell you how long the ownership would last. With leasehold property it is the lease which will tell us that. The particulars should therefore refer to the physical property. Here the reference can be a brief description followed by a reference to the property as being, for example, 'the property comprised in a lease dated 1 May 1970 and made between P. Church (1) and B. Cobb (2) together with the rights contained in the said lease'. The description should state also:

(1)   The total length of the term of the lease.
(2)   The date the term commenced (which is not always the same date as the date of the lease).
(3)   The rent payable under the lease.

(iv)   In registered leasehold title much the same details are needed but the drafting of the particulars is much simpler as a simple physical description of the property and a reference to the property as comprised in a title number will be adequate reference to the details of the lease.

Special conditions   Many of the matters which should be considered here are the same as for freehold title. The property should be expressed to be sold subject to the covenants and restrictions contained in the lease.

There are certain open contract rules and Standard Conditions which relate to leasehold property and which should be understood so that they can be amended by the inclusion of a special condition if needed. These include:

(a)   *Disclosure of the lease.* Standard Condition 8.1.2 provides that the sellers must, before exchange of contracts, provide the buyers with full details of the lease and that this having been done the buyers purchase with full knowledge of the terms of the lease.

(b)   *Title to be shown.* The open contract rule is that if the title is unregistered the sellers must provide the lease and all dispositions of the lease for at least the last 15 years. Obviously this is only appropriate if the lease is at least 15 years old. If the lease is less than 15 years old then all the dispositions of the lease must be shown. The open contract rule if the title is registered is that the copy lease and the documents specified in the Land Registration Act 1925, s. 110, must be provided. This means that, amongst other things, the sellers must provide copies of the entries on the register.

Whether the property is registered or unregistered title the open contract rules do not provide for the buyer to be given any of the freehold title. If the property is registered and it has absolute leasehold title then this is not a problem as the buyer can rest assured that the registrar has checked the freehold title. In any other situation the open contract rules are unsatisfactory to buyers and the buyers' solicitors are likely to ask for some special condition to cover the point.

The Standard Conditions go to the other extreme. The open contract having denied the buyers the right to any freehold title at all, Standard Condition 8.1.3 provides that the sellers shall produce sufficient title to enable the buyers to register the lease with absolute title. This means that the sellers have to be able to provide evidence of the freehold title which is certified as examined with the original documents and which shows that the freehold title is technically in order. If the sellers are unable to do this, even if, for example, the problem is that they have only photocopies rather than examined copies of the freehold title, a special condition must be included in the contract to override the Standard Condition and oblige the sellers to show only that title which they have.

(c)   *Condition of the property.* Whatever the capacity in which the sellers sell leasehold property there will be two covenants for title, additional to those in freehold title, which will be implied into the purchase deed. These two covenants for title are:

(i)   that the lease is valid and subsisting, and
(ii)   that the rent has been paid and all the covenants and obligations under the lease have been performed.

Usually the lease will contain some covenants or obligations with regard to the repair of the property and its physical condition. The effect of the implied covenants for title is usually, therefore, that the sellers will be covenanting with the buyers regarding the state of repair of the property. If this were left unmodified the effect would be that the buyers could sue the sellers if, after completion, they found that the physical state of the property was worse than that required by the lease. Standard Condition 8.1.5 provides that the purchase deed is to include a statement that the implied covenants for title shall not make the sellers liable to the buyers in respect of any breach in the terms of the lease regarding the physical condition of the property.

Perusing and approving the draft contract

The considerations here depend on the terms of the lease itself and any special conditions which the sellers' solicitors have included in the draft contract. So far as the terms of the lease are concerned, they should be checked through carefully with the buyers to ensure that they are acceptable. If they are not acceptable then the buyers should be advised not to buy the property as any term in the lease which relates to the property will be enforceable directly against the buyers if they go ahead and buy the property.

So far as the Standard Conditions and open contract rules are concerned, the matters looked at above need to be considered from the point of view of the buyers rather than the sellers. For example, if the contract were to include a special condition excluding Standard Condition 8.1.3, the buyers should be advised to think very carefully about buying the property. Not only will there be a risk that the purported landlord did not in fact have a good right to grant the lease but also the property may not be readily resaleable as building societies and banks may be unwilling to provide mortgage finance in the face of the possible risks.

Pre-contract enquiries and searches

These enquiries will be much the same as the enquiries made when purchasing a freehold title. The enquiries of the sellers will be made on the additional property information form which includes questions regarding service charges, complaints, disputes and alterations to the property. Enquiries of the sellers should include enquiries about whether all the covenants in the lease have been performed. Particular problems should be considered such as whether any alterations or additions to the property have been made and, if so, whether the landlord's consent was obtained.

In addition, the buyers might consider asking that, if the landlord's consent to the sale is needed, it is obtained before exchange of contracts. The Standard Conditions contain provision for either party to withdraw from the contract in the event of consent being refused. However, if your clients propose to enter into a contract for sale of their existing property at the same time, they do not want to find themselves able to withdraw from their purchase, but bound to complete the sale, particularly when everyone could have been sure of the position if steps had been taken to obtain the consent before the contract was entered into.

Deducing and investigating title

What title the buyers are to be entitled to see should have been considered carefully by both solicitors at the stage of drafting and approving the contract. However much title to the leasehold (and freehold) is provided, the buyers should investigate title using the same methods as for freehold property. In unregistered title this will involve investigating all the documents of title (and making all necessary pre-completion searches and inspections). The leasehold title must, of course, be investigated and if evidence of the freehold title is provided that must be investigated also. It helps, I think, to look at the investigation of leasehold title as if the freehold and the leasehold are on two levels. They are really two separate titles which you are investigating and the only connecting link, which you must always have, is the lease itself (see table 17.1).

Table 17.1

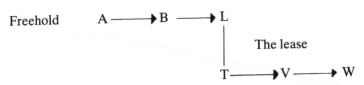

In registered title the investigation of title involves checking the copy lease, checking that the provisions accord with the details disclosed by the sellers prior to exchange of contracts and checking copies of entries on the register in accordance with the Land Registration Act 1925, s. 110. If the title is absolute leasehold then that and the pre-completion searches and inspections are all that are required. If the title to the property is, for example, good leasehold then if the sellers are bound to provide evidence of the freehold title as well (as they would be if Standard Condition 8.1.3 were included in the contract), this must be investigated.

One further matter should be mentioned in respect of checking the documents of title. When checking the lease itself do not be misled by the fact that the lease is executed only by the lessor. A lease is prepared in two identical parts. The lease, which is executed by the lessor only and becomes part of the lessee's title document, and a 'counterpart lease' which is executed by the lessee only and is retained by the lessor.

Drafting the purchase deed

When the contract is for the sale of an existing lease, the purchase deed will be called an assignment rather than a conveyance. If the title is registered then a form of transfer will be used.

The contents of an assignment are much the same as a conveyance:

(a)   If recitals are included they can be used to recite the creation of the lease, any assignments of the lease and, if appropriate, the consent of the landlord to the assignment.

(b)   The description of the property. The same problem arises here as we have just looked at in drafting the contract. When dealing with freehold land it is sufficient to refer to the property as freehold or as being the fee simple. In the case of leasehold you must go further than that and describe the property by reference to the lease, mentioning the term, the commencement date and the rent reserved by the lease. In the simple form of draft conveyance which we looked at in chapter 10 the parcels clause could be enlarged to include this information.

(c)   Covenants for title. Certain covenants for title will be implied into the purchase deed depending on the capacity in which the seller conveys. Remember that for leasehold property there are two additional covenants. If the Standard Conditions have been used the assignment should recite the limitation on the covenant concerning the observance of the terms and conditions of the lease, so far as the physical condition of the property is concerned, which is contained in Standard Condition 8.1.5.

(d)   Indemnity covenants. Where leasehold property is being sold there is no need to include an indemnity covenant in the assignment in respect of matters contained in the lease. The covenant for indemnity will be implied in any event by the Law of Property Act 1925, s. 77. (If the assignment were not on the occasion of a sale this would not be implied, and express indemnities would have to be given.)

The contents of the transfer are almost the same as a transfer of registered freehold title. In addition, though, the need to modify the covenants for title (if Standard Condition 8.1.5 is included in the contract) should be remembered and again there will be no need for indemnity covenants in respect of the provisions in the lease (Land Registration Act 1925, s. 24).

Searches and inspections before completion

The searches and inspections which are needed for leasehold property are much the same as for freehold property. If the property is unregistered, a Central Land Charges search (and if appropriate a company search) will be needed against each owner of the lease in the title and if the freehold title is being shown a search against each freehold owner should also be obtained.

If the leasehold is registered with absolute title, a Land Registry search on form 94A should be undertaken in the same way as for registered freehold title.

If the leasehold is registered with good leasehold title and the buyers have no right to the deduction of the freehold title then an ordinary form 94A search should be done. If the buyers are entitled to see the unregistered freehold title then a form 94A search should be done in respect of the registered leasehold title but in addition a Central Land Charges search (and company search if appropriate) should be undertaken against each freehold owner.

In the case of both registered and unregistered title, an inspection of the property must be carried out as for freehold title.

Preparation for completion

There are usually two additional matters which should be considered in preparing for completion where the property is leasehold.

Apportionments   In preparing for completion in freehold title we looked at the need to apportion any amounts paid by the sellers in respect of the property. In the case of leasehold property the rent paid (and if appropriate any service charge paid) should be apportioned so that the buyers reimburse the sellers for any rent which the sellers have paid which relates to a period after the completion of the sale to the buyers. (If the rent is payable in arrear then the apportionment will need to give credit to the buyers for the proportion of the rent due from the sellers for their period of ownership up to completion.)

Statement to client   In the statement to your clients showing the amount due to or from them you should remember to include additional fees arising out of the lease. The sellers' solicitors should remember to include the costs incurred by them (and if payable, by the landlord's solicitor) in obtaining the landlord's consent to the assignment. The buyers' solicitors should remember that the buyers may be required to give notices to the landlord for which a fee may be required. For example, leases quite commonly require the buyers to give notice of the purchase of the property and any mortgage to the landlord's solicitors and to pay a fee to cover the costs of recording the notices. This amount should be included on the clients' statement.

Completion

On completion the buyers' solicitors will wish to inspect the receipts for ground rent both to confirm that the sellers have paid the rent for which they are claiming an apportionment but also as an indication that the covenants under the lease have been performed.

    The buyers' solicitors will also expect to receive certain documents. What the documents are will depend on whether the title to the lease is registered or unregistered and whether the freehold title is required, under the contract, to be produced.

Unregistered title   The buyers' solicitor will expect to receive:

(a)   The original lease.
(b)   Any assignments of the lease over at least the last 15 years.
(c)   Duplicates of any notices given in the past in connection with the assignments etc.
(d)   Any mortgages endorsed with receipts (or, if not available, an undertaking by the sellers' solicitors to repay the mortgage and forward the receipted mortgage deed).
(e)   The properly executed assignment to the buyers.
(f)   Landlord's consent to the assignment where appropriate.
(g)   Executed share transfer form and share certificate in respect of residents' management company where appropriate.
(h)   Marked abstract of the freehold title where appropriate.

Registered title   The buyers' solicitors will expect to receive:

(a)   The original lease.

(b)   The land certificate (or charge certificate if the property is subject to the mortgage).

(c)   Duplicates of any notice given in the past in connection with the assignments etc.

(d)   Receipted form 53 in respect of any mortgages (or if not available an undertaking by the sellers' solicitors to repay the mortgage and forward the receipted form 53 (and charge certificate if not already in the sellers' solicitors' possession).

(e)   The properly executed transfer to the buyers.

(f)   Landlord's consent to assign where appropriate.

(g)   Executed share transfer form and share certificate in respect of residents' management company where appropriate.

(h)   Marked abstract of the unregistered freehold title where appropriate, i.e., if title is good leasehold and the requirement to show evidence of the freehold title has not been excluded.

After completion

There are various matters which must be attended to after completion which are either in addition to or differ slightly from the matters to be dealt following the completion of a sale of the freehold:

(a)   *Stamping*. As with freehold title two different stamps must be considered. *Ad valorem* duty will not be payable if the consideration does not exceed £30,000 *and* the assignment or transfer contains a certificate of value. Otherwise *ad valorem* duty is payable at 1 per cent of the total consideration. A particulars delivered stamp is required if the assignment is on sale and the lease was granted for a term of seven years or more. The timing and other considerations as to stamping are the same for leasehold as for freehold property.

(b)   *Notice of dealings*. The lease must be checked for the requirement to give notice to the landlord of any dealings in the property. Often the lease will require notice to be given of both the assignment of the lease and the mortgage of the property by the buyers. A fee will usually be payable and a time-limit for the giving of the notice prescribed.

(c)   *Registration*. If the title to the lease is unregistered the assignment on sale of a lease with over 21 years left to run will give rise to the need for first registration. If the leasehold title is already registered, application for registration of the dealing in registered property must be made to the Land Registry within the priority period of the Land Registry search.

Common examination problem areas

I can hear you saying it: 'Never mind problem *areas* the whole of leases is a problem'. Your first hurdle is to overcome the psychological problem. Remember what I said at the beginning of the chapter. The basic difference between leasehold and freehold is the length of the period of ownership. Once you have looked at it in that light (and calmed yourself down), what are the common points to remember?

(a)   *The length of the term.* How long is the period of ownership?

(b)   *The particular provisions of the lease.* It is all too easy in the panic of the exam to ignore the actual provisions of the lease. Read the lease carefully. Note the obligations of the tenant.

Some obligations will deal with procedural matters such as giving notice to the lessor of any dealing with the property. These are not problematic but you must remember to comply with them. Others may be more problematic. They might, for example, prevent the buyers from doing what they want to do with the property or they might impose a very heavy financial burden on the buyers. All the provisions of the lease should be noted and dealt with appropriately. Remember also that covenants in leases are usually directly enforceable by the lessor against the current owner of the lease.

(c)   *The title.* Title seems to cause people terrible nightmares. Exactly what documents of title are needed depends on the terms of the contract between the sellers and the buyers. Try to break the thing down, at least at first, into very simple ideas. Where the title to the leasehold property is unregistered, to be sure that the lease is in order the buyers must check:

(i)   The lease itself.

(ii)   The chain of transactions sufficient to show that the sellers are the current owners of the leasehold property. (This is where you can usually rely on 15 years of transactions involving the lease. Obviously if the lease is only 10 years old you cannot 'magic' 15 years and simply providing all the transactions will be acceptable.)

(iii)   Sufficient evidence of the freehold title to be sure that the lessor was the owner of the freehold and so had the right to grant the lease. The checks which you are making here are in fact very similar to those you would make if you were buying the freehold. If you were buying the freehold title and would accept the evidence you have been given then it is likely to be acceptable as part of the leasehold title. (If the lessor was the owner of a lease rather than the freehold there would be an additional parallel title to check, see table 17.2. You must check each parallel title and the links between them which are the leases.)

Table 17.2

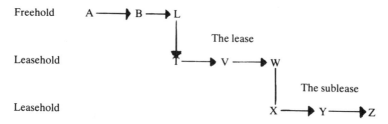

Remember also that, in the absence of a special condition, the Standard Conditions entitle the buyers to receive such evidence of title as will enable them to register the lease with absolute leasehold title.

In registered title, if the leasehold title is absolute then issues of title become much less awesome and the property can be dealt with in much the same way as a registered freehold property. If, however, the title is good leasehold, realise that you are again in effect checking two titles, the registered leasehold title and the unregistered freehold title. Pretend that you are buying both titles and consider what matters would concern you in *each* of the transctions.

Whatever you do, even if you are still unhappy about leases when you get to the exam, do not disintegrate because you find that leases are on the paper. The first step is to keep calm. The second step is not to be bamboozled into rushing into the thing. Think all the time about basic principles. I have seldom had occasion to criticise a conveyancing paper for being correct but too simplistic. It is far more common that candidates attempt complicated answers and in doing so tie themselves up in knots!

EIGHTEEN

TRANSACTION PROTOCOL

In March 1990 the Law Society introduced the National Conveyancing Protocol which is called Transaction. The protocol is a set of procedures which are designed to speed up the domestic conveyancing process. The procedures under the protocol differ, in places, from the standard conveyancing procedures which we have looked at so far. This chapter is not designed to substitute for a careful reading of the National Protocol and the Law Society Council Statement but rather to provide you with an overview of a transaction when using the protocol.

Status of the National Protocol

The protocol was described in the Law Society Council Statement as 'preferred practice'. It is not compulsory to adopt the protocol in every domestic conveyancing transaction but it is obligatory to inform the solicitors acting for the other party whether or not it is proposed to adopt the protocol.

If the protocol is adopted it has specifically been stated that the obligations of the protocol should not be regarded as undertakings.

Effect of the National Protocol

Adopting the protocol will mean not only following standard procedures, but also using certain standardised documentation. Included in the documentation are the following:

(a) *The property information form.* This form takes the place of the standard form of pre-contract enquiries which, in a non-protocol transaction, the buyers' solicitors would have sent to the sellers' solicitors before exchange of contracts. Even where the protocol is not adopted this form may be used. It includes information regarding such matters as: boundaries, disputes, guarantees (e.g., NHBC or timber treatment), routes of services and the interests of occupiers.

(b) *The additional property information form.* This is, like the property information form, the information which passes between the sellers' solicitors and the buyers' solicitors. It is used where the property is leasehold as it includes standard questions which are peculiar to leasehold property. It includes questions about such matters as insurance, service charges and management companies.

(c) *The property information questionnaire*. This form is designed to be completed by the sellers to provide the sellers' solicitors with information which the buyers may want to know. The information will form the basis of the replies to the property information form.

(d) *The leasehold questionnaire*. This form is designed to be completed by the sellers and provides the information necessary to complete the additional property information form.

(e) *The fixtures, fittings and contents form*. This form is to be completed by the sellers. If any chattels are to be included in the sale or fixtures to be removed it may be incorporated by reference into the contract. A special condition will be used to make it clear which fixtures are being removed by the sellers and/or chattels included in the sale but the reference to and incorporation of the form saves an otherwise lengthy repetition of the items in the special condition itself. The items listed are extensive and range from the television aerial and fitted kitchen units to spice rack and clothes line!

Apart from the use of the standard documentation, how does adopting the protocol affect the standard procedures?

Sellers' solicitors: taking instructions

The protocol assumes that as soon as the sellers have taken the decision to put their house on the market they will also instruct solicitors. The solicitors must obtain specific information and documentation from the sellers including:

(a) Sufficient information to complete the property information form and a completed fixtures and fittings form.
(b) The originals of any guarantees, planning permissions etc.
(c) Details of any mortgages affecting the property.
(d) The identity of any adults living in the property and whether or not they have made any contribution to the purchase or improvement of the property.

Sellers' solicitors: action to be taken following instructions

The sellers' solicitors must assemble a package of information for the buyers' solicitors. Many of the enquiries which the sellers' solicitors must make when actually taking the instructions are no different from those a sensible solicitor would make when the protocol is not being used. So too with the matters to be attended to. (For example, the protocol says that sellers' solicitors must locate and obtain the title deeds!) There are, however, some matters which would not necessarily be dealt with if the protocol were not being used:

(a)   The sellers' solicitors must carry out:

   (i)   A local search and additional enquiries of the local authority.
   (ii)   A commons search (if appropriate).
   (iii) Mining enquiries (if appropriate).
   (iv)   A search of the Public Index Map (unregistered title only).

This is a departure from the procedure which we have looked at so far. In a traditional conveyancing transction these searches are carried out by the buyers' solicitors. The advantage of the protocol method is that the searches are sent off as soon as the sellers place the property on the market. A buyer may not be found for the property for some weeks, by which time (hopefully) the search will have returned and the transaction will not be further delayed by the buyers' solicitors having to send off, and wait for, the searches.

   (b)   If the title to the property is unregistered the sellers' solicitors must also provide (and if not in their possession carry out) a land charges search against every holder of the legal title since and including the root of title. This includes a search against the sellers themselves. Under a non-protocol transaction the buyers' solicitors would carry out a search against the sellers provide. Under a non-protocol transaction these *could* be dealt with at this stage but in any event (whether or not the protocol is adopted) the search against the sellers will have to be repeated immediately before completion.

   (c)   The sellers' solicitors must provide a package of information and documentation. The property information form provides the standard replies to what, in a non-protocol transaction, would have been enquiries before contract sent by the buyers' solicitors. The sellers' solicitors must also, before exchange of contracts, provide evidence of title in the form of an epitome in unregistered title or office copies and relevant copy documents in registered title.

Buyers' solicitors: taking instructions

As soon as the buyers' solicitors are instructed they should ask the buyers whether the purchase is dependent on the sale of any property and, if so, what stage the related sale has reached. If the buyers are agreeable the solicitors must disclose this information to the sellers' solicitors.

   Note that normally, if there is to be any departure from protocol procedures the solicitor is under a duty to give notice to the solicitor acting for the other party. The Law Society Council Statement makes it clear that throughout the protocol the duty of confidentiality to the client is paramount and that a failure to disclose details of a related transaction because the clients refuse their authority does not give rise to the requirement to give notice.

   The buyers' solicitors should now consider the draft contract and documentation and the searches which the sellers' solicitors has provided.

Note that although it is the sellers' solicitors responsibility to carry out the searches, the buyers' solicitors must satisfy themselves that the searches are satisfactory. If the buyers' solicitors consider any to be unsatisfactory, or that any should have been done which have not been, then the buyers must repeat the search or make additional searches. The buyers' solicitors should, at this stage, also consider using the Law Society Search Validation Scheme. For a small premium a local search which is a little out of date can be insured against entries made between the date of the search and exchange of contracts.

If the buyers' solicitors are unhappy with any of the information given on the property information form or require extra information then pre-contract enquiries can be raised. The protocol, though, specifically states that no questions should be asked about the structure of the building where the information could be obtained from the buyers' own inspection or survey.

After exchange of contracts

Although the protocol provides for delivery of the evidence of the sellers' title before exchange of contracts it anticipates that requisitions will be raised after exchange.

The protocol specifically provides for the use of the Law Society's Code if completion takes place by post.

Solicitors' overriding duty to their own clients' interests

The Law Society Council Statement, in addition to describing the protocol as 'preferred practice' also expressly stated that the protocol must always be considered in the context of solicitors' overriding duty to their own clients' interests. This presumably allows for the variation of the protocol (subject to the requirement to give notice) whenever the interests of the clients require it.

Dealing with the National Protocol in examinations

Whether or not your syllabus requires you to be familiar with the workings of the National Protocol, you should nevertheless ensure that you are familiar with the documentation which is used widely even in transactions where the protocol is not adopted.

If the National Protocol does form part of your syllabus then you must know the detail of the provisions and of the Law Society Council Statement. This book has concentrated on the procedures for a simple sale of freehold property. Try when you study the Protocol to look at it in two ways:

(a)   How it will alter the procedures with which you are by now familiar.
(b)   The problems and uncertainties which are inherent in the protocol itself. With regard to this you may find the professional journals a useful source of commentary.

NINETEEN

CONCLUSION

There are now two possibilities. First of all it could be that you have flicked to the end of this book like I do when reading a novel. If you are a 'flicker' then my advice is to go back to where you should be and read steadily through. Attempting to rush conveyancing is a sure recipe for disaster!

The second possibility is that you have actually read this book right the way through. If you have, Congratulations! I hope that you will now not be totally at sea with conveyancing. Don't be dismayed, though, if you are still a little unsure of yourself. Competence can be developed quite quickly by serious study. Confidence, on the other hand, can take quite some time to acquire. Practice at dealing with old exam questions and, where possible, real conveyancing problems, is one of the best ways to do it.

There are three thoughts which I would like to leave you with.

First, don't expect not to make mistakes. We all do our best to avoid them but we are all human. Sooner or later, whether it is in an exam or in practice, you will make a mistake. It's annoying but it's not the end of the world and it does not necessarily mean you are a bad lawyer.

Secondly, don't expect to open the exam paper and be able to do it. Part of the psychological reaction to exams is to feel unsure of yourself. When I first started to teach law I astonished myself. I had gone to work early to check through an exam paper before the exam. My immediate reaction was that I couldn't do it! I had to remind myself that I had lectured the course *and* set the paper. It is amazing how, in a state of nerves, your mind can play tricks on you.

Thirdly, don't expect that once you have gained more confidence you won't, on occasions, lose it again. Not long ago I was handed the deeds to a property which belonged to a client who had just died. I had to prepare an abstract of title because the property was being put on the market. My first attempt to sort out the deeds left me feeling as I did in my student days. I had attempted to do it in a hurry and had succeeded in confusing myself. A quarter of an hour set aside at lunch-time, with a clear desk and a large piece of paper for notes restored my confidence. Reducing the title to basic principles soon put me back on the right track.

I wish you confident and successful conveyancing!

GLOSSARY

Abstract of title. A document written in a form of shorthand which details the main points from the documents and events of title.

Ad valorem. In proportion to value. Where *ad valorem* stamp duty is payable the amount payable will vary directly in relation to the amount of the consideration.

Administrator. Person who, usually in the absence of the deceased having made a will appointing executors, is entitled under the statutory rules to apply for and has applied for a grant of administration.

Assent. The agreement of an executor or administrator giving the legatee the property bequeathed to him or her. An assent in respect of land must be either in the form of a deed or in writing.

Assignment. A transfer of property. (The term is particularly used in respect of the transfer of existing leases and the charging of endowment policies in connection with a mortgage.)

Certificate of value. A written declaration of the consideration paid in respect of the transaction (or series of transactions) which either reduces the amount of *ad valorem* duty payable or exempts the document from a charge to *ad valorem* stamp duty.

Chain. The term is used in a transaction where there is a series of sales and purchases which are dependent on each other.

Cleared funds. Funds which are in the possession of the account holder and are not dependent on the honouring of any cheque or promise.

Co-ownership. Ownership where two or more people are entitled to the property concurrently rather than consecutively.

Conveyance. Deed in a prescribed form used to transfer title in unregistered title.

Covenant. A promise made in a deed to do or refrain from doing something.

Deed of gift. A deed transferring an interest in property for which no consideration is paid.

Defect in title. Some problem which suggests the owner of the property might be dispossessed or sued without any redress.

Disbursement. A fee or charge which is paid out (e.g., by solicitors on behalf of a client).

Easement. The right which belongs to the owner for the time being of one piece of land to use another piece of land (e.g., right of way, drainage, light).

Engrossment. The final version of a deed produced on good paper.

Epitome of title. A list of the documents and events of title usually accompanied by photocopy documents.

Equity of redemption. The interest of a mortgagor in mortgaged property.

Estate contract. A contract to create or convey a legal estate.

Fee simple absolute in possession. One of the two legal estates, commonly called the 'freehold', which will continue until the current owner dies without leaving the property by will and with no living relatives.

Floating charge. A type of charge which may affect property belonging to a company. The charge affects a class of property but will not be a charge upon individual properties within the class unless or until the charge crystallises. After crystallisation the charge has broadly the same effect as a fixed charge or mortgage.

Frontager. Someone whose property adjoins another piece of property, particularly a road or a river.

General conditions. Printed conditions which are incorporated into the contract intended to apply to all transactions unless specifically excluded or modified by a special condition.

Grant of probate. A grant of representation which is made to executors where the deceased left a will. It confirms the authority of the executors and the validity of the deceased's will.

Grant of representation. An order of the High Court which establishes the authority of the personal representative.

Grant of administration. A grant of representation which is made to administrators usually where the deceased died either leaving a will which did not appoint executors or without a will. The grant establishes the authority of the administrators to act and either the validity of the will or that the deceased died without leaving a will.

Joint tenancy. A form of ownership which, on the death of one of the co-owners entitles the surviving co-owners to the whole of the property.

Land charge. A third-party interest affecting land. It may be either a 'local land charge' or a land charge as defined by s. 2 of the Land Charges Act 1972.

Legal interest. An interest defined by s. 1(2) of the Law of Property Act 1925.

Legal estate. A right of ownership of property for a period of time. Only two legal estates exist: the fee simple absolute in possession and the term of years absolute.

Mortgage. A charge on property securing the repayment of money.

National Protocol. A series of procedures recommended by the Law Society for adoption in domestic conveyancing transactions. The objective of the National Protocol is to minimise delay in such transactions.

Open contract rules. Rules of law which apply to regulate the relationship between a buyer and seller of land in the absence of a special or general condition in the contract.

Option to renew. A contract (often contained in a lease) giving the lessee of the property the right to a further lease at the end of the current term.

Option to purchase. A contract which obliges the owner of property to convey the legal estate to the other party if the other party should request it.

Personal representative. The executor or administrator of a deceased person.

Positive covenant. A covenant which obliges the covenantor to do something (e.g., a covenant to paint the exterior of property). The substance rather than the wording is important. For example, a covenant 'not to allow fence to fall into disrepair' is a positive covenant because in substance it requires the covenantor 'to maintain' the fence.

Postal rule. The rule that a contract is made when the acceptance is put in the post not when it is received by the offeror.

Puisne mortgage. In unregistered title, a legal mortgage which is not protected by deposit of title deeds.

Purchase deed. Deed transferring the interest in land to the purchasers.

Restrictive covenant. A covenant whereby the covenantor agrees to refrain from doing something (e.g., a covenant not to use premises for business purposes). The substance rather than the wording of the covenant is important in determining whether it is positive or restrictive.

Right of pre-emption. A contract whereby if the estate owner were to decide to sell the property the property must first be offered for sale to the grantee of the right. The grantee of the right must be given the opportunity of first refusal.

Severance. The conversion by a joint tenant of his or her interest into that of a tenant in common.

Special conditions. Conditions of a contract which are peculiar to that particular transction.

Standard Conditions. A form of general conditions prepared by the Law Society (1990).

Tenancy in common. A form of co-ownership only applicable to equitable co-owners. On the death of one of the co-owners the deceased co-owner's interest will pass according to his or her will or intestacy.

Term of years absolute (leasehold). One of the two legal estates in land. It gives to the lessee the right to exclusive possession of the land for a fixed term usually in return for the payment of rent.

Third-party right. The right of someone other than the owner of the legal estate to own, occupy, use, or control the use of, land of which the third party is not the legal freehold owner.

Title deeds. The documents evidencing the transfers of ownership from party to party.

Trust for sale. A trust which imposes a *duty* to sell on the trustees. The duty may be modified by a *power* to postpone the sale or a requirement that the trustee obtain the consents of certain people before the sale.

Trustee of the legal estate. An owner of the legal estate who is either not the sole equitable owner of the property or has no equitable interest in the property at all.

INDEX

TITLE IN THE SERIES

SWOT Law of Torts
SWOT Law of Evidence
SWOT Company Law
SWOT Law of Contract
SWOT Revenue Law
SWOT Family Law
SWOT Land Law
SWOT Criminal Law
SWOT English Legal System
SWOT Equity and Trusts
SWOT Commercial and Consumer Law
SWOT A Level Law
SWOT Constitutional and Administrative Law
SWOT Employment Law
SWOT Jurisprudence
SWOT Conveyancing
SWOT EEC Law